THE WORLD'S
MYTHOLOGY
IN COLOUR

THE WORLD'S
MYTHOLOGY
IN COLOUR

Veronica Ions
Introduction by Jacquetta Hawkes

Hamlyn
London · New York · Sydney · Toronto

Front cover

Heracles and Nereus, seen on a Greek amphora of the fifth century BC. Nereus knew the way to the Garden of the Hesperides but was reluctant to tell: but Heracles managed to extract the knowledge from the god who was called 'The Old Man of the Sea'. British Museum.

Half title

Kuan Yin, the female Chinese form of the Bodhisattva Avalokitesvara, who postponed Buddhahood in order to help mankind. She was identified with the Taoist Tou Mu, goddess of the north star and ruler over life and death. Red amber. Wellcome Medical Museum.

Frontispiece

Etruscan amphora in the Villa Giulia, Rome, depicting a Triton, a minor sea god from Greek mythology. The Etruscans borrowed not only Greek art forms but their beliefs: and Rome, dedicated from foundation to resist the Etruscans, yet took Greek ideas via Etruria.

Published by
The Hamlyn Publishing Group Limited
London · New York · Sydney · Toronto
Astronaut House, Hounslow Road,
Feltham, Middlesex
England
© Copyright The Hamlyn Publishing Group Limited 1974

ISBN 0 600 31301 8

Printed in Hong Kong by Lee Fung

Contents

Introduction
Myth and Mankind by
Jacquetta Hawkes

It is rare for a word to retain two precisely opposite meanings, each being selected according to the beliefs and prejudices of the user. Myth is such a word. Thinkers of many different disciplines have found that at all times myth represents an absolute truth, affords insight 'into the indescribable realities of the soul', or, as Malinowski says 'is not in the nature of an invention...but a living reality'. Such vital interpretations look like winning the day, yet their victory is far from complete. Thus in the august pages of the Oxford English Dictionary myth is defined as 'A purely fictitious narrative usually involving supernatural persons, actions or events and embodying some popular idea concerning natural history or historical phenomena.' This supercilious O.E.D. attitude is conspicuously maintained in everyday talk and journalism.

The use of the term myth as synonymous with fiction comes to us from nineteenth-century positivism and rationalism. Comte's famous Law of the Three States laid it down that the nature of man's thought had at first been theological, then philosophical and was now entering its rational scientific or Positivist state of enlightenment. The most extreme of the rationalist interpreters was to be Max Muller who suggested that myth was 'a disease of language', an abnormality of the human mind caused by an inability to express abstract ideas except by metaphor. He saw it as a disease that was at its worst in the early stages of human thought, but which had never been completely cured.

The early theorists might seek the origin of the mythical figures of religion through a linguistic study of the historic mythologies of the Indian Veda, the Iranian Avesta, of Homer and the Norse Edda. Soon, however, there was a new generation of pioneers in anthropology and archaeology to add the beliefs and rites of non-literate peoples past and present as subjects of study and speculation. After Darwin, evolutionary ideas based on biological rather than historical models were, of course, greatly strengthened, and so, too, was hostility between those who accepted divine revelation and those who subjected it to rationalist vivisection.

Among the founding fathers of anthropology, R.B. Tylor, influenced by Comte and later involved in Darwinian disputes, was above all an anti-theological evolutionist who sought to apply scientific laws to man's emergence, step by regular step, from prehistoric darkness into modern European light. In particular he taught that the 'primitive' peoples of the contemporary world were indeed survivals from the savage or barbaric phases of the past and so could illuminate the beliefs and practices of early man. This view, later consigned to a dishonoured grave, is now being offered a cautious hand for resurrection.

Towards the end of the nineteenth century the evolutionary approach tended to be displaced by the sociological. It was Émile Durkheim who probably did most to break out from a narrow rationalism by recognizing religion, with its expression in myths and symbols, as a reality in itself, a force that existed and would always exist, enabling human beings to relate themselves to the external world and to the order of society. He went so far as to say that religious forms were the primeval matrix out of which both culture and society had grown, and which, in spite of ever sharper division from the secular, they could never do without.

With the fully developed functionalist school of social anthropology all concern for historical change was set aside in the hope of obtaining a static, but all-inclusive picture of individual societies and cultures—as though they could be revealed by the camera of a spy satellite. In practice, however, the great virtue of their method was that it took the functionalists into the field to live at close quarters with native communities. It was his experience among the Trobriand Islanders that obliged Malinowski to see that their myths were neither primarily symbolic in meaning nor stories invented to satisfy curiosity as to 'how things began'. He wrote:

'The myth in a primitive society, that is in its original living form, is not a mere tale told but a reality lived. For the native these stories are the assertion of an original, greater, more important reality through which the present life, fate and work of mankind are governed and the knowledge of which provides men on the one hand with motives for ritual and moral acts, on the other with directions for their performance.'

This was a recognition of the social reality of myths: at much the same time a totally new approach began to reveal their psychological reality. Hitherto theorists had studied myths in time and space, historically, culturally, socially.

But always they had looked at them objectively and in their external affects. Freud taught us to look within at that psychic groundwork of our being, that mysterious source from which the myths have flowed, that invisible force mighty enough to raise temples, ziggurats and pyramids to exalt its divinities.

Freud had much influence on Malinowski and others concerned with mythology: ideas such as that embodied in the Oedipus complex were an obvious challenge. Yet the doctrine that creative images within the psyche were largely to be attributed to the sexual repressions of individuals was not to prove generally illuminating or appropriate to the evidence. Carl Jung parted company with Freud primarily over his concept of the collective unconscious. Significantly, this concept originated in his discovery that the dreams, visions and fantasies of his patients were related to widespread and recurring figures and themes of mythology.

From such empirical evidence Jung became convinced that just as all men inherit similar bodily parts from the human and pre-human past, so, too, they have a common mental inheritance in the archaic depths of the unconscious. These primordial images or archetypes, in certain ways analogous to instincts, being universal forms, part of 'the inherited structure of the psyche', can manifest themselves anywhere and at any time. Jung emphasises that they have no determinable content of their own. He has likened them both to empty stream beds ready for the water of different cultures to flow through them, and to 'the axial system of a crystal, which, as it were, preforms the crystalline structure in the mother liquid although it has no material structure of its own.' It would seem that this thesis is well illustrated by the rich variety, yet similarity, of figures, situations and events of the mythologies presented in this book.

Of their very nature, archetypal forms must remain elusive. Among the most emotive and persistent figures, however, it is possible to name the Divine Child (who, as in the story of the Christ Child with St Christopher, can be smaller than small and bigger than big); the Wise Old Man; the Great Goddess and Earth Mother; the Maiden-Mother; the Sky or Sun God. Then there are sacred features such as the cosmic tree or tree of life; the mountain and the cave; the Golden Age or Paradise. Among recurrent events and situations are the descent to the underworld; the quest; the exotic origins of the hero; great transits and initiations–from life to death and regeneration. Above and below them all, and often investing them with its tremendous duality, lurks the primordial image of day and night; the children of light and the children of darkness; angels and devils; intellect and the unconscious.

It is obvious that if the Jungian concept of the collective unconscious is accepted it is of the utmost importance within the disputed problem of diffusion versus independent origins that includes so many aspects of culture, including mythology. No one would deny that historical continuity and diffusion were sometimes dominant–as in the spread of religious myths between the many peoples of the ancient Near East and the handing on of at least some elements to the Hebrews, Greeks and Christians. On the other hand the existence of archetypal forms in a collective unconscious would vastly increase the likelihood of similar religious myths and rituals arising independently. It is at least a possibility that deserves far more attention than it usually gets in arguments for and against diffusionism.

During the long course of western man's attempt to learn and understand more about mythology, a pursuit that led him deep into himself, there have been many disputes among theologians, historians, anthropologists, sociologists and psychologists. Inevitably each faction saw itself as children of light and its opponents as children of darkness. Yet in spite of so much disagreement, understanding has vastly increased over the past century and a half. A little should be said about the findings that have been made with so much toil and passion.

First of all it is greatly to be hoped that anyone reading this book is by now prepared to accept the view that myths are to be distinguished from legends, folk tales and other fictions in having a fundamental reality. For some thinkers it may be social, for others psychological and for others again spiritual and transcendental, yet all accept this reality and its immense importance for the well-being of mankind.

Myths tell of sacred beings, human or animal, and of semi-divine heroes. Sometimes they may have been historical figures, but they are absorbed into the archetypal forms of myths. Themes usually concern beginnings, the coming into being of all things from the cosmos and mankind to the smallest details of everyday life.

Another of their most significant characteristics is that myths belong to sacred time, to eternity – what the Australian hunters so beautifully named the Dream Time. Then, too, their power and meaning tends to centre on a sacred place, perhaps a tree, a rock, a fissure whence the ancestors have come from the nether regions, or where a divinity was born, died or created the world. Among simple societies these holy places are often natural features within their own territories. Sometimes there is an historical origin – as for example in Greece where very many of the myths of classical times centre on important sites of the Mycenaean Bronze Age. Local sacred centres might be enhanced by enclosure within a sanctuary, perhaps a rough stone circle, perhaps a great temple. More significantly, a fane might represent the sacred place anywhere – as Egyptian temples stood where the Sun God created the world on the first hillock to rise from the waters of chaos, and as Christian churches stand upon Golgotha. In the same way participants re-enter sacred time with every rite and festival, being once more a part of the eternal beginning of the mythical world.

A festival that illustrates with particular force the inter-penetration of myth and rite, of man and nature and the divine, of the social order and the divine order, is that of the Babylonian New Year. The succession of rites and celebrations that occupied eleven days are known mainly from late Babylonian times but certainly went back at least to the beginning of the 2nd millennium BC. At the heart of its meaning was the annual reinforcement, based on the *Enuma elish* myth of creation, of the defeat of chaos by the forces of order, led by the supreme god of the state. Yet the idea of renewal – of the rebirth of the god, of man, of vegetation and the year – was also central, the god being liberated from confinement in the underword; on a later day the king, his representative, enacted the sacred marriage, probably with a high priestess representing the goddess. The fact that the gods of subject city states were escorted by their kings to Babylon to take their due order of precedence in the festival, reveals the correspondence of divine and earthly hierarchies. The participation of all the people appears in their mourning for the god while he is lost in the underworld, and in the wild rejoicing at his resurrection. Above all the essential part played by myth in the structuring of the festival is emphasised by the reading of the *Enuma elish* as the principal event on the fourth day.

This Babylonian festival was celebrated with tremendous pomp, with kings, orders of priests, officials, specialist crafts-men, all filling their appointed roles. Yet the creation story itself, with the gods shaping the cosmos out of the body of their mother, a being of the primeval waters of chaos, and mankind from one of her lieutenants, is primitive enough. Such contrasts illustrate the dangers of arranging mytholo-gies and their religious expression in an historic scheme. Nevertheless, as already hinted, progressive change can to some extent be identified with evolving types of society.

This book also deals with the myths of non-literate peoples past or present. It can be said that they tend to be more deeply involved with nature than those of more advanced societies, the sacred beings changing freely from animal into human shape and back again. In totemism, too, men trace their origins in the beginnings of sacred time to animal, plant and other natural forms. Yet there is often much subtle spiritual meaning behind such animal ancestors and deities – as, for example, in the Mantis creator spirit of the Bushmen. Indeed, these myths flowing directly from intuitions and archetypal promptings unaffected by conscious elaboration are nearer to pure psychic reality than those of more advanced societies.

Among barbarian peoples, best represented here by the Scandinavians and Celts, animals are still important but have often become the attributes or epiphanies of gods in human form. The mythical stories are likely to make much use of battle, warrior heroes and deities, and the values of an heroic society. Thor is a perfectly appropriate god for such peoples. Yet there, too, are the unchanging archetypes: the tree of life, the serpent, the satanic god, Loki.

In the high civilizations of the Bronze Age world, such as those of Egypt and Mesopotamia, the myths might be affected by conscious speculations concerning origins, identifications with natural forces and so forth. These more evolved myths might then figure in religious rite, as we have seen in Babylonia, or take a more literary form as in the epic of Gilgamesh, in the *Iliad* and *Odyssey* and the biblical *Genesis*.

Another characteristic of the mythologies of the ancient

high civilization, and to some extent those of the New World also, is that they revealed the hierarchical earthly state as a counterpart of the divine cosmos. With this went a tendency for celestial to dominate earthly and chthonic deities, and for the rulers of great states and empires to be identified with sun gods.

While any attempt to relate mythologies to different stages of social evolution is bound to be excessively rough and beset with anomalies (such as the strange persistence of animals in Egyptian religion) one phase at least is quite sharply distinct: that of the present day.

Whatever his point of view, no one can reasonably deny that Christianity supported the spiritual life of Western man on a mythical structure that comprised both historical figures and the greatest of primordial images. Now, largely through the impact of science, these forms have lost their inner potency and the mythology on which we have depended for so long lies shattered.

Often before now myths that once expressed reality have lost their power within men's minds and degenerated into legends, folk tales and superstitions. Yet always, unless the peoples themselves died out, they were replaced by new realities, probably by more exalted ones. Now the collapse is of a different order, brought about not by a quiet withering away that can nourish a fresh growth, but by a positive and devastating attack.

Even now, as Kerenyi has put it, 'Mythology, like the severed head of Orpheus, goes on singing even in death and from afar.' The primordial forms re-appear in secular dress, some of them trivial, some of great moment. The most momentous can be found in communist states where revolution has at once stirred the depths of the psyche and given expression to relatively simple minds. There is no mistaking the proletariat as the host of the children of light, or the devilish aspect of the capitalist. Marx is perhaps one of those supreme sky gods who become remote from everyday affairs, while Lenin with his sacred tomb and his countless idols and ikons is the undisguised father-creator god. These divinities are leading the children of light towards a golden age, a paradise, that is now set in the future. The incident of Chairman Mao swimming in the Yangtse is the very stuff of the minor mythological story.

While their potency lasts, these myths give a strength to communism that is lacking in the disenchanted West. Here we live with a motley of survivals, revivals and archetypal projections that can hardly maintain the eternal struggle against chaos. There is what survives of Christianity; there is the deliberate or unconscious use of mythical themes in literature and the cinema; the faint aura of the sacred that still surrounds royalty, traditional ceremonies and certain charismatic individuals. Although the many divine names incorporated in it are almost forgotten, our calendar still has some power to give shape and meaning to weeks, months and seasons. In this it is noticeable that with the people the (Christmas) tree of life at midwinter and the spring egg of regeneration outlast Christian symbols. New Year rituals, though trivial, still bring some hope of renewal and the return to beginnings.

Among projections, folk heroes like James Dean may be made into dying gods, the pop singer with his rout of tranced or frenzied females is Dionysiac, while 'sex symbols' from full-breasted to twiggy are aspects of the mother-maid goddesses. The desire to identify real places with Atlantis, prevalent even among scholars, surely relates to paradisiacal longings, while the biologists' fondness for drawing evolutionary trees that rise from primeval slime to *Homo sapiens* must be another manifestation of the tree of life.

Cravings left unsatisfied by the disintegration of myth and ritual may find more dangerous satisfactions. Drug-taking can be seen as a drive to attain the Dream Time without effort, and to activate the images of the unconscious without order or meaning. Then there is the revival of superstition and occult magic – from the harmless horoscope to the return of covens and other cultic sects, with animal, and even human, sacrifice. Orpheus' head indeed, but it can sing some dark songs.

The reader of Introductions, if such a person exists, should not be delayed any longer from the great mythologies of the past, so finely presented in words and works of art. These may do more than show the marvellous variety of cultural dress in which the great mythical forms have been clad. Perhaps if he truly yields himself, the reader will find a living response in the depths of his own mind.

The Near East

Mesopotamia

The Sumerians, who first settled southern Mesopotamia about 3400 BC, found themselves in a land of great natural fertility but open to the parching sun and winds and to unpredictable flooding from the rivers Tigris and Euphrates. The condition of their survival and advancement was the ordering of the destructive forces of nature, and the main theme of their mythology thus became the struggle between order and chaos. They organised themselves into theocratic city states under the leadership of the chief priest of the city-god or, in time of emergency, under an appointed ruler. Among the threats to their settled agricultural civilisation, the Sumerians saw the Semitic nomad shepherds and caravaneers from the desert edges of northeast Arabia, represented in myth by Enkidu, and the Iranian highlanders to the east, whose destructive raids were identified with Enlil the storm-god. The last of these, under Cyrus the Great, brought an end to the ancient Mesopotamian civilisation, with the fall of Babylon under the Aramaeans or Chaldeans in 538 BC. Before

then, however, the greatest influence had been Semitic, with the domination of Sargon of Akkad (2242–2186) and his dynasty, until the revival of Sumerian power in the Third Dynasty of Ur in 2044. The next Semitic domination was that of the Amorites (1826–1526). Both Akkadians and Amorites were more inclined to adopt the mythology of the conquered peoples than to supplant it, and this was true too of the Assyrian Empire in northern Mesopotamia (c. 1200 BC till the fall of Nineveh in 612 BC). Indeed, the conquerors spread Mesopotamian ideas throughout the ancient Near East.

The Mesopotamian pantheon was huge and many-faceted, reflecting every aspect of life. But as in real life, it was governed by a supreme hierarchy. At its head was Anu, god of the sky, home of sun and rain clouds, and supreme king, source of order. Anu's executive on earth was Enlil, prototype of the earthly ruler, mediator between the supreme king and the people, bringing them both the benefits of order and calamitous punishment. Enlil was identified with the wind, which in Meso-

potamia brings fertilising rain and dries the floodwaters, but at other times brings dust-storms and locust-swarms to ruin the crops. By extension, Enlil was also identified with the destruction caused by enemies from the steppes or the Iranian highlands.

Enki, god of water, also had a dual character. His union with Ninhursag, mother-earth or cosmic mountain, produced agriculture and its benefits, but these benefits were threatened when Ninhursag cursed her husband for his incestuous adventures with his daughters, various mother-goddesses, and he descended to the underworld, leaving earth parched. Only the intervention of the council of heaven persuaded Ninhursag partially to relent, thus creating the seasonal cycle. The miracle of fertilisation by water led to Enki's being considered god of magic, of wisdom and of justice. In a form of trial by ordeal, people were thrown into the river, and the guilty sank, as did a sacrificial sheep charged with the sins of the community which was annually cast into the waters.

Enki's role as god of wisdom was taken over to some extent under the Amorite domination by Shamash, god of the sun, the all-seeing who daily traversed the firmament and the underworld and defended all against wrongdoers. Sin, the moon-god, was chiefly revered as the measurer of time, the main cult centres being Ur in the south and in the north Harran, on the desert caravan trade route.

As in all civilisations based precariously on herds and agriculture, the mother-goddess was an important figure. Inanna was her Sumerian form, later identified with the Semitic Ishtar, and the celebration of her sacred marriage with the spring vegetation-god Tammuz assured the Sumerians of crop, animal and human fertility. The violence of her love annually destroyed Tammuz and the other lovers who inadequately replaced him (by irrigation) in the dry season. Each year Ishtar sought Tammuz in the underworld to revive him, and with him the fertility of the natural cycle destroyed by their absence in the nether regions. Ishtar's violence was seen too in her role as warrior-goddess, whose cult animal was the lion and who was associated by the warlike Assyrians with their national god Ashur.

In her search for Tammuz, Ishtar escaped from the bondage of the goddess of the underworld, Ereshkigal or Allatu, through a ruse of Ea. Ereshkigal in her turn was

left
Eagle with a lion's head in the 'Tree of Life' pose between two stags, symbols of fertility. The lion was the cult animal of the mother-goddess Innana or Ishtar. Temple lintel from al-Ubaid, near Ur, early second millenium BC. British Museum.

above
Pazuzu, a composite lion and eagle-monster. Such demons were said to populate the desert fringes of civilisation. Some were set to guard the Tree of Life from mortals' approach, others to visit disaster and disease upon men. Bronze amulet. Louvre.

Ishtar, Semitic form of the fertility-goddess. Sculpture from Mari of the early Amorite period, depicting the goddess with a jar: her womb is the never-ending source of the water of life—a role imitated by kings. National Museum, Aleppo.

far right
Adad, Assyrian form of Enlil. He is depicted in this relief as an Assyrian warrior-king mounted on his cult animal, the bull; as storm-god, his weapons are thunderbolts. Like Marduk, he was associated with the Assyrian national god Ashur. Louvre.

dethroned by and married to the solar deity Nergal, who with his weapons of heat, hot desert winds, lightning and plague, symbolised mass slaughter by plague and war.

These deities contrast with the beneficent Nebo, heavenly messenger and god of speech and of writing, which the Sumerians developed, on clay tablets, as early as the middle of the fourth millenium BC. His symbol was the wedge or stylus used in writing on clay.

Another beneficent deity was Marduk. Originally the city-god of Babylon under the Amorites, in the south he took over the functions of Enlil as divine executive and defender of order. (In the north, Adad incorporated Enlil's role under the Amorites, as did Ashur under the Assyrians.) In the spring, the crisis-point of the Mesopotamian agricultural year, the New Year festival of *enuma elish* reflected man's awareness of his limitations in the face of nature, and his assertion that by upholding the divine order god's royal representatives on earth ensured control over the forces of chaos. Marduk (or Enlil) was said each year to be confined by the cosmic forces of disorder in the underworld. His eventual release by the divine advocate Nebo followed upon rites of atonement by the whole people, and abasement and abdication of the king. The rites culminated in Marduk's reinvestiture as king by the council of the gods, his ceremonial union with the fertility-goddess, and the re-establishment of order in nature and in society under the guidance of Marduk's earthly representative.

This order was that determined by the myth of creation, which related how the primordial forces of chaos Apsu and Mother Tiamat bore the other, active, gods of the Mesopotamian pantheon who named (and thus created) the heaven and the earth, parting the waters and creating dry land. After overcoming Apsu by magic, Ea fathered Marduk, who came to be chosen by the divine court as their champion against resentful vengeance of the monstrous forces of chaos. These were assembled by Tiamat under the leadership of Kingu, who held the Tablets of Destiny. After an epic combat, using his weapons of storm-god, Marduk ripped apart Tiamat and seized the Tablets of Destiny from Kingu. Then he completed creation, making half Tiamat's body into the sky, allocating their abodes to the great gods Anu, Enlil and Ea, creating stars and moon and the measurement of time. From the blood of Kingu he created man for the service of the gods, to liberate them from all labour once they had constructed Marduk's great temple-palace on the ziggurat of Babylon (Tower of Babel).

The potentialities and limitations of man, compounded of divine blood but existing for the service of the gods, is reflected in other Mesopotamian myths. Thus Adapa, a priest of Ea, had been taught wisdom by his divine master. When Adapa used his skill to curse the south wind, Anu, incensed that Ea should impart divine wisdom to a mortal, summoned him before the divine court. Ea advised him that the refreshment offered would bring death; but when Adapa refused it, it was revealed that Anu had in fact offered the bread and water of life. Through subtlety and caution—imperfect wisdom—Adapa forfeited the chance of immortality.

Most clearly exemplifying the theme is the myth cycle of Gilgamesh, based on a historical Sumerian king of Uruk about 2850 BC and said to be two-thirds god and one-third man. The companion of his heroic exploits was also of divine origin, the creation of a goddess who fashioned him of clay in the image of the supreme god Anu. But Enkidu was a wild man, living among the beasts of the steppe, until Gilgamesh brought him within the ambit of civilised city life, first socialising him by sending him a temple prostitute with whom to mate, and then overcoming him in an epic wrestling match, after which Enkidu acknowledged Gilgamesh's right to rule and become his friend. Together and with the aid of Shamash, the patron of Gilgamesh, they overcame the giant Huwawa, who guarded the cedars (of Lebanon) growing on the volcanic seat of the gods. After this exploit, Ishtar wooed Gilgamesh, but he resisted her entreaties, knowing that the love of a goddess destroys a mortal man, and that Ishtar's love had even killed the god Tammuz. The goddess spurned persuaded Anu to send a seven-year drought and famine in the form of the Bull of Heaven, the destructive power of Nergal, and threatened to release the dead from the underworld to consume the living. But Gilgamesh demonstrated his power as king to ensure fertility for his kingdom. With Enkidu, he killed and dismembered the Bull of Heaven, offering its heart to his patron Shamash, and returned to Uruk and the celebration of his triumph by chanting women. Enlil and the council of the gods avenged the Bull of Heaven by striking Enkidu with mortal sickness. The hero thus entered Irkalla, the place of no return, not nobly in heroic exploit, but ingloriously by disease.

In mourning his friend, Gilgamesh turned to the quest for immortal life. He made the arduous journey to the outflowing of the rivers at the edge of the world to visit the former king Utnapishtim and his wife. They had been granted eternal life by Ea as a token of the wisdom he had taught Utnapishtim. This had enabled him to obey Ea's instructions for secret construction of an ark and thereby save himself and his household, wild and tame animals, together with seeds from a flood sent by Enlil to destroy mankind and terrorise the gods. Though Utnapishtim had saved life on earth, Enlil insisted that he and his wife alone of mortals should be granted immortal life, and that it should be lived in remote exile. Gilgamesh therefore had many obstacles to surmount on his journey: the scorpion-men guarding the mountains at the edge of the earth; the mountain forests with their jewelled trees; the blandishments of a woman met by the seashore beyond the mountains who urged contentment with the pleasures of the flesh; the waters of death which skill and the help of the ferryman Urshanabi enabled him to traverse unharmed. All in vain: Utnapishtim too advised Gilgamesh to abandon his quest—his own eternal life was one of inactivity and boredom. Man is not made for immortality, and Utnapishtim proved it by challenging Gilgamesh to remain awake for a week. Of all his ordeals, Gilgamesh could not triumph here: and he who cannot defy sleep cannot defy death. Utnapishtim nevertheless told Gilgamesh how to obtain from beneath the waters a plant of rejuvenation. This he obtained but it was promptly stolen from him by a serpent. Thus snakes acquired the power to be born anew by sloughing their skin. The tragic irony of man's aspirations was underlined. Finally, unable to bring Enkidu the plant of life, Gilgamesh sought him in the underworld, but the task was impossible. Through Ea's help, Enkidu was brought to a final meeting with his friend, but his dismal message was that the horrors of Irkalla were mitigated for the valorous only by the presence of parents and wife.

Kings, alone of mortals, partook to some extent in divine power, for their claim to rule (especially when they had come to the throne by inheritance rather than because of military or political choice) depended on proving their ability to channel divine benefits to the people. The king was not considered divine himself; and he had to prove his merit before the gods, as did Etana, who flew up to heaven on an eagle to present himself and to seek the 'plant of birth'. When the gods recognised the king's claims they commissioned him to establish law and justice in his kingdom, as a condition of his power. Sargon of Akkad claimed to have been recognised by and received the love of Ishtar (perhaps in reality he was favoured by a priestess of Ishtar) while employed as

temple gardener. It may be that he was 'gardener' of the Tree of Life, sometimes used as Ishtar's symbol, sometimes as that of Tammuz. His legend would thus confirm his potency in a Mesopotamian king's most important role in assuring fertility and abundance in his land.

Canaan

The land known in the Bible as Canaan consisted of Palestine and Syria, including its coastal area, Phoenicia–a constellation of trading ports linking and receiving the influence of the cultural centres of Egypt and Mesopotamia. In terms of belief and myth the greater influence came from Mesopotamia, where related Semitic peoples absorbed Sumerian culture. The mountainous inland topography fostered tribal dislocation and independence, with small city-states centred on pockets of fertile land watered by heavy winter rains and summer dews, and with numerous springs for local irrigation. Natural crops included wild wheat, vines, olives and pine and cedar forests. Life cannot be easy in any primitive agricultural community, but it was less subject to cataclysm than in Mesopotamia, and this is reflected in a less dramatic mythology. The Canaanites were less concerned to understand cosmic forces than to placate the gods and ensure agricultural and human fertility.

At the head of the heavenly court held on the Mount of Assembly (Armageddon) was El the Creator, known as the Bull and also as the Compassionate, supreme fount of justice, and called the father of the king. This refers to his devolution of power to Baal, the executive of heaven especially in the workings of nature. Baal's relationship to El was the prototype for that of the earthly king to the gods. Except in mythology determining social relationships and the maintenance of order, El was inactive.

Baal, 'He who mounts the Clouds', was seen as a warrior actively bestriding the world, and the heavens. As the Thunderer, god of winter storms and lightning, his helmet bore the horns of a bull, his mace a sprouting cedar tree, as befitted a rain-god bringing fertility, son of the corn-god Dagan. He was also known as Hadad, identified with the Mesopotamian Adad or Enlil. Like Tammuz, he was a dying and rising god of vegetation.

Nergal, a solar deity, who conquered Ereshkigal in her underworld kingdom, becoming god of mass death by war and plague. His breath, the desert wind, and the monstrous Bull of Heaven aided him in destruction. Terracotta relief from Kish. Ashmolean Museum.

The New Year festival in Canaan was held in the autumn. It corresponded to the crisis-point in Canaanite agriculture, when after five months of summer drought, with the final harvesting completed, thoughts turned to prospects for the next year's crops, and the necessity of heavy rain to soften the ground for early sowing. Without such rain, there could be no prosperity next year: fertility and order in nature would be overcome by sterility. Baal as prototype king was chief protagonist in the mythological struggle between these forces, and his role was played by the human king in rites designed to ensure fertility.

In this struggle, as recounted in the texts discovered at Ras Shamra (ancient Ugarit), the authority of El and his heavenly council was challenged by the overweening Yamm, Prince Sea and Ocean Current, representing primordial chaos. El was so far cowed that he agreed to hand over Baal in tribute to the upstart, thus admitting that his royal executive was incapable of imposing divine order on the universe. But Baal as the active god would not submit so easily: supported only by the divine artificer, who fashioned weapons dedicated to the overthrow of Yamm, he engaged in epic combat with the enemy of divine order, slew Lotan (Leviathan), the seven-headed primeval serpent of the depths, conquered Yamm, and diverted the waters to fruitful use. His victory was hailed by the goddess Athtarat or Astarte, Canaanite counterpart of Ishtar. Baal had subjugated nature to fertility, he had proved his efficacy as king for one more year. At the instance of Asherah, the mother-goddess who in Canaanite imagery takes the place of the Tree of Life, his power was celebrated with the building of his House on Mount Saphon by the divine artificer, using the cedars of Lebanon, precious stones, gold and silver. The building was completed with the installation of Baal and the opening of the roof shutter, whereupon the heavens opened, thunder announced the onset of the heavy autumn rains. Baal proclaimed his might, threatening to rout Mot, god of death and sterility.

But Baal's triumph was not assured: with the spring sirocco heralding summer drought, he yielded to his enemy. After mating with a heifer (the bull was his cult animal), he descended to Mot's underworld kingdom, taking with him to the House of Corruption his clouds and his rain, and three daughters or concubines, plump abundance, dew and rain. Mourning for the death of Baal, similar to that for Tammuz in Mesopotamia, was led by El and by Baal's sister Anat, who like Ishtar

combined the roles of fertility-goddess and goddess of war. Guided by Shapash, the sun-goddess, on her nightly journey through the underworld, Anat sought and found the body of Baal for burial. Athtar, god of the Venus-star and of irrigation, originally a deity of Syrian desert tribes, was installed on Baal's vacant throne on Mount Saphon, but could not fill the great god's role, and was demoted. Anat once more descended to the underworld, begging Mot to release Baal, but he refused. At this crisis-point Anat became an avenging fury, seizing Mot, killing, dismembering and grinding him with a millstone, then scattering the remains to be devoured by the birds and wild animals. Baal was revived and wrought further destruction in the underworld, while Anat continued in gory exultation by slaughtering hordes of young warriors in her temple. Death and destruction were the prelude to fertility, to the celebration of a successful harvest, when Baal returned from the underworld. Then the skies rained oil, the wadis ran with honey, the mountains dripped sweet wine, and the hills flowed with milk. Even this victory was not secure: just as Baal overcame death, so Mot renewed his challenge every year, and especially on the seventh, perhaps a sabbatical year when the fields lay fallow and the forces of sterility were allowed to exhaust themselves.

Fertility could never be taken for granted, in agriculture, or in human life. Misfortune in the royal house was particularly serious. Thus King Krt, when all his offspring died, begot another family, the eldest, heir to the throne, being suckled by the goddesses Athirat and Anat. But he offended Athirat and was struck ill, so that injustice and sterility stalked the land. Only the intervention of El restored the king to health and brought divine order to the kingdom.

In the myth of King Daniel (Dn'il), the childless king was granted the blessing of a son by El, through the intercession of Baal, so that the son might maintain the traditions and cohesion of the community and the link through established ritual with the gods and the benefits they brought. Aqht, the ideal prince, was born, and on reaching manhood received a bow created by the Divine Artificer. The goddess Anat, coveting the bow, offered Aqht first money and then immortality in return for it, but he did not believe her promises and refused. Spurned, the fertility-goddess brought about the death of Aqht and loss of the bow, followed by a seven-year drought and famine, the period of mourning underlined rather than expurgated by the bloody vengeance wreaked upon

Anat's assassin by Aqht's sister, the Maiden. The resolution of the country's misfortunes came not from this but from King Daniel's ability to dispense justice in accordance with divine law as son of El, and his success was marked by the birth of a new heir. Thereafter, he could sit at the outflowing of the two streams (the fount of abundance), on the holy mountain, the earthly executive of El, the wise and the just. His throne, at the right hand of Baal, was guarded by winged sphinxes like those guarding the Tree of Life, and like the cherubim in Hebrew mythology.

Israel

That monotheism does not preclude an active mythology is amply attested by an examination of themes in the Bible. Indeed, the mythology of the Hebrews relating both to history and to messianic hopes is so manifold and so well known through the scriptures that space permits examples only to be given here. These myths were partly derived from the cultural heritage of the component peoples of the Hebrew nation, partly picked up from surrounding peoples in their wanderings and after their settlement in Palestine. They explain the changes of political fortune of the Hebrews; but equally their elaboration was encouraged by developing belief in the transcendance of God and growth of mythology surrounding his representatives on earth.

The patriarchs of Israel originated among the Aramaeans in northern Mesopotamia. They belonged to nomad tribes, and had intermarried with Kenites (smiths). After their expulsion from Mesopotamia they wandered south, bringing with them Mesopotamian ideas about the origins of the universe, about the Flood, and mythology laying patterns for social and political relationships, and especially kingship. These origins coloured many early beliefs about God: like Mesopotamian and Canaanite deities, He manifested his power by miracles affecting nature. Thus in Exodus He appeared at Sinai as a pillar of cloud, smoke and earthquake (perhaps partly under the influence of the Kenites, for as smiths their livelihood depended on fire); in rescuing the Hebrews from the pursuit of the Egyptians, He parted the waters of the Red Sea (Sea of Papyrus Reeds); and He prolonged the hours of daylight and cast down stones from heaven to annihilate the Amorites fleeing from Joshua (*Joshua* 10).

Their personal experiences on expulsion from Mesopotamia also affected the emphasis given to certain mythological themes. For example, the theme of Adam (primeval man); the Tree of Life and the Tree of Knowledge; the temptation by the serpent (incarnation of the powers of chaos in Canaanite belief); and the expulsion from Eden (denial of divine wisdom to

man, as in the myth of Adapa, but also an image of their own exile from the settled prosperity of Mesopotamia). The story of Cain and Abel reflects the hostility of settled farmers and nomad herdsmen and smiths, 'Cain' being related to 'Kenite'. Later references to the Tower of Babel (a Babylonian ziggurat) may be interpreted as sour grapes.

Events experienced by the Hebrews alone were of even greater importance. The deliverance from slavery in Egypt, accompanied by natural portents marking out the Hebrews as the Chosen People, such as their exemption from the plagues affecting fertility of land, beasts, and the Egyptian people and the parting of the Red Sea, was dramatically portrayed as the confrontation between the Pharaoh representing evil and Moses as leader of God's people. The Hebrews' special position was crystallised in the theophany at Sinai (probably really elsewhere) and the Covenant, in which a code of laws, moral, political and social, was linked to the promise of a fertile homeland. Historical experience, dramatised for those who had not experienced it personally or in their own family, thus became a mythological basis for national cohesion.

The Deliverance and Covenant were celebrated at the Feast of Tabernacles in the autumn. Corresponding in time to the Canaanite New Year festival, this cele-

left
Amorite king about to perform a sacrifice.
The importance of the king's role in
transmitting divine benefits is shown by
his size, though Mesopotamian kings
were not themselves considered divine.
Eighteenth-century BC fresco from the
palace at Mari, on the mid-Euphrates.
Louvre.

right
Worshipper praying for Hammurabi
(1724–1682), most famous king of
Babylon of the Amorite period, who was
commissioned to institute his code of laws
by the sun-god Shamash as a token of
his right to rule. Gold-covered bronze
statuette. Louvre.

Sargon of Akkad, who justified his assumption of power by claiming to be the son of an *enitum*, or sacred prostitute, presumably by the king taking the god's role in a sacred marriage—thus claiming royal descent and divine association. Iraq Museum.

opposite
Statuette of a king presenting a sacrifice. At the spring New Year festival in which the king impersonated Marduk as champion of order against chaos, atonement through sacrifice was the prelude to renewal of just rule and abundance. Louvre.

bration had and has many features of a fertility rite. Thus, as in the Baal myth, God's goodwill manifested itself in abundance, in the 'land of milk and honey'. The New Year was the 'Day of the Lord', when He prevailed over the forces of Chaos. In early belief, God Himself was made manifest: thus in Job, the sign that His effective rule was once more established was a great thunderstorm. With the establishment of the dynasty of the House of David, the power of God was invested in the Kings of Judah, and the Feast of Tabernacles reaffirmed God's support of the Hebrews through their royal house.

When the Kingdom fell, this imagery was gradually transferred to a more purely spiritual plane, especially under the leadership of the high priests. The contrast of the Chosen People and their opponents grew from political opposition into a conflict of good and evil. God was thought to rule in heaven with a council of angels, including sixty-three who each represented a nation (Michael represented Israel) and four Archangels surrounding his throne: Michael, bringer of good tidings and opponent of Sammael (Satan);

Gabriel, God's strength; Raphael, the power of healing; and Uriel, God's radiance, who ruled over hell. The essence of angels was fire, and of the ninefold hierarchy, seraphim were angels of love, light and purity and cherubim were angels of knowledge who guarded the gates of Paradise, excluding man from Eden. Angels fed upon manna, the food of Adam and Eve before the Fall. This heavenly host, mediators and messengers between God and man, were supported on earth by heroes such as Samson, whose exploits against the political and religious enemies of Israel can be likened to those of Gilgamesh and Heracles.

Ranged against the forces of good were the personifications of evil such as Beelzebub (Baal), Leviathan (primeval chaos), and above all Satan. Evil was equated with Israel's political enemies, for example by Nahum with Assyrian Nineveh, and with their gods. Satan, a late development of the third century BC, was originally one of the 'heavenly host'—derived from gods worshipped by other peoples. At first considered merely inferior to the God of Israel, they were made his executives; but when they were later branded as ineffective, presumptuous, false gods, they were consigned to the infernal pit. Thus Satan was later described as a seraph charged by God to put temptation in men's way, to test them and to give them freedom of choice. Satan's effectiveness in leading men astray led to his fall. To maintain his ultimate purpose God intervened, relegating Satan to the depths of Sheol (hell).

A mythological structure of stark polarities developed, perhaps due to influence of similar notions in Egyptian and Zoroastrian mythology. God's moral ascendency was still described in terms of nature imagery: thus lightning triumphed over the black waters and the creatures of the watery depths, such as Leviathan (Lotan), converting them into beneficent agents of fertility; or He was described as light shining in the darkness. Nevertheless, the Feast of Tabernacles now celebrated God's general support in the vicissitudes of history: proof was not needed in yearly fertility. The stage was set for the development of messianic and apocalyptic beliefs.

According to these, the reign of the Messiah, the anointed representative on earth of God the Divine King, will see the eclipse of the political enemies of Israel and the forces of evil. The 'beast' will be thrown into a lake of fiery brimstone, his minions consumed by the birds, and Satan, the serpent, cast in chains into the bottomless pit. Those faithful ones who

have died before this judgment of God and establishment of His order will become the subjects of the Messianic kingdom in the First Resurrection. This will continue for a thousand years, after which Satan will rise again. He will muster the powers of evil and destruction under Gog and Magog, but in a great conflict these will be finally routed by fire from heaven. Alternatively, the Messiah and his subjects will die and silence will reign until a new creation: a new heaven, a new hell (the fiery Gehenna to which unrepentant sinners are once more to be consigned), and a new earth, where the virtuous will enjoy the Garden of Eden, where the Tree of Life which will bring peace to nations will grow by the source of living water. The new Jerusalem will be a city of eternal light and peace.

The Kingdom of God in Christian imagery

Historically, the kings and judges of Israel justified their rule by their support of the Covenant, which recognised equal consideration for all members of the sacred community. Their power was upheld by assent of the elders and prophets, especially at times of crisis. The ruler thus identified himself with God's purpose, as God's representative on earth in the struggle against the powers of Chaos and evil. The kings of the House of David 'stood at the right hand of God': their task was to maintain social order and justice, to defend the weak, and to maintain the physical wellbeing (fertility) of the land. To do this the king acted as representative of the people, 'Son of Man', leading them to knowledge of God's will and in rites of atonement and fasting.

The development of this tradition in Christianity is obvious, as are also the survivals of nature mythology derived from other peoples in the sort of miracles whereby Jesus Christ demonstrated his identity – the power of God to supply food and drink, to calm the waters, to heal the sick, etc. The Messianic priest-ruler as 'Son of Man' or archetypal man, Adam, tends the Tree of Life in the divine garden. He celebrates the triumph of his rule by feasting with the virtuous, sometimes upon the flesh of Behemoth the hippopotamus and Leviathan, the crocodile or primeval serpent, incarnating the forces of evil, as in Egyptian and other mythologies. Here mythological imagery supports religious belief in conveying hopes of an ineffable Divine Order.

right
Ram reaching up to the fruits of the Tree of Life, symbol of Ishtar. Figurine from the royal graves of Ur. Featuring often in palace architecture, the Tree of Life symbol seeks to achieve and attests the king's potency in fertility rites.
British Museum.

below
Royal investiture, from the Amorite palace at Mari. The date palms represent the Tree of Life, guarded by winged genii. Between them, Ishtar grants the king his power to promote fertility, while beneath gush the four streams of living water.
Louvre.

left, above
The Tree of Life, with the combined motifs of Mesopotamian date palm and Egyptian lotus, tended by a figure with Egyptian royal headdress. The king as guardian of fertility is a motif common to many mythologies. Phoenician ivory from the Assyrian palace at Nimrud. British Museum.

left, below
Phoenician ivory plaque from the Assyrian palace at Nimrud. Assyrian conquests in Canaan, and then in Egypt, and Phoenicia's far-flung trading colonies—contributing the ivory—made Tyre and Sidon cultural entrepôts. British Museum.

below
Female head of Phoenician workmanship found at Nimrud, depicting the fertility-goddess, known almost interchangeably in Canaan as Astarte-Athtarat (whose cult centre was the timber port Byblos), as Anat, avenger of Baal, and as Asherah, the fount of life.

23

right
The capture of a wild bull. Instead of the Mesopotamian and Hittite stag, the Canaanites and other Mediterranean peoples chose the bull as fertility symbol. Both El and Baal were associated with the animal. Greek gold cup, c. 1500 BC. National Museum, Athens.

above
Boar adorning an axe found at Ras Shamra (Ugarit). In his descent to the underworld, Baal was accompanied by seven boar-hunters. The boar was accursed in Semitic mythology for killing Tammuz (the Greek Adonis). Probably Mitannian, c. 1600 BC. National Museum, Aleppo.

below
Excavated ruins of a Canaanite temple of the fourteenth century BC. The establishment of the god in his house or palace, in the case of Baal on Mount Saphon (Jebel al-Agra in north Syria), was the apogee of the New Year fertility rites, and heralded the welcome autumn rains.

below, right
The spring of Jericho where, in a motif common to all ancient Near Eastern beliefs, God through his prophet Elisha manifested his power by creating sweet waters, saying 'there shall not be from thence any more death or barren land'. (*2 Kings II*. 19–22)

left
Looking across the Gulf of Aqaba to Midian in the northern Hejaz, the nearest volcanic area to Sinai. Moses married a woman of a Midianite tribe of nomad smiths (Kenites), and thus may have imported the notion of a volcanic holy mountain.

below
Hebrew slaves moulding bricks in Egypt. Fifteenth-century BC mural painting from the tomb of Rekhmire near Thebes. Memory of this bondage, reducing all Hebrews ('displaced persons') to equality, was the cohesive force binding the new nation after their escape.

right

Palace of Ahab, King of Israel during the early ninth century BC., when the capital was Samaria in northern Palestine. The introduction of Baal-worship was made through his wife, the Phoenician Jezebel, and he notably lacked prophetic support for his rule.

below

The resurrection of the 'dry bones' of the virtuous dead of Israel, and their reception into the Messianic kingdom, a second creation where God's purpose would not be frustrated by evil, as visualised by Ezekiel (*Ezekiel* 37). From the synagogue at Dura Europos, northern Mesopotamia (2nd century AD).

27

Egypt

Ancient Egypt, which can be defined as that part of the Nile valley made fertile by the annual floods, was a natural geographical enclave shut off to the east and west by deserts. Given political organisation, especially necessary in the south, it was potentially a land of abundance, of the good life–contrasting starkly with the sterility of the desert, which the Egyptians saw as the land of the dead, where the hot sand naturally preserved the bodies of the departed. The most salient features of Egyptian mythology reflect the effort to preserve the benefits of life after death and the need to maintain a social organisation that could reap the benefits of the Nile. Agriculture could flourish along the whole length of the river, and could support a number of different cities, each with its own cult centre. Shifts of political power over a long history had their reflection in corresponding changes in mythology, the tendency being to syncretism rather than to suppression of one cult by another.

Throughout history, however, true prosperity existed only when Upper and Lower Egypt were united. The first historical unification and founding of the First Dynasty occurred about 3000 BC under Narmer of Menes, king of Upper Egypt and follower of the falcon-god Horus, identified with the sky and considered a leader and protector in war. The so-called 'animal deities' were very early anthropomorphised: worshipped for the qualities the Egyptians imagined them to possess. Menes made his first capital Thinis in Middle Egypt, near Abydos, the cult centre of Osiris, god of fertility and of the dead, who was already worshipped throughout Egypt. Menes later built a new capital, Memphis, in Lower Egypt, near Heliopolis, cult centre of the sun-god Ra, whose followers had apparently achieved a unification also, in prehistoric times. Mythology soon connected Horus, Osiris and Ra, linking them closely with the pharaoh as divinely appointed intermediary with the gods, dispenser of justice and of a social code that would assure fertility.

In Egyptian ritual, gods were treated like kings; soon kings came to be treated like gods, and the outward forms surrounding them, and the artistic representation of ritual, were fixed as early as the Second Dynasty. The early mythology supporting this ritual had to relate all gods, of whatever provenance, to the welfare of an agricultural people. And it had to explain the connection of Ra, god of the sun, considered the enemy of the farmer, to the pharaoh who as chief priest assured the fertility of the land, good order on earth being the guarantee of similar blessings in the afterlife–and vice versa. Thus the welfare of the pharaoh's soul after death was of capital importance for all his former subjects, and much of Egyptian mythology was concerned with bolstering the pharaoh's authority through the earthly hierarchy and the system of land tenure. The earthly hierarchy was chosen from among the priesthood, high priests of the various cult centres standing in for the pharaoh both in religious cult and in secular function as governors of provinces. The hereditary priesthood of Amon-Ra in Upper Egypt, having claimed virtual autonomy in the Eighteenth Dynasty, were brought to heel only after many centuries by the imposition of the pharaohs' eldest sons as high priests.

The task of mythology was to relate all gods of national importance to fertility, to the sun as royal emblem, and to creation. For the most part, the priesthood of the different cult centres asserted superiority by declaring their own god as both connected with the sun cult of the royal house and as central to creation. Their god could therefore claim suzerainty by virtue of heredity, as did the pharaoh on earth. The mythology to support these claims mostly centres on the nature-gods, 'Gods of the First Time', or golden age when men and gods lived together on earth.

In the beginning a primordial ocean called Nun, a featureless expanse of stagnant water, filled the universe, like a cosmic egg. Just as the Nile floodwaters receded, leaving behind fertile land, so a primeval hill rose out of Nun. Each cult centre claimed to be sited on this hill, the creation mythologies being essentially variants of that evolved at Heliopolis in support of Ra, the sun climbing to its zenith. According to this Atum (a predynastic sun-god, later depicted as an old man and identified with the setting sun) was that hill, or created it. Merged at Heliopolis as Ra-Atum, he was described as a Bennu-bird or phoenix, who alighted on the benben stone, represented as an obelisk, to disperse the darkness of Nun. Atum's cult animal was the bull

Mnevis, as befitted a creator. He created a son, Shu, god of wind or air, the life principle, and a daughter, Shu's consort Tefnut, goddess of lifegiving dew and the principle of world order, also known as Mayet (though in a fierce solar form represented as a lioness).

One day, Ra-Atum lost Shu and Tefnut in the dark wastes of Nun. He sent his Eye, which was physically separable from him, to search for them. By the time the Eye returned with Shu and Tefnut, Ra-Atum had replaced it with another. To mollify the fury of the first Eye, he placed it on his forehead where it could rule the whole world he was about to create. This fierce Eye, or *udjat*, an aspect of the burning sun, was associated with the cobra-goddess Buto or Edjo from Lower Egypt, protectress of the kingdom and shown in the form of the *uraeus* on the foreheads of the pharaohs. Atum's tears of joy at regaining his children became men, who were to populate the world.

Shu and Tefnut begot the twins Geb and Nut. Nut was the sky-goddess, who was pictured as a cow standing over the earth and supported by other deities, with the barque of the sun sailing along her starry belly; or as an elongated woman bending over the earth, Geb, and separated from him by her father Shu. Geb, the earth-god, lay prone with vegetation sprouting from his back, in the centre of a circular ocean; or reaching up to Tefnut and thus forming the mountains. The ocean, or Nile, flowed through his black fertile lands surrounded by red desert, and into the underworld, abode of the dead, through which the night-barque of the sun sailed. Geb was sometimes called the goose that laid the cosmic egg. Nut, originally a mother-goddess, was said as the heavenly cow to bear the sun anew each morning. This rising sun was symbolised by Khepri, a great scarab beetle rolling before it a ball of dung in which it had laid its eggs and from which would burst forth life. From this association, Nut became protectress of the dead. She was the mother by Geb of

The vulture-goddess Mut. During the New Kingdom her temple at Luxor was the scene of an annual sacred marriage ceremony with Amon-Ra, who sailed from his temple at Karnak to visit her. Late Eighteenth Dynasty. Cairo Museum.

four of the principal deities of the First
Time: Osiris, Set, Isis and Nephthys.
Horus, archetype of the pharaohs, was the
son of Isis and Osiris, or was sometimes
called the son of Nut.

The priests of Memphis, whose high god
was Ptah, adapted the Heliopolitan cosmogony by calling each of the great gods
of the First Time an aspect of Ptah, who
was not only the creator of the world, but
the primeval mound itself. Memphite
belief sometimes replaced Ra entirely as
the agent of Ptah's will by Thoth, god of
the moon and of wisdom, whom they
called the Tongue, and Horus, who was
the Heart. Egyptians considered the heart
to be the seat of the mind or intelligence,

and the tongue to be the seat of command
or power. Ptah was thus seen at Memphis
as the establisher of moral order and of
royal power. He was generally considered
patron of craftsmen, artists and magicians.

At Hermopolis in Upper Egypt, aspects
of watery chaos depicted as frogs and
serpents were said to have created the
world and ruled over it during a golden
age; their power continued after their
death, for they caused the Nile to flow
and the sun to rise. The Hermopolitans
held that the world hatched from an egg
laid by Geb as a goose, or by Thoth as
an ibis; or from a lotus flower bearing Ra,
or Khepri. As the lotus opens and closes
every day, it symbolised the sun.

The Theban cosmogony was evolved late, in support of Amon, chiefly known as Amon-Ra, the high god of Thebes in Upper Egypt when it came to prominence about 2000 BC and in the New Kingdom (1546–1085 BC) when it was capital of reunited Egypt after the expulsion of the Hyksos. Amon was associated with the air as an invisible, dynamic force; like Ptah, he was made into a supreme and invisible creator, incorporating the powers of all the other gods. Thebes was said to be the first city and model for all others, and as the Eye of Ra oversaw and ruled them; it was also claimed as birthplace of Osiris. As creator-god, Amon was associated with the virile goose and the ram. Later, as

political and military leader, he incorporated Mont, with his bull symbol, together with the solar attributes of Ra, as father of the pharaohs and 'king of the gods'. Amon-Ra was also known as vizier of the poor, and accorded a personal worship as upholder of justice and compassionate father unusual in Egyptian tradition. The extremes of this and of the wealth and influence of the Amon-Ra priesthood led to the famous reaction under Akhenaten, who introduced state worship of an abstract force symbolised by the Aten, the sun-disk, forsaking the numerous and magnificent temples dedicated to Amon-Ra. Though Amon-Ra was later reinstated, especially under the

soldier-pharaoh Horemheb, no single god was ever again singled out for exclusive worship by the pharaohs. Military expansion and foreign influence weakened the old order and the solar cult of the pharaohs; the personal faith of Osirianism gained ground. Amon-Ra's consort was the Theban vulture-goddess Mut, Great Sorceress, sometimes confused with another vulture-goddess Nekhebet, protectress of Upper Egypt, also a mother-goddess and consort of Hapi, the Nile.

Other male deities were locally described as creator-gods, such as Khnum the Divine Potter at Elephantine; and Min, rain-god of the delta, Hapi, god of the Nile, and Bes, a Sudanese patron of women and

childbirth, were generally worshipped as fertility-gods. But mother-goddesses presented more important alternatives to the cosmogonies of the great cult centres. Among the oldest was Neith from Sais in the Delta, mother of the gods as personification of the waters of chaos, wife of Khnum, guardian of men in life and in death, sorceress and arbitrator of the gods and, in the Twenty-sixth Dynasty when she became chief state deity, mother of the pharaohs.

More important throughout history was Hathor, a great sky-goddess represented as a cow. The daughter and wife of Ra, she was confused with her mother Nut and was popular as goddess of music, joy, love and motherhood, and later welcomed souls to the underworld and sustained them on their journey to the Hall of Judgment. She derived dynastic associations from being wife of Horus the Elder at Edfu and mother of Horus the Younger. Hathor was also feared: as the Eye of Ra, she had taken the form of the lioness-deity Sekhmet to punish rebellious mankind, and would have destroyed the entire race if Ra had not made her drunk.

This was but one incident in the reign of Ra as first king and founder of a divine dynasty which laid the pattern for earthly rule. In his prime, Ra successfully reigned as upholder of good order and justice, symbolised by Mayet. During this golden age he maintained a constant presence on earth. But when he became old, gods and

then men rebelled against him. Having re-established order with the help of Hathor, he withdrew to the heavens on Nut's back, handing over the throne to Thoth, god of the moon and of wisdom and writing, who had been herald and judge in his kingdom.

Thereafter, Ra's daily routine was immutable. Rising in the morning from the mountains bounding the earth, he traversed the heavens in a boat manned by other gods, including Geb and Thoth. Each day Apep, the serpent of chaos, tried to obstruct the solar barque, but was overcome, sometimes, it was said, by Set, who later himself personified evil in Osirian belief. Storms or eclipses were interpreted as temporary victories of Apep. At the approach to the western horizon Ra grew old, as he had during his reign on earth. He then changed to another boat, the night-barque of the sun, manned by stars, the souls of the dead, and at the prow the wolf-god Upuaut, Opener of the Ways. Ra became ram-headed Auf, the dead sun-king, during a twelve-hour journey through the provinces of the underworld. During it he was challenged by the monstrous serpents and demons who threatened the existence of the dead, and once more by his eternal enemy the serpent Apep, who was eventually pierced with knives and bound in chains. Steadily Auf passed from cavern to cavern, shedding brief light on the inhabitants of the underworld, who after his departure fell back

into the agony of darkness. Finally at dawn he emerged to be reunited with Khepri and to traverse the heavens once more.

Ra's death and rebirth were taken as symbolic of life and death and inevitable rebirth for the pharaohs, especially after the Fifth Dynasty when pharaohs were considered to be actual sons of Ra (by union with the wife of a priest of Ra). And just as it was essential for the well-being of Egypt that the sun should rise every morning, so it was essential that by prayer the people should ensure safe passage through the perils of the underworld for the soul of the pharaoh, their mediator with Ra. Thus was laid the mythological pattern for the all-important relationship between pharaoh and people.

Ra's immediate successors as king were divine. The first was either Thoth, or more commonly Shu, whose chief activity was in building temples to the gods throughout the land. Apep and his sons, who dwelt in the desert, were unable to storm these shrines, but after their repulse by the gods Shu lost his sight and misfortunes befell the kingdom. Finally Geb violated his mother Tefnut, Shu's wife, and seized the kingdom. Darkness and storms filled the land for nine days, but finally Geb was acknowledged king. He remained weak, however, and was advised to place the *uraeus* serpent, Ra's Eye, on his head as symbol of royal might. But the *uraeus* killed Geb's attendants and afflicted him with fever, incurable except with the *aart* of Ra (later transformed into the crocodile-god Sebek). Thereafter, Geb resolved to reign justly: he constructed temples, established nomes and settlements, and built towns, walls, and irrigation works. After living 1,773 years, Geb abdicated in favour of his sons Osiris and Set, the North being assigned to Osiris and the South to Set.

Osiris, an ancient corn-deity, probably from Syria, instructed his subjects, who were still barbarous cannibals, in the ways of civilisation, teaching them what to eat and how to raise crops. He drew up laws and religious rites for them, helped by his scribe Thoth, who invented arts and sciences and gave names to things. Then he decided to bring civilisation to other countries, and embarked on peaceful conquest, leaving his wife Isis to rule in his place. Isis was a skilled enchantress and at the end of Ra's reign had extorted from him his secret name, and thus his power, causing it to be transmitted to her son Horus (to become archetype of the pharaoh). She had helped in her husband's civilising mission by teaching women the domestic arts and by instituting marriage. Her wise rule during her husband's absence was resented by her scheming brother, the warlike Set, who coveted the entire kingdom. At the celebrations on Osiris' return, Set inveigled him into a chest, which he cast into the Nile floodwaters. Isis sought the chest and eventually found it at Byblos in Phoenicia, where a tamarisk tree which had grown round it formed the pillar of the king's palace. By her magic arts she recovered Osiris' body and conceived a son while mourning over it in the form of a kite. This son, Horus, assured the succession to the throne of Lower Egypt.

Before his birth, however, Set discovered the body of Osiris hidden in the marsh reeds of the Delta, and cast it in fourteen pieces along the length of the

Nile. Again, patiently, Isis sought out the dismembered body, and found every piece except the phallus, eaten by the accursed Nile crab. With the help of Thoth, her sister Nephthys, who had fled her husband Set, and the jackal-headed Anubis, son of Nephthys and Osiris, whom Isis had adopted, Isis restored her husband to life by the rites of embalmment. But Osiris now preferred eternal life as king of the underworld, leaving the earthly throne to his son Horus.

Horus, originally a falcon-deity representing the sky, was early solarised as royal god and called son of Ra, or most commonly Ra-Harakhte. The winged sun-disk over temple gates symbolised his role as Horus of Edfu or Horus Behdety, when he slew plotters against Ra. The solar Horus was known as Horus the Elder to distinguish him from Horus the son of Osiris, Harsiesis; but the two forms were constantly confused as Osirianism became the paramount faith, and Horus of Edfu became the vanquisher also of Set. When Horus succeeded to the throne of Osiris, the old enmity imagined between Set and Horus son of Ra was transferred. According to this Geb had adjudged Set a bad ruler and had reassigned Upper Egypt to Horus. After an epic battle, the case had gone to arbitration by the gods, Ra sup-

porting Set as powerful and experienced defender of the throne, and the other gods supporting the young Horus against Set's accusations of illegitimacy. Horus won, for Isis cheated Set into admission of guilt, and Set was exiled to the heavens where as Great Bear he became god of winds and storm; or to the desert borders, as personification of aridity and god of foreigners (he became the warlike god of the Hyksos pharaohs who ruled 1678–1570). Horus re-established the reign of justice and was the model for all pharaohs thereafter, each taking the title 'Living Horus'.

The final argument that had decided the tribunal of the gods in favour of Horus was brought by Osiris, pointing out the benefits of his line in bringing civilisation and fertility to Egypt and, from his position as lord of the underworld, threatening gods and mortals with the 'savage-faced messengers' which he could send to fetch the hearts of evildoers. Gradually, however, the belief in an underworld of horrors was transmuted into a cult of redemption. The Osiris myth gave promise of eternal life, which by embalmment and other rites performed by the grieving family on the Osirian model, became a prospect for ordinary men as well as for the pharaoh.

Nevertheless, old beliefs about the judgment of the dead were not discarded. Osiris

above
The Great Sphinx at Giza, a representation of Harmakhis (Horus of the Horizon), symbolising resurrection, and a portrait of Khephren, the Fourth Dynasty pharaoh. Behind are the pyramids of Khephren and Cheops, massive symbols of the primeval hill symbolising hopes of rebirth.

opposite
Ra-Harakhte, enthroned like a pharaoh. His was the form of Horus with which the pharaohs closely identified themselves. On his falcon-head he wears the solar disk surrounded by the *uraeus*. Above him are two *udjats*, Eyes of Ra, and the symbol of eternity.

took over or doubled the role of Ra as judge in the underworld, when the soul of the deceased, his *ka* or protective genius, represented as a mummy, was brought to the Hall of Judgment, having previously been placed upright for the Opening of the Mouth ceremony, part of the burial rite, which prepared the way for the rebirth of the *ka*. In the Hall of Judgment the soul had to recite the ancient 'negative confession' admitting to no sin, and answer questions from forty-two judges, presided over by Ra. In the second part of the hear-

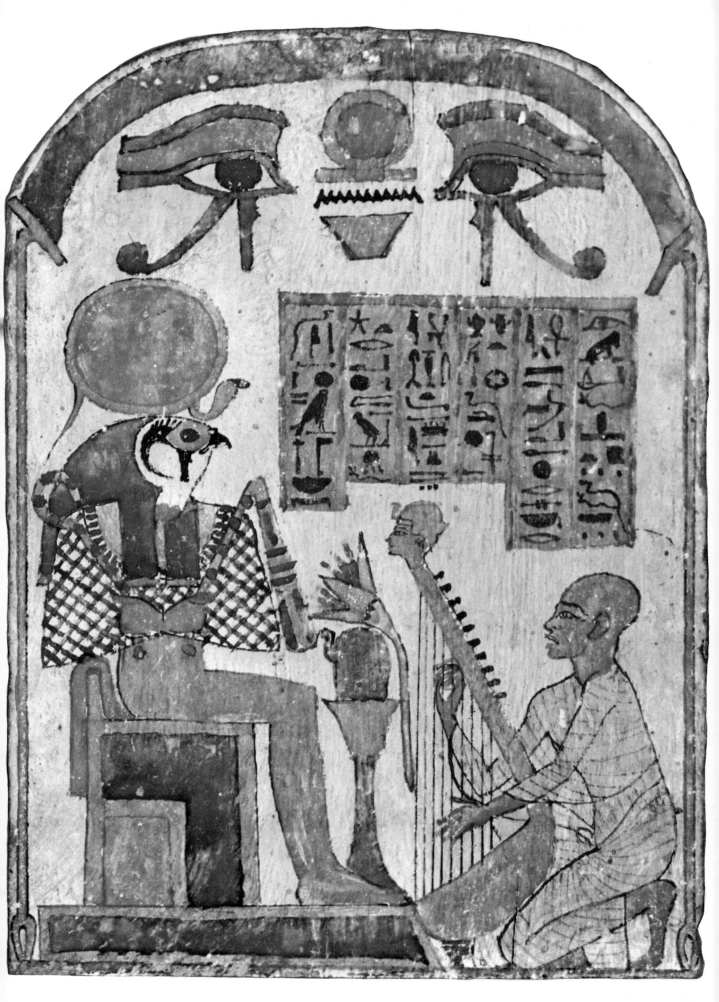

ing, presided over by Thoth as a baboon, the soul was put in a balance by Anubis and weighed against Mayet, the spirit of world order, sometimes represented by an ostrich feather. A soul found not 'true of voice' was devoured by Ammut, while a virtuous soul was dressed in feathers like Osiris, and presented to the supreme judge by Horus. Osiris declared that he might lead a life of eternal bliss among the gods and spirits, assigning to *ushabtis*, the servant figures placed in his tomb, his duties in tilling the lands of Osiris and maintaining order in his domains (a mirror of his duty on earth to the pharaoh).

opposite
Isis wearing the feather headdress and *uraeus* as queen of the underworld, and bearing the symbols of Hathor: cow's horns surrounding the solar disk, and in her hand the sistrum, with Hathor's broad cow-face. From Seti I's temple at Abydos. Nineteenth Dynasty.

above
Haroeris, the solar 'Horus of Two Eyes', with his wife Tafner, a form of Hathor, receiving a libation from Ptolemy VIII Euergetes II (170–116 BC). The royal sun cult continued in Ptolemaic Egypt, though Osirianism was at its peak. Temple at Kom Ombos.

above
The pharaoh Rameses II embraced by a goddess, probably Isis, as queen of the goddesses wearing the *uraeus* and the double crown or *pschent* that symbolised the unification and strength of the kingdom. Coloured relief from the Great Temple at Abu Simbel.

opposite
The young pharaoh Amenhotep II of the Eighteenth Dynasty, suckled by Hathor as a cow. The green spots are stars—gods of the First Time or, under Osirian influence, the souls of the dead. Hathor suckled not only the pharaoh but all souls entering the underworld.

page 40
Amon as a ram, wearing the triple crown. As the most powerful deity of the pharaohs during the New Kingdom, he is protected by the snake-goddess Buto hovering above, with the symbol of protection between her wings. Facing him is Mayet.

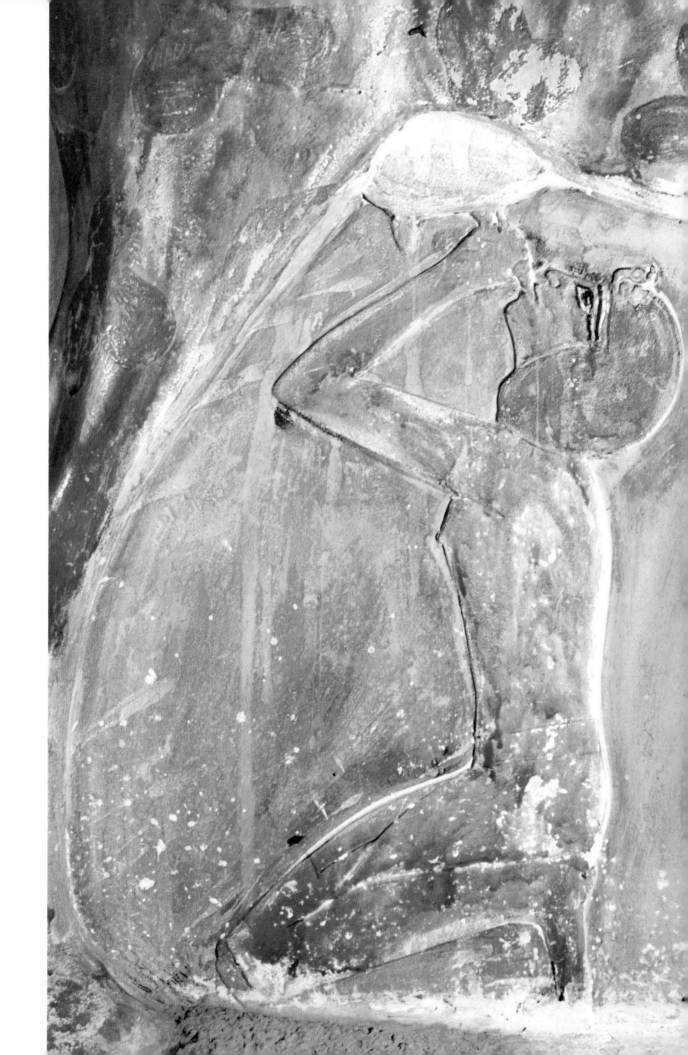

page 41
Ptah of Memphis embracing Sesostris I,
second pharaoh of the Middle Kingdom
(Twelfth Dynasty). Theban princes had
reunited Egypt after lengthy civil strife, but
pharaohs were still crowned at Memphis.
In the Middle Kingdom divine benefits
were democratised.

below
The hypostyle hall at Karnak near Thebes,
begun as part of the continuing
'reparations' to Amon-Ra after
Akhenaten and completed and decorated
by Rameses II the Great (1304–1237 BC).
It was the largest columned hall ever
constructed. Nineteenth Dynasty.

opposite
Rameses II dedicating a statue. Coloured
relief from his temple at Abydos. Under
the dominance of Amon-Ra and Thebes
in the Eighteenth Dynasty, Osirian Abydos
had been abandoned as a royal burial
place for the Theban Valley of the Kings,
but Rameses II made his capital in the
Delta.

The Nile-god Hapi, with offering tray of
food for the gods. By providing the
fertilising floodwaters of the Nile, he
upheld creation and the divine order. He
helped resurrect Osiris by suckling him.
Sandstone pillar relief from temple of
Rameses II at Abydos.

below
Selket, the protective scorpion-deity, standing at one corner of the gilded wooden shrine of Tutankhamun. She guarded one of the four gates of the underworld, whence flowed the Nile, so was a goddess of fertility and death, standing with Isis at the foot of coffins.

page 46
The deceased as Osiris, enthroned in mummy wrappings and bearing the *djed* column, possibly a cedar from Syria, where Osiris probably originated as fertility-god. From the Great Temple at Abu Simbel, built partly by captives of the expanding empire, such as the Nubians and Hebrews.

page 47
Mayet, goddess of truth and justice and personification of the divine order, wearing her symbol, an ostrich feather. Mayet accompanied her father Ra in the solar barque, for without her creation could not be sustained. The pharaoh was her chief upholder.

opposite
Ra, with the falcon-head of Horus and the sun-disk and *uraeus*, wearing mummy wrappings for the night voyage through the twelve provinces of the underworld. The herd of heaven, seven cows and a bull, provided his sustenance. Papyrus of Ani, Nineteenth Dynasty. British Museum.

below
Amon-Ra, wearing the tall plumed headdress of Mont, the war-god he absorbed, receiving offerings from Seti I. Seti I (c. 1319–1304) largely won back the Asiatic empire lost during Akhenaten's reign, and built part of the hypostyle hall at Karnak. Nineteenth Dynasty.

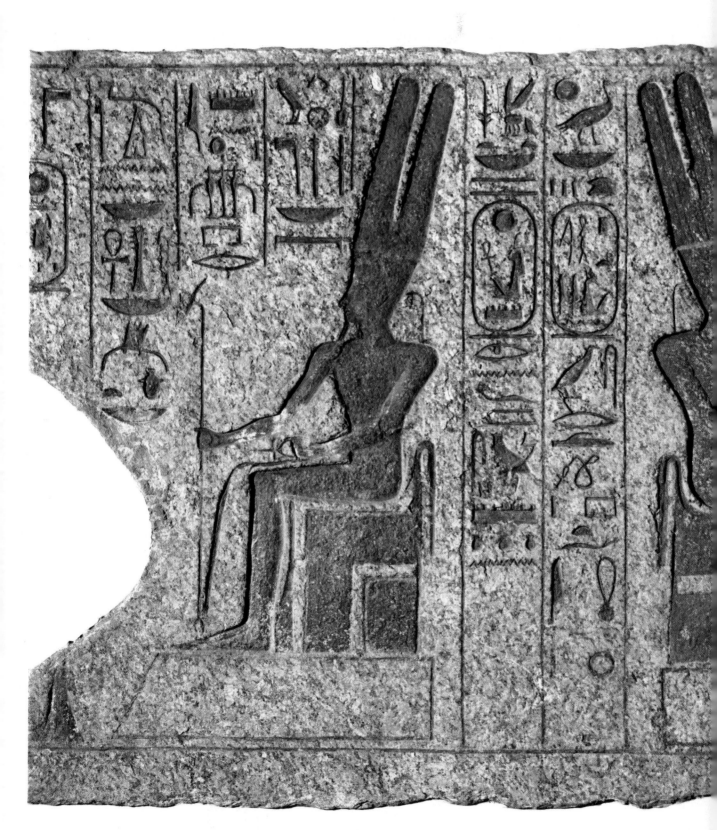

The judgment of the dead. The heart of
the deceased is weighed against Mayet
by jackal-headed Anubis, announcer and
god of death, who in ancient times may
have brought ritual death to the pharaohs
by snake-poison. Ibis-headed Thoth
records the result on his scribe's palette.
Twentieth Dynasty funerary casket.

Attendants at a burial rite. Professional mourning women were employed at funerals to mimic the mourning of Isis over Osiris, in the hope of identifying the deceased with Osiris' resurrection. Wall engraving from the tomb of Pennut at Miam, Nubia.

opposite
Stela depicting scenes from the judgment of the dead. In the upper panel the suppliant worships Osiris, a dark-faced mummy bearing flail, crook and *atef* crown. The red colour represents earth, and the green vegetation. Behind are Isis and Horus. British Museum.

Sennofer, keeper of the royal parks during the magnificent reign of Thuthmosis III, when the empire's tribute poured into Thebes. He sits amid the Tree of Heaven, whose fruits give the gods immortality (a Near Eastern borrowing). From Sennofer's tomb at Thebes.

Persia

Persia, or Iran, is a mountainous land bound on three sides by the high ranges of the Zagros, Elburz and Hindu Kush, and containing two deserts on the central plateau. Nevertheless, it has in history been open to outside influences, and has spread its own culture to east and west through the great empires built up by its hardy people. Though one might imagine nature to be unremittingly harsh in such a land, under a southern sun, in fact pockets of fertility, even tropical luxuriance, have supported the traditional agricultural life and high civilisations, characteristically mirroring their surroundings with belief centred on stark contrast.

The earliest known inhabitants were the Aryans, that branch of the Indo-Europeans from Central Asia who came to Persia and northern India as nomads and warriors and dominated Persia by about 800 BC. Their beliefs, their celebration and fear of nature, are known from the Persian hymns called Yashts and, in variant forms, from ancient Hindu scriptures, the Vedas. The first great Persian empire, the Achaemenian, was founded by Cyrus the Great, who united Persia itself, invaded Egypt, Lydia, and India, and conquered Babylon in 539, twelve years after the traditional

death of Zoroaster. This priest and prophet of a new religion, otherwise known as Zarathustra, probably came from Media. His doctrines, embodied in hymns he wrote called the *Gathas*, and personified in mythological representations of abstract philosophy, seem to have been accepted by Darius (521–486), who succeeded Cyrus, and his successor Xerxes (486–65). Ahura Mazda was glorified at the expense of earlier gods.

The Achaemenian empire fell to Alexander the Great (333–28) and Persia remained under Hellenic domination for two centuries until the rise of the Parthians (Pahlavas) from Scythia under Mithridates. Under the Parthians Manichaeism and Mithraism became important. In AD 224 the Parthian Empire was overthrown in turn by the truly Persian Sassanians, who pushed the empire east to India and west to Syria and Cappadocia. The peoples of the empire were mostly accorded religious toleration, so that many faiths coexisted and to some extent influenced each other, though Zoroastrianism was confirmed as the state religion. From this period dates the other great source for Persian mythology, Avestan texts on the creation and its purpose, known as the

Bundahishn. The King of Kings came to be seen as defender of divine purpose in that creation, especially during the glorious reign of Khusrow I (Chosroes), 531–79, who consolidated the monarchy and stabilised the empire after a period of internal and external disruption, introducing far-reaching reforms. He was regarded as semi-divine–a hero who would return at the end of the world with an army to defeat the demon enemies of Persia.

Nevertheless, stagnant through centuries of power, the great Persian empire fell to Islam in 651, and the majority of the people were converted. One of the greatest sources for Persian myth and legend despite this comes from the Moslem period. It is the *Shah name*, 'The Book of Kings', a mythological history by the poet Firdausi, writing at the court of Mahmud of Ghazni about 1000.

The earliest beliefs in Persia featured the so-called 'pagan' deities, and a mythology reflecting the life of warriors, and of nomads beginning to turn to agriculture as they settled and became a homogeneous people in Persia. The deities represented the universal cosmic forces of nature, both beneficent and fearful. The cult, celebrated close to nature, in the open air and often

left
Lion's head, symbol of royal power, surmounting a column at the great palace at Persepolis built by the Achaemenid king Darius (521–486 BC). Darius was the first king of kings to acknowledge Ahura Mazda as the source of his power and success.

opposite
Bull's head (the horns are lost) surmounting a column at Persepolis. Persepolis was known as the Throne of Jamshid (Yima), who as prototype king lost his 'Glory' (charisma) through sacrificing a bull, a fertility rite conferring immortality that was the prerogative of the gods.

on mountain-tops as the nomads wandered, was in itself the subject of myth. Among its celebrants were the famed Magi, apparently fire-priests of Median origin, later considered great sages to whom the coming of Zarathustra and the saviours was revealed.

Ancient Persian beliefs about creation gave a central position to the new homeland, with Mount Alburz considered the cosmic mountain. It had grown for eight hundred years, until its peak touched the sky, a hard shell enclosing the round and previously flat, featureless earth. From its peak stretched the Chinvat bridge, the route of souls to heaven or hell, and from its base another gateway to hell and meeting-place of demons. The impetus to this creation of the earth as it now is was evil, which crashed through the sky, stirring up the previously peaceful and harmonious waters and land masses, and causing the heavenly bodies to revolve round the earth. They entered and left the sky daily through apertures on Mount Alburz. The earth itself was divided into seven parts—Khwanirath in the centre, surrounded by six Keshvars. To pass from one part to another men rode on the heavenly ox Srishok, who would ultimately be sacrificed at the 'renovation' when men would be made immortal. Other beneficent animals were a mountainous ass with three legs, nine mouths, six eyes, and a horn, who destroyed pests and disease; and ten fish ceaselessly guarding the Gaokerena tree, source of the elixir of immortality, from the attacks of an evil lizard.

Vayu, the wind-god, formed the cosmic ocean beyond the peak of Mount Alburz by blowing together the rains. His was an ambivalent nature, a warrior bringing life-giving water and pitiless death by storm. The wind moved through the world of good and the world of evil, and received sacrifice from the creator-god, from the incarnation of evil, and from men. The rains themselves were formed by Tishtrya, source of fertility, taking the forms successively of a man at the ideal age of fifteen, a bull and a splendid white horse. In the last form, he engaged in cosmic battle with Apaosha, demon of drought, as a black horse. After an epic but inconclusive struggle, the creator intervened and by offering sacrifice to Tishtrya (which men had been neglecting), strengthened him to vanquish the demon and allow the waters to flow. The flowing waters themselves, together with mother's milk, male seed and female wombs, were purified by the noble, beautiful and beloved goddess Anahita. Her undefiled springs were a thousand lakes within the

cosmic ocean, beside which stood not only the two trees of many seeds, origin of all other trees, but also the Gaokerena, otherwise known as the White Hom.

The fruit of this tree, ultimately to bring immortality, was represented in the cult by the juice of a mountain plant, and in mythology by a god, called Haoma. In addition, Haoma was the divine priest, and when sacrificed and offered to the gods gave them life and strength. The pressing of Haoma as a sacrificial offering, and its consecration in ritual, gave it additional power, and the first four men to press Haoma were blessed with heroic sons: Yima, Thraetona, Keresaspa and Zoroaster. The other deified element of the cult was Fire, Atar, which received the sacrifice and transmitted it to the gods, thus enabling them to uphold creation against the forces of evil and darkness. In Zoroastrian belief, Fire was adopted as symbol of the creator Ahura Mazda. As defender of creation, Atar fought the

three-mouthed monster of destruction, Dahak, attempting to seize the Divine Glory to keep it from Dahak. But neither could gain it, and it remained unattainable. In early belief, an associated cosmic god was Rapithwin, Lord of the Noon-day Heat and of the ideal world, for the sun stood at its zenith in the ideal world before creation (and while Ahura Mazda performed the creative sacrifice) and would do so again to preside over the 'renovation' and defeat of evil at the end of time. This time was foreshadowed by Rapithwin's annual return each spring after his retreat underground to keep the waters warm, leaving the demon winter to hold brief sway above.

The gods thus far considered represent productive nature and the priesthood or cult. The final major god of early belief represents the third element of the so-called tripartite division of Indo-Iranian society (also seen, elaborated, in the Indian caste system). This god is Verethragna,

were the slaves of mankind, but danger
threatened in the form of three winters of
desolation. Yima, warned that these would
destroy all men and animals, constructed a
vast cavern, his *vara*, and preserved in it the
best of all mankind, of animals and of seeds.
The *vara* was enclosed with Yima's golden
ring, his token of leadership, and its inhabitants lived in warmth and comfort, with
inexhaustible food. Through an aperture
in the roof the men and creatures within
saw the heavenly bodies once a year, which
seemed like every day; every forty years
each couple bore a male and a female child.
It was a life of eternal harmony, but in
another interpretation it was the land of the
virtuous dead. Yima was also considered a
sinner, for he had tried to seize the prerogative of the gods in performing a bull
sacrifice to make men immortal. Perhaps
for this he was relegated to the land of the
dead. In early belief he was cut in two by
his brother Spityura; but later he was
thought to have been killed and supplanted
as king by the tyrant Dahak, elsewhere the
demon of evil.

Dahak in the shape of a three-headed,
three-jawed, six-eyed dragon, the lie-
demon created to destroy men's virtue
and their habitations and to bring them
disease and fever, was engaged in a mighty
battle in the heavens, Varena, by the hero
Thraetona, later known as Faridun.
Having failed to kill Dahak with his club,
Thraetona stabbed him, but from his
wounds came snakes, scorpions, lizards,
toads, frogs and tortoises. Afraid these
loathsome creatures might overrun the
world, Thraetona bound Dahak in chains
and imprisoned him in Mount Demavend.
Thraetona, by thus defending the world
against violence and disease, 'seized the
khwarenah' (glory or charisma) of Yima.
The hero Thrita likewise protected men
against pain, disease and death, for not
only was he the third man to prepare
Haoma for men, but his prayers also
brought them the healing plants that grew
near the Gaokerena tree. A third hero to
catch Yima's *khwarenah* was the youthful,
club-wielding Keresaspa, who battled nine
days and nights in the cosmic ocean with
Gandarewa, a monster who could swallow
twelve men at once and whose head rose
to the sun, and who also killed Kamak, a
bird whose enormous wings prevented the
rain falling. It was thought that at the
end of the world the demon Dahak would
break out of Mount Demavend and wreak
havoc and that to save creation and mankind, Keresaspa would be resurrected to
slay him with his club. His own renown
made Keresaspa careless of his religious
duties, however, and at his death he was
almost refused admission to heaven.

dynamic, aggresive Victory, whose cult
was popular among soldiers and therefore
spread wide in the empire. An irresistible
god, he defeated the malice of men and
demons. Like Tishtrya, and strikingly like
Vishnu in Hindu mythology, Verethragna
assumed ten successive incarnations in
order to accomplish his work: a strong
wind, a bull with golden horns, a white
horse, a camel, a fierce boar, a youth of
fifteen, a raven, a wild ram, a fighting
buck, and a man holding a golden sword.
The manifestations as boar and as bird,
whence superstitions about ravens'
feathers, were most popular.

Semi-divine rulers also fall into the third
category of the tripartite system, but they
are to be regarded less as gods than as
legendary heroes, each of whom had some
flaw in his character. Yima, the Great
Shepherd (known as Jamshid in Firdausi)
was the prototype of kings and of priests
who ruled over earth for a thousand years
of peace and such prosperity that the earth
had to be enlarged to support the growing
numbers of mankind. Yima established the
social divisions and allotted tasks to each
class. Falsehood, hunger, sickness and
death were unknown, for the demons

below
Buddhist fresco from Bamiyan, Afghanistan. After the Persians pushed east under Shapur I (240–72), there was an exchange of religious imagery and ideas. The mythology of Buddha's and Zoroaster's birth, childhood, revelation and mission are strikingly similar.

bottom
Illustration from Firdausi's mythological history of Persia, showing the king Bahram Gur fighting a dragon. Firdausi's accounts cannot necessarily be taken as accurate representations of ancient mythology, since they were tailored not to offend a Moslem audience.

opposite
Kalki, final avatar of the Hindu creator-god Vishnu as a white horse, led by Vishnu himself, ready to slay the wicked in a degenerate age in preparation for a renewed creation. There are clear parallels with the myth of Verethragna and Zoroastrian saviour figures.

In some ways similar to the primeval heroes was the god Mithra, who came to prominence in Persia with the Parthians (Arsacid dynasty), for he was the victorious warrior hero smiting demons in defence of creation. Though conceived specifically as god of the sun, living in a palace of light and purity, and drawn across the sky in his chariot by four swift white horses, he was, like Ahura Mazda, seen primarily as unconquerable light. As the marker of time, Mithra the sun was drawn into the Zoroastrian pendulum swings of good and evil. And as the overseer of all deeds, he was one of the judges of the soul at death. Under Zoroastrianism Mithra enjoyed great popularity, especially among the soldiers, who spread his worship. It became rooted throughout Asia Minor and elsewhere. As Mithras, he became a major god at Rome, his austere cult as warrior and judge remaining, though his attributes as slayer of the bull in a fertility rite, vegetation cascading with the blood, were added.

Under Zoroastrianism, the ancient gods Vayu, Anahita, Haoma, Atar, Verethragna, Rapithwin and Mithra became Yazatas, or Worshipful Ones, sorts of saints. Each of the innumerable Yazatas is associated with a specific day or month and able to intercede for men on small personal matters. They are third in the heavenly hierarchy. At its head is the creator Ahura Mazda, later known as Ohrmazd. From his robe shines the stars and his eye is the 'swift-horsed sun'. His

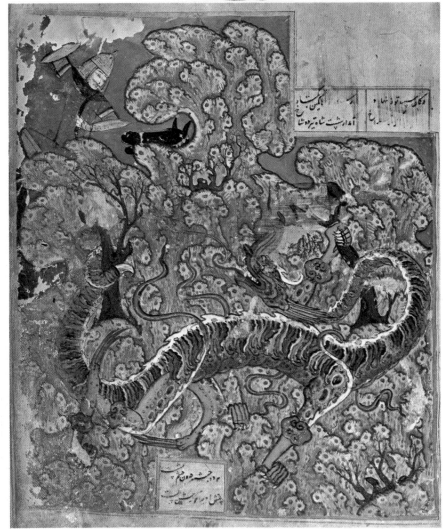

opposite
Illustration from the *Shah name* showing king Takhmoruw, father of Yima, slaying demons. He particularly attacked idolatry and magic, and had the spirit of Angra Mainyu transferred to a horse, which he rode round the world during his thirty-year reign.

left
Persian knotted wool carpet of the fourth or third century BC. The motif in the central panel is a four-rayed star, characteristic of Luristan. Apart from their symbolic motifs, carpets were identified with aesthetic pleasure and were said to furnish each stage of heaven.

below
Gold rhyton or drinking vessel of the fifth century, supported by a winged lion. As in many civilisations, gold had a symbolic value. It was associated with the first quarter of the final three thousand years of the world, when the Good Religion was revealed to Zoroaster.

most beautiful form is as the sun, for he represents and is the source of all that is good and positive: light, beauty, truth, life, health and happiness. He brings the divine order to mankind, and his power supports every just ruler. It is the duty of man to seek righteousness by emulating each of Ahura Mazda's aspects or characteristics, except his first, Spenta Mainyu or Bounteous Spirit, which characterises him as creator. Ahura Mazda requires the support of men through worship and righteousness in his cosmic struggle with evil, darkness, disease, death, which characterise the Lie or Disorder, called Angra Mainyu. The Zurvanite heresy held that Good and Evil were themselves two aspects of an ultimate creator, Zurvan; but orthodox Zoroastrianism maintains total polarity between the two, with no contact except constant battle and vigilance. Thus Ahura Mazda is not responsible for the creation of evil or suffering, and though he is the chief god and is immortal, he is not omnipotent, for until his final triumph his power is limited by Angra Mainyu.

Second in the Zoroastrian hierarchy are the seven personified aspects of Ahura Mazda, the Amesha Spentas. These children of god sit on golden thrones beside him in the heavenly House of Song, the abode of the righteous dead. They protect creation against attack by the demonic battalions of Evil, and against men who have espoused the cause of evil. After Spenta Mainyu, the first is Vohu Manah, Good Mind, or Wisdom, the

creator's adviser and protector of useful animals, who keeps a record of men's deeds and through whom they can attain integrity and immortality in the Kingdom. His demonic adversaries include Akah Manah, Discord, and Aeshma, Fury. Second is Asha, Truth, upholder of the moral order on earth, whose great enemy is Indra, Apostasy, who brings decay, fiends and sorcerers into the world. Third is Kshathra Varya, the Desired Kingdom, representing God's power, through whom men will receive final judgment at the end of the world, whose helper is Mithra, the sun, and whose enemy is Saura, Misgovernment and Drunkenness. Fourth is the creator's daughter Armaiti, Devotion, representing righteous obedience, and giving pasture to cattle, who contends against Presumption and Deviousness. Fifth and sixth are the daughters Harvatat and Ameretat, Integrity and Immortality, the vigorous sources of life and growth, whose enemies are Hunger and Thirst.

The figure representing worship in Zoroastrian mythology is Sraosha, Obedience, who took the seventh throne in the House of Song when Spenta Mainyu became identified as sole prerogative of Ahura. He is seen as an obedient and forceful warrior in the fight against Evil, who invented the potent rite of spreading sacred twigs, barsom, and first offered prayers and hymns to Ahura Mazda. He is pictured living on a mountain-top, in a brightly lit house with a thousand pillars and surveying the world from a chariot drawn by four white horses with golden feet, on constant look-out for demons, whose heads he smashes with his battle-axe. His chief enemies are Aeshma, Fury, whose destructive activity he deflects from the Good Creation to his own, Evil Creation; and Angra Mainyu, later known as Ahriman, leader of the demons and creator of the world of Evil, the negative mirror of each detail of the Good Creation, who attempted to seduce Zoroaster himself and is known as Druj, Lie or Deceit. One of the cohorts of Druj was the powerful Azhi Dahak, whose story from the ancient beliefs was elaborated with tales of attempted seduction of Vayu and Anahita to collaborate in his destructive plans, and, when sacrifice proved useless, his effort to extinguish the sacred flame. Though Yima intervened to save the flame, Dahak's vengeance caused Yima's fall.

Zoroastrianism incorporated the ancient creation myth, but prefaced it with a confrontation between Ohrmazd, who in the beginning dwelt on high in endless light, and Ahriman, who dwelt in the depths in darkness, with the void separating them. After three thousand years of this

opposite
A Mede carrying a bundle of barsom twigs, depicted on a gold plaque from the Oxus treasure. The barsom twigs were an essential part of the Persian ritual, so that this figure is indicated as a priest. The spreading of the twigs was taught mankind by Sraosha.

above
Mount Demavend, chief peak of the Elburz mountains, the Persian cosmic mountain. Mount Demavend was the place where Thraetona (Faridun) imprisoned the demon Dahak, and whence he will escape in a final upsurge of evil before the renovation.

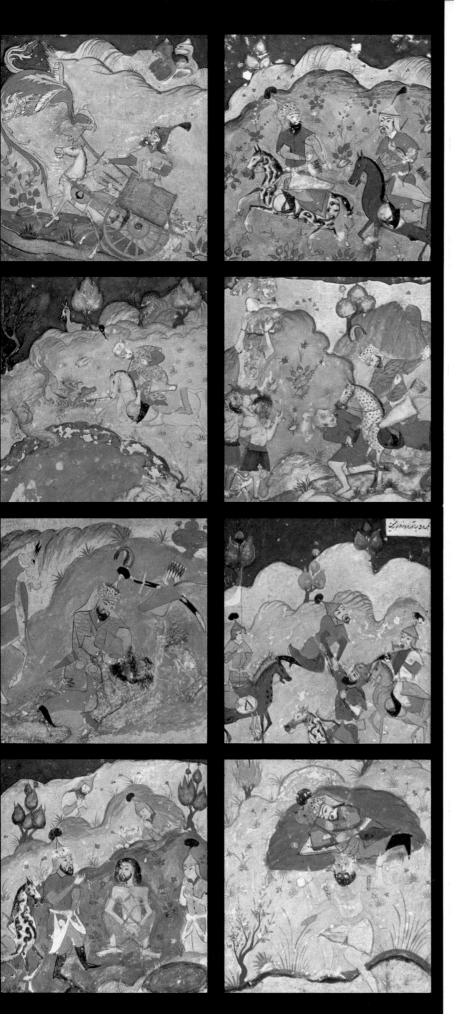

spiritual world Ohrmazd offered Ahriman peace, but Ahriman refused, wishing to envelop all in destruction, though he agreed to a time limit for battle; when he realised that by agreeing to open declaration of war he had ensured his own ultimate downfall he retreated in impotence to hell, leaving Ohrmazd to create an ideal material world and to rule in peace for a further three thousand years. At the end of this period, Ahriman was roused by Jahi, spirit of female impurity, who promised to corrupt the holy man, Gayomart, and the ox with such suffering they would rue life. Rising to the attack, Ahriman made Jahi desirable. So successful was this assault that Ahriman appeared the victor. But having shattered creation and killed man, Ahriman wished to return to his native darkness—and he found himself a prisoner in the world, bound by the hard shell of the sky, personified as a warrior in armour, aided by men's fravashis, their just souls. Ahriman was captive on earth, forced to coexist there for the third three thousand years of existence with Good. Good had not been defeated: from the slaughtered ox came corn, medicinal herbs and animals; and from the dead man came metals and, from his seed, the first human couple, Mashye and Mashyane. Thus Ahriman could win individual battles, but never the war.

Mashye and Mashyane first grew as a plant with fifteen leaves (the ideal number). From its fruits grew the ten races of

left
The hero Rustam, who like his main opponent performed seven superhuman labours, illustrating the simurgh bird (vulture), which saved the life of his father Zal, Rustam's fabulous horse, his exploits in saving kings against demons and the Turanians (Turkestan and China), and his temporary capture by a demon.

right, above
Fire-temple near Isfahan. Each of the three classes of fire, corresponding to the classes in society—priests, warriors and productive workers, came from a different mountain, and was carried on the back of the heavenly ox Srishok. Yima installed fire in temples.

right
Reconstruction of the Carrawburgh Mithraeum at Newcastle. The Roman legionaries spread their version of the Persian god (a bringer of fertility rather than a judge) throughout the empire. The temple represented the cave in which Mithras slew the bull.

mankind. When they had taken human form, Ohrmazd instructed them in their duties; but they were seduced into evildoing by Ahriman, who persuaded them to declare that he was the creator. Thereafter, their sacrifices to the gods and their work produced nothing but discord. When they began to worship demons they lost sexual desire, so committing another sin by failing to populate the world. After fifty years they did have children, but ate them until Ohrmazd made them less sweet. Finally, they begot the human race, to help Ohrmazd in his struggle against evil.

This struggle is perpetual, for God and for men during life. Even after death, for the first three days and nights, demons lie in wait to attack the soul, especially that of a virtuous man. Sraosha, with the aid of relatives' prayers, protects it. Relatives must not bewail their loss too much, however, for the river of their tears forms a barrier for all souls on their passage through the afterlife. After three days the soul is judged by weighing in scales watched by Sraosha, Rashnu and Mithra. The virtuous are guided by a beautiful maiden and a fragrant wind across the broad Chinvat bridge to heaven, which is divided into four 'stations', of ascending height, each designed for pleasure and furnished with fine carpets and cushions. An old hag and foul smell lead the wicked, chased by their evil deeds in the shape of a wild beast, to the Chinvat bridge, which becomes tortuous and from which they plummet into the abyss of hell. If the good deeds and the evil deeds of the soul in life balance, it is consigned to an intermediate place, Hamestagen. Apart from the general miseries of hell – congestion, foul smell, heat, cold, darkness, dragging time, fiendish creatures – each soul is subjected to corrective punishment to match its sins. For hell is not eternal, and this punishment will make all men fit to partake in the final resurrection.

The ultimate triumph of Good was assured with the birth of Ahura Mazda's son Zoroaster to a virgin. The birth, foretold to the heavenly ox and Yima, was accompanied by miraculous portents. Zoroaster's revelation and his mission to teach the true doctrine could not be

The magi bringing gifts to the new-born Christ. Byzantine mosaic from San Apollinare Nuovo in Ravenna, with an accurate portrayal of Parthian dress. The magi were famed in the West as far back as the time of Plato, less as fire-priests than as sages. The archetypal magus was Zoroaster.

swayed by temptations from the demons. By performing a healing miracle. he successfully converted King Vishtaspa, whose rule thereby received divine protection.

The pendulum swings of good and evil are to be repeated three times during the period after the revelation of Zoroaster, at thousand-year intervals. In each cycle a son of Zoroaster will be born to a virgin. In the first two cycles evil will nearly destroy the world, but creation will be saved by the slaying of an arch-demon. In the third, the saviour Soshyant will preside over the final triumph of good, with the death of Dahak at the hands of Keresaspa. Men's souls will be resurrected and reunited with their bodies so that they may pass to final judgment as whole men. A stream of pure molten metal will restore earth to its primeval state, and will pass over men too. They will receive immortality from Soshyant celebrating a final sacrifice—an ox, man's servant. The elixir will be prepared from the ox fat and White Hom. All demons will be killed except Ahriman and Az, who will flee to hell and be confined there for ever by the molten metal, the barrier weighted by the souls of sinners. The pristine universe will be restored, 'renovated', in every particular, except that Evil will be wiped out for ever.

right
Lion attacking a bull. Relief from Persepolis, where the Nauruz festival, celebrating the return of Rapithwin after the winter, was held. The lion may symbolise the sun and the bull the rains, so that the scene is reminiscent of Mesopotamian seasonal mythology.

right, below
Scenes of a king hunting a boar from a relief at Taq-i Bustan, dating probably from the reign of Khusrow II (590–628), when the king of kings, though not a god, maintained his indispensability as executive of God on earth—indicated by his size and halo or *khwarenah* (charisma).

below
Ohrmazd, on the right, presenting the diadem and the symbol of kingship to Ardeshir I (AD 224–41). Ohrmazd tramples on Ahriman; Ardeshir, founder of the Sassanid dynasty, semi-divine champion of Zoroastrianism, tramples his Parthian predecessor. Rock relief from Naqsh-i Rustem.

left
Genii, protective spirits, beneath the winged symbol of Ahura Mazda, who was represented in this abstract form during the Achaemenid period. Glazed brick decoration from the exterior of Darius' palace at Susa, showing Mesopotamian influence.

below
Lion griffin in glazed brick from Susa. It was an appropriate symbol of fierce majesty decorating one of the palaces of Darius, who consolidated and greatly extended the Achaemenian empire. The other palaces were at Persepolis, Hamadan (Ecbatana), and Babylon.

opposite
Gayomart, illustrated in a manuscript of the *Shah name*. In Firdausi, Gayomart becomes the first king, ruling in the mountains and clothed in leopard skins. He discovered food and clothing and the reverence accorded him was the fount of religion.

ذكر كيومرث

سروح كه تاريخ دهقان كرد ياد	زگفتار دهقان چنين كرد ياد	كه تاكرد بنياد كنتى خداى	زشاهان باوفرو هندكورى
نخستين خديوى كه كشور گشود	سرنامداران كيومرث به تاج	جو بنشست رخت به نهاد تاج	بنداخت بر مرد دهقان خراج

بداد و هش خلق راوعده كرد جهان را به نام نكو عهد كرد راوبان آمار از آن پادشاه كه ما را خبار جنين كرده اند
كه كيومرث از اسباط مهلائيل بود و زنج الانساب فرزند صلبى آدمكه است و امام حجة الاسلام محمد بن القرائحة
در كتاب نصيحة الملوك آورده است كه كيومرث برادر زشيث بود و بعضى كويند از اولاد نوح است و در رغم طائفه ازمغا
كيومرث خود آدم على الجملة تا اختلاف انساب اتفاق ارند كه نخستين پادشاهى است از پادشاهان جهان و معنى كومر
بلغت سريانى حى ناطق است يعنى زنده كويا و حقيقت اسم او با مسمى مطابق ارد باوجود سبطنت ملك و كثرت سباه و وقار
از مشعوف بود بسياحت و منازل و مراحل رحمت قدم آوردن و شها كرد و و شت كشتن و بربخار و برستو راحل كه دشتن
و جون تقدير ملك و مصالح زبرد راحتى رغبت بيزرد راحتى در زشعان مهاوى مهيب و شعاب شوايح عظيم ما و ساحتى و شبها و روزها
سبوحه و عبادت كله انبدى جون زقاب بكردنكشان در زقيه عهد و بيان وطوق عبودت و قومان آورد و بديوان و مرده و عفاريت شياطين مجازيا زرد
و سلاح و جوب و فلاختى بود و لباس او زبوست او زيوست اكرى جبين كويدكه ديو ورى در او ايل رنبى كه مراشكار كه دكر كه دكره

ودوستى و دشمنى وحرب باد مهردى تا بوقت نوح بعد از طوفان زخلق نابديد بيشده در بام كيومرث لباس آدميان ناز حلود
حيوانات بود و مردمان از ديوان در زحمت بودند و خلايق را از ظلم ايشان خلاص داد و ديوان را از آدميان براند و حجاج عدل
و احسان بر سرنى آدم بكستر د و در كشف ظلامت مظلمان و قضاء حوايج ملهوف را مبا لعنت بود وكفت اما ملك الارض ابرز لله
مزبادشاه زمين و نكاه دارن زمين زخلق ام قهرمان خداى تعالى ولقب او كشاه بود بنشستن نكاه خود نزد بك دماوند ساخت
وبعايت خوب صورت بود و باقر ورد و فرزند آمد وراد نام نهاد مشى مذكر و مشانه مونث و بعضى كويد بديد بيدمشك
اول ... فرزند وشت و مشى بعايت زاهد و متعبد بود و روزى از ديو برسيد كه ازكارها جه بهتر بدبرشكت كه ازارى
مردمان و برستش خداى عزوجل كفت سى از آزرى شوان بود و مكر خبا بود از ايشان وطاعت نتوان كرد مكرتها و دين
سبب از خلا يق كراه كوفت و دركه اسرى بود كامى بد زد بدين او بى و بدين بدر آمدى بس زاين

71

left

The tyrant Zahak, otherwise the demon Dahak, who overthrew Yima and reigned a thousand years. Originally a brave prince, he was corrupted by the Evil One through vanity, so that from his shoulders sprouted snakes which daily fed on two human brains.

opposite

King Faridun (Thraetona), with his two sons. He overcame the tyrant Zahak at his palace at Jerusalem, smashing Zahak's helmet with an ox-headed mace. Having imprisoned him, he devoted his reign to overcoming pestilence through improved farming.

India

Complexity is perhaps the dominant feature of Indian mythology. It is preeminently a mythology that reflects and supports a social structure, and over a long history it has had to make many adaptations, usually conflating earlier beliefs either with those of new rulers or new cults, or explaining a new turn in a chequered history. This adaptability is one reason for the fact that Indian mythology is part of the living culture today, in different ways for the illiterate masses and for the educated—but not just by way of literary allusion, as has happened in the West.

Some changes in mythology hinge not on political factors but on deliberate innovations by the Brahmins, the priestly grade of a tripartite society which the Aryans of India shared with those of Persia. In India this division was transmuted into a theoretically rigid stratification of society (with the addition of a fourth caste, the Sudras, servants or slaves—probably formed of the indigenous people—and later of the untouchables or outcastes). By mythology the Brahmins justified their own privileged position and explained developments of religious philosophy. One of the most important was the idea of reincarnation, unknown in the Vedic age, which allowed any new god to be identified as an old one in a new birth. The social aspect of these interpretations helped maintain their position of influence through the vicissitudes of the period 300 BC to AD 1000, which saw the rise of two new faiths, Buddhism and Jainism, each introduced by a member of the 'royal' warrior caste, the Kshatriyas. It helped them gain the trust of foreign rulers, especially after AD 1000 and the establishment of the Moghuls in the north.

This is not to say that the common people, the peasant caste or Vaisyas, have not contributed to the growth of myths: in many an anti-Brahmin feeling can be seen. Other contributions were made by the aboriginal inhabitants of India, and may be divined from the myths of isolated hill tribes today. Their supplanters, the dark-skinned Dravidian peoples, in turn driven south by the Aryan invasions about 1700 BC, became the demons, rakshasas, of Hindu myth. The earliest beliefs may have sprung from a fertility cult, as did those of an advanced civilisation in the Indus valley centred at Harappa and Mohenjodaro,

which seems to have been of Mesopotamian, possibly Chaldean origin. There were two main elements in the cult of this agricultural people: phallic worship, and the propitiation of mother-goddesses. The yogic crosslegged posture of the Hindu god Shiva resembles that of the bull-horned god of the Harappa seals, while Shiva's consort in her association with bloody sacrifice resembles the ancient mother-goddess surrounded by animal and human sacrificial victims. Thus a resurgence of old beliefs may have helped in the overthrow of the Aryan gods, often called the Vedic gods from the chief scriptures of the age, the Vedas, a collection of hymns completed about 800 BC.

The gods brought by the Aryans when they overthrew the Indus valley civilisation about 1700 BC reflected their own values as hard-drinking, fair-skinned conquerors, who knew little of settled agricultural life. They were warriors who respected skill with horse, chariot and sword. Thus their most important god was Indra, god of the storm, whose weapon was the thunderbolt, Vajra, and who rode across the sky on a horse or in a golden chariot. He was the son of Prithivi, the earth, and Dyaus, the sky or heaven, earlier fertility-deities said to be the parents of all the gods and of men. Varuna, guardian of the cosmic law and universal monarch, was at first the most powerful of the gods. Having created the universe by exercise of his creative will, maya, using the sun as his instrument, he continued in his creative function, sustaining his creatures by causing rain to fall and rivers to flow. Maya was also the principle of truth and justice, and with his eye, the sun, Varuna surveyed men from his thousand-pillared mansion in the heavens, judging and punishing them according to rta. As this divine law was unknowable to men, their only course was to exercise extreme circumspection in dealings with Varuna. His functions and nature were early shared with another god, Mitra, whose realm became the day, while Varuna's was the night. Together with Aryaman they formed a triad, the Adityas, or Celestial Deities.

At the time of Indra's birth these priest-gods had been failing mankind, for they had allowed the demon Vritra to steal the cloud-cattle, thus reducing men to starvation through drought. Indra sprang from his mother's side, a golden warrior full of

energy and impulsiveness, seized and drank the enormous quantity of soma that men were offering in sacrifice to the gods and, fortified by this intoxicating drink, set off to do battle against Vritra. After storming the demon's ninety-nine fortresses, Indra overcame Vritra himself with his thunderbolt and let loose the cloud-cattle. By this exploit the Kshatriya Indra became king of the gods, and with his natural prowess in a tireless battle against demons heightened by the prayers and sacrifice of men, he annually thereafter released the pent-up waters after the summer drought. Indra consolidated his position as bringer of fertility by killing his father. Varuna too had to concede his supreme position, based on law and magic power, to the personal might of Indra supported by man. Instead of bowing to an inscrutable god, men could henceforth hope to affect or even to direct the flow of benefits from a supreme god partially dependent on them for his strength.

Indra assumed Varuna's role as creator, building, or better rearranging, the universe like a house, propping up the heavens, regulating time and the seasons. Indra reigned in his heaven, Swarga, built for him by his brother and former rival Tvashtri, an artisan-god and earlier fount of all created forms, who made Indra's thunderbolt, Vajra, and a magic bowl for the gods, constantly replenished with soma, source of their strength. Tvashtri's daughter Saranyu was married to Vayu, the wind-god, whose breath gave life to gods and men, but it was by Indra that she bore her sons, the Ribhus, minor artisan-gods who among other things created a cow of plenty which dwelt in Indra's heaven.

Agni, god of fire, complemented the role of Indra, and was said to be his brother. Born fully matured, he immediately began to feed upon his parents, and when he had consumed them fed upon the

The tower of the Parthasarathi Temple at Triplicane. The multiplicity, vigour and dramatic stance of the innumerable figures of gods, demons, holy animals and animals incarnating evil, aptly conveys the extreme complexity of a mythology elaborated over centuries.

offerings of clarified butter poured on the sacrificial fire. He had seven tongues to lick up the butter. Agni symbolised the vital spark in all nature: he consumed in order to vivify, and as initiator of sacrificial rites, was the archetypal priest, mediator between gods and men. He was also a mighty slayer of demons and renowned for his truthfulness. The other deity associated with sacrifice was Soma, as with the Persian Haoma both victim and priest in the rite. A milky fermented liquor pressed from a mountain plant, Soma was an integral part of all Vedic sacrifices, symbolising the vital fluid in all beings and in some ways superior to Indra, since he derived his strength from the juice, also called amrita (ambrosia). Soma became identified with the moon, Chandra, source of fertility, and in later times this was the only form in which he survived, for the use of intoxicants was forbidden, allegedly because, drunk with soma, Brahma had committed incest with his daughter.

Equally benevolent were the various deities of the sun: Vivasvat, the rising sun, father of Yama and Yami, the first man and woman, and of the twin Aswins, divine horsemen who brought men medicines; Savitri, the sun in its morning and evening aspects, the stimulator bestowing longevity on men and immortality on the gods; and Surya, chief sun-god after he had absorbed the functions of the other two, who was son of Dyaus and sometimes father of Soma or Chandra. Another child of Dyaus, Ushas, the eternally young and welcomed dawn, bringer of wealth and light, was the sister of Agni and of Ratri, gentle night.

The last two Vedic deities to be considered owe their importance to the way they later developed. They are Rudra, god of storm and winds and father of Indra's companions the Maruts, who with their golden armour and chariot wheels gleaming rode on the whirlwind directing the storm, alternately fierce warriors fighting demons to create rain, and gay, carefree youths. Similarly Rudra had a terrible aspect as wild-tempered robber-god, the divine archer whose arrows brought death and disease; and a beneficent role as lord of cattle, the bountiful lord of song and sacrifices and divine physician. This mixture of characteristics was to develop in the Hindu god Shiva.

The tenth-century Rajarani temple at Bhubaneswar, a ruined city in Orissa sacred to Shiva. The main architectural motif is the lingam or phallus, a form in which Shiva was cursed to be worshipped by a slighted sage, Bhrigu – one of Shiva's many quarrels.

The second deity was Vishnu, a benevolent manifestation of the sun's energy, who with three steps measured the seven worlds, thus taking part in its creation. He helped Indra in battle against demons, was connected with Agni as intermediary between gods and men, and welcomed the faithful to heaven.

There were three Vedic heavens. Indra's was on Mount Meru, the cosmic mountain, centre of the universe, inhabited by the major gods, sages and saints, and by the spirits of nature – a place of joy and light where recreation was provided by the singing and dancing of Apsaras and Gandharvas, which was the permanent or temporary home of fallen warriors. The second heaven was Varuna's, situated in the sea when Varuna had been demoted to Lord of the Ocean. Its inhabitants were the minor deities: the Adityas (celestial deities), Nagas (serpents), Daityas and Danavas (ocean demons), the spirits of rivers and other waters, and of the cardinal points and mountains. The third heaven was that of Yama, the first man and pathfinder for the human race. As the first man to die, he had discovered the 'path of the fathers' (Manes or Pitris) – later presided over by Agni through cremation – and became king of the dead and, with Varuna, their judge, Dharmaraja. To the virtuous he gave soma conferring immortality, while the guilty were consigned to annihilation or to hell, Put. At first all men who had children to perform sacrifices for them were received either in Indra's heaven or, if less virtuous, in Yama's. Later popular belief made Yama's kingdom a series of hells, places of refined torture for the wicked.

Towards the end of the Vedic age an increasing trend to pantheism, with speculation about the identity and nature of a universal spirit, *Brahman*, and a growth in the power of the Brahmins and the value given to sacrifice, had two important reflections in mythology. The first was an elaboration of creation myths and cyclic time systems; and the second was the idea that priests through sacrifice, and later sages and ascetics through their holy power, created forces ensuring the continuance of the universal cycles which regulated the existence of the gods. In Hinduism this was crystallised in the cycle of life, death and rebirth represented by the great triad of Brahma (Creator), Vishnu (Preserver), and Shiva (Destroyer). The age also produced two new religions, Buddhism and Jainism.

Brahma, officially the All-god of the Hindu triad, closely identified with *Brahman* and considered the chief Brahmin or priest, is in mythology a somewhat passive

god, since creation is less a matter of origination than of reorganisation. Each complete cosmic cycle represents one hundred years in the life of Brahma, followed by dissolution of the entire universe, including the gods and Brahma himself in a Great Cataclysm, Mahapralaya, and a hundred years of chaos after which a new Brahma is born. The Kalpa, one day in Brahma's life, equals 4,320 million years on earth. At its end, while Brahma sleeps, the three worlds are destroyed and all beings whose virtue has not brought them liberation from the cycle are judged, and must prepare for rebirth according to their deserts, *karma*, when Brahma wakes. Each Kalpa is further subdivided into a thousand Mahayugas, each Mahayuga seeing steady moral deterioration and the weakening of Dharma, god of justice and duty. According to this pessimistic scheme, we are now living at the end of a Mahayuga. The prelude to destruction is drought, followed by fire, followed by flood.

In Vedic times a golden cosmic egg representing fire contained the universal spirit, which took the form of the first man, Purusha. Sometimes the gods were said to have sacrificed Purusha in order to create the cosmos and men in their castes. Most creation myths describe Brahma sleeping within a lotus floating on the floodwaters of chaos. When he woke and set about creation, he at first made several mistakes. From ignorance issued the Beings of Darkness, who tried to devour him. The worst of these became the rakshasas, enemies of men, while the less bloodthirsty became yakshas. Thereafter, Brahma completed creation. Reflecting the increasing importance attached to the notion that sages could acquire powers superior to the gods themselves, for they could become absorbed into the universal world spirit, the Laws of Manu maintained that the sage Manu survived the destruction of one Mahayuga and was Brahma's efficient agent in the next creation.

Despite his official title as god of wisdom, many myths show Brahma as victim of a sage or demon, who forces him to create a situation that Vishnu or Shiva must set right. Vishnu as Preserver and Shiva as Destroyer have more active roles to play, and more devotees to claim that their god plays the key part. As destroyer of Brahma's creation, Shiva is known as Mahadeva or Iswara, Supreme Lord. His weapon of destruction is the fire of his third eye, created when his wife Parvati once covered his eyes and so plunged the world into darkness. His other weapons include a lightning trident and the three snakes twined about his neck. In addition to periodic destruction of the universe,

Shiva is celebrated for his constant battles against demons, and this beneficent destruction is part of his role as fertility-god, distributor of the seven holy rivers formed as the Ganges cascades down from Brahma's city on Mount Meru. As the personification of sexual energy, he is worshipped as the lingam, phallus, while his consort is worshipped as the yoni, also known as Shiva's shakti, or female energy. With the basic form of this consort, Devi, he dances as god of rhythm symbolising the eternal movement of the universe. This includes dancing in order to destroy: over the body of a slain demon or by the Tandava dance, annihilating the world. The consort herself also enjoys most popular worship in fierce forms: as Kali, based on primitive bloodthirsty mother-deities, and as Durga, herself a fearsome demon-slayer. In his connection with agricultural fertility Shiva is accompanied by the bull Nandi, whose symbol, the crescent moon, he wears on his forehead.

The source of Shiva's strength was the austerities he performed, originally in penance as a Brahminicide, for in order to assert his superiority to Brahma, he had struck off Brahma's fifth head. Shiva alone of the gods was able to give Indra strength to overcome the demon Vritra who, also by the practice of yoga, had acquired strength to create illusions, endless energy, and power over the gods. Shiva was the special strengthener and helper of warriors, ready to dispense magic weapons, and god of medicine too. Once while meditating he was interrupted by and killed Kama, god of love. The fruit of his delayed desire was Karttikeya, god of war.

Shiva's first wife was Sati, daughter of the sage Daksha, the son of Brahma. She had married him against the wishes of her father, who subsequently berated him in front of the assembled gods as a flouter of divine ordinances who had abolished ancient rites (sacrifice), haunted cemeteries, and looked like a madman in his yogic aspect. Later Daksha invited all the gods except Shiva to a sacrifice, whereupon Sati, to vindicate Shiva's honour, threw herself into the sacrificial flames and was consumed. (The practice of 'suttee' arose from this.) Shiva's grief at her death threatened the divine order, and ultimately she was reborn as Parvati.

The mythology surrounding Vishnu is linked with samsara, the idea that every man is born many times over, each life representing a punishment or reward for his previous life. If he performs his duty, dharma, he progresses upwards until he becomes a saint or god. If he has not done his duty, he slips downwards towards life as a demon. Good and evil, opposite poles, are both active in the world, but if evil becomes dominant the ladder of samsara becomes too difficult for men. It is then Vishnu's function to intervene: as preserver he descends to earth in an incarnation or avatar.

The first avatar, borrowed from the mythology of Brahma, was as a fish, Matsya, who helped save the sage Vaivaswata, an Indian Noah, and progenitor of the human race. The second was as a tortoise, Kurma, when, after a periodic deluge, various precious things had been lost. Most important was the source of the gods' strength, amrita, the cream of the milk ocean. Using Mount Mandara as a churning stick, the serpent Vasuki as a rope, and Kurma's back as a pivot, the gods churned the milk ocean and recovered the precious things. The third avatar was as Varaha, a boar as large as a mountain and the only creature able to kill Hiranyaksha. This demon had induced Brahma to grant him the boon of invulnerability (but had forgotten to mention boars) and had seized the Vedas and dragged the earth down into his watery abode. The fourth avatar was Narasinha, a man-lion, who evaded the conditions of a boon granted by Brahma to the demon Hiranyakasipu, who had been laying waste the world and persecuting his son Prahlada, a devotee of Vishnu. The fifth avatar, Vamana, had the task of curbing a king, Bali, who by sacrifice and austerities had gained the power to oust Indra from his heaven. Born a dwarf, Vamana asked Bali for the gift of three paces of land. The gift granted, Vamana grew to enormous size: his first two paces covered all earth and the heavens; but Bali's merits had to be recognised, so he was given dominion over the nether regions, Patala. The sixth avatar, Parasurama, born the son of a Brahmin hermit, defended his parents against the arrogance of a king and all his Kshatriya caste. Having exterminated them in twenty-one campaigns, he gave the earth into the care of a Brahmin sage, Kasyapa.

The seventh and eighth avatars, Ramachandra (Rama) and Krishna, are the most famous and have been elaborated in literature, but space does not permit details. Rama was born a human prince to overcome Ravana, the most powerful demon king yet, who had so propitiated Brahma and Shiva that he was free to persecute gods and men; but this rakshasa king of Lanka (Ceylon) had been too proud to ask immunity from the attacks of men. While Rama was living in the forest in exile from his father's court with his half-brother Lakshmana and his wife Sita (incarnation of Vishnu's wife Lakshmi),

Ravana had Sita abducted. Rama made an alliance with the monkey-king Sugriva, son of Indra. Under the generalship of the monkey-god Hanuman, who as son of Vayu, the wind, could fly, they attacked Lanka and its massive fortifications. After a mighty battle all the rakshasa generals were killed. Rama faced Ravana in single combat. He struck off Ravana's ten heads one after the other, but each was replaced by another until Rama brought forth the Brahma weapon fashioned by the sage Agastya, which slew the demon.

In the eighth incarnation, as Krishna, the task was to kill Kansa, the tyrannical king of the Yadavas at Mathura in northern India. Kansa, forewarned of his future killer's birth, ordered all newborn males to be slaughtered; but by exchange of babies, Krishna escaped and grew up in secrecy among cowherds, a delightful, mischievous boy, except when attacked by demons sent in different forms by Kansa, which he overcame by strength or ruse. The second phase of his life was a celebration of sexual love, in which women's frenzied devotion to Krishna was most notably expressed in a dance of consummated love with the gopis or cowgirls. While dallying with the cowgirls Krishna continued to slay demons sent by Kansa, and finally accepted Kansa's invitation to his court. There, forewarned of Kansa's plot, he broke the bow of Shiva, and with his brother Balarama overcame a mighty elephant and a wrestler posted to crush them, and then killed Kansa and his eight brothers. Further demons came forward to avenge Kansa, and Krishna remained on earth as a sort of feudal prince. The struggle continued, with wave after wave of demons slaughtered. Krishna finally built a fortress city, Dwarka, and married Rukmini, another incarnation of Lakshmi, and seven more wives, then a further sixteen thousand one hundred girls—each marriage marking the conquest of yet more demons. His son by Rukmini was Pradyumna, a reincarnation of the god of erotic love Kama, whose death at the hands of Shiva had made nature languish. The climax of Krishna's long battle with evil was in the epic struggle between the Pandavas and Kauravas, related in the *Mahabharata*, in which Krishna acted as adviser rather than as warrior. The chief

Central image of Shiva representing him as Great Lord, serene universal spirit, from the triple image in the seventh-century rock carving at Elephanta. The face on the right represents his virility and willpower, and a third, out of view, shows his feminine aspect.

advice was that all is illusion, maya, including battle, but that men must do their duty, leaving the higher perspective to the gods, in order to ascend the moral ladder through samsara; but also that there was, in addition to yoga and austerities, another way to escape samsara and obtain release, *moksha*, and fusion with the universal spirit. This was by *bhakti*, devotion to a particular god, with concentration on him and repetition of his name. (Those who endlessly chant Hari-Krishna in the West are latter-day exponents of the theory.) For obvious reasons the worship of Krishna was and is enormously popular, and he is sometimes called a god in his own right, with Balarama considered the eighth avatar of Vishnu.

The ninth avatar was as Buddha, a Buddha seen through Hindu eyes as a hedonistic subverter of divine truth, a devil's advocate whose ideas would weaken the opponents of the gods and lead them back ultimately to the traditional gods. In a sense, Buddhism really did this: during the millenium when Buddhism was the religion of the ruling classes, popular imagination created a Buddhist mythology based on the ancient gods, and pantheistic confusion continued in popular mythology even after the resurgence of Hinduism.

Vishnu's last avatar is yet to come, at the lowest point of degeneration of the present Mahayuga, when civilisation will have crumbled away. He will be incarnated in a white horse, Kalki, and riding it with his drawn sword blazing like a comet, will accomplish the final destruction of the wicked, so preparing for the resurgence of virtue in the next Mahayuga.

The Vedic gods, demoted under Hinduism, lent elements of their mythology to the great triad, and developed some new myths. Indra is still god of storms, but less a warrior than a king, mounted on an elephant (elephants were created from shavings of the sun). Through his weakness for soma and women, he loses power and is worsted by demons, sages and others. However, he is chief of the eight 'world guardians'. The other seven are Yama, now a fearsome messenger of death riding a buffalo; Varuna, who keeps watch over the demons of the ocean darkness; Agni, purifier of sacrificial offerings; Surya; Vayu, intemperate slayer of demons and seducer of women; Soma or Chandra, now entirely identified with the moon, and afflicted with recurrent consumption (the phases of the moon) by a curse of his father-in-law, the sage Daksha; and a jewel-laden god of riches, Kubera, a dwarf and in the Vedas chief of the evil beings, who had become a god by virtue of

austerities and who was the father of Ravana. Apart from Dharma, duty personified, the other important and popular new deity was the elephant-headed son of Parvati, Ganesa, god of wisdom and the remover of obstacles, whose original head had been struck off by Shiva and replaced with the first available substitute.

Buddhist mythology
The mythology of Buddhists, as opposed to that concerning Buddha within Hinduism, sought to place the historic teacher of a highly abstract philosophical creed in a pattern of previous incarnations familiar to Indian believers, and to prove his divine origin. The Jataka tales relating his previous lives begin with his seeing the glory of Dipankara, the Buddha of the age before ours, and determining himself to become a Boddhisattva. In his many lives, among them as a hare, as an elephant, as various priests and ascetics, and as a prince, he sacrificed himself in order to preach the virtues of patience and submission to fate, so impressing Sakra (Indra) that he gave him aid to perform miracles.

As Buddha he was born to King Suddhodana of Kapilavastu and Queen Mahamaya, who conceived him after dreaming of a white elephant entering her womb. He was born beneath a Sal tree, in full awareness and looking like the young sun. At each of his first seven footfalls a lotus sprang up, and gods and men acknowledged him. It was predicted he would either become a great king or an ascetic, and he was named Siddhartha. To ensure that he would not renounce the world, his father shut him off from life outside, even after his marriage to Yasodhara, so that his boyhood and youth were a time of careless pleasure sheltered from all knowledge of sickness and death.

In time the gods filled the universe with the thought that it was time to go forth, and Siddhartha persuaded his father to allow him four chariot rides outside the palace. The gods thwarted the king's precautions and presented Siddhartha with the Four Signs, an old man, a sick man, a dead man, and a monk, detached and peaceful. He learnt that renunciation was the path of salvation. Shortly afterwards, his son born, he escaped from the palace, divested himself of his princely jewels, cut off his hair, and began to search for enlightenment. First he sat at the feet of the philosophers and found them wanting; then he became an ascetic, but found physical weakness was an impediment to the spirit. After seven years, almost despairing, he sat beneath a pipal tree in contemplation, resolved not to rise until he had achieved enlightenment. For twenty-eight days he remained in meditation, ignoring

the nightly efforts of Mara, the Evil One, to distract him, and on the twenty-eighth day he rose triumphant, lord of the three worlds.

At the entreaty of Brahma, Buddha remained on earth to preach – that attachment to life and desire are the cause of sorrow, and that detachment may be achieved by following the Holy Eightfold Path. His first exposition of this Law (Dharma) took place in the Deer Park in Benares and is referred to as the first turning of the Wheel of the Law. Thereafter he preached at his father's court, where he converted his wife, his brother Ananda and his son Rahula, who continued to spread the word, while Buddha ascended to heaven for three months to convert his mother and the gods. The only opponent to Buddha was his cousin Devadatta, who mounted several attacks, but was finally consumed by flames shooting out of the earth. After a ministry of forty-five years Buddha gave up the desire for life, adopted a position of yogic concentration, and shook off the life remaining to him. Before his death he journeyed to Kusinagra, where before expiring he received kings, noblemen and Brahmins in a grove of Sal trees. As his soul entered Nirvana earth trembled in darkness, while the heavens were lit up. Winds raged and the rivers boiled. On the seventh day the body was cremated, the fire lighting itself, and leaving behind a heap of pearls, divided into eight parts and taken into kingdoms near and far.

In addition to the mythology surrounding Buddha himself, popular Buddhism added a pantheon adapted from the Hindu, but drastically altering the roles of the deities. Thus Shiva and Parvati are Buddha's doorkeepers, while Kubera is his bodyguard. The goddesses of Buddhism mostly resemble the fierce aspects of Shiva's consort, though Tara, the most revered, is perhaps more fearsome.

Jain mythology
Mahavira, the great teacher of Jainism in the present age and a contemporary of Buddha, was born in Benares to Jain parents worshipping a previous Tirthankara, Parshva, who had taught resistance to the urge to kill. His mother Trisala had

Shiva Nataraja, Lord of the Dance, trampling a dwarf demon. Shiva's dancing symbolises and perpetuates the movement of the universe, representing cosmic truth and the destruction of the illusory world of maya. The halo represents the universal cycle. Madras bronze, tenth century. Victoria & Albert Museum.

below
Shiva Bhuteswara, haunter of
cemeteries. Helped by Ganesa and
watched by Parvati, the infant
Karttikeya and the bull Nandi, he strings
together the skulls of the dead at the
cremation ground. Nandi's symbol, the
crescent moon, surmounts Shiva's third
eye. Kangra painting, 1790. Victoria &
Albert Museum.
opposite
 Detail from a sixth-century Khmer
sandstone statue of Harihara, Vishnu and
Shiva seen as complementary aspects of
the universal spirit. On the left Shiva's
tangled hair and lightning trident; on the
right, Vishnu's cylindrical headdress and
discus weapon.

a dream in which sixteen images foretold the birth of a great emperor or of a great saint. The gods transferred the unborn child from the womb of Devananda, a Brahmin's wife, to Trisala's, and the child was duly born and named Vardhamana. Endowed with beauty and with physical and spiritual strength, when only a boy he overcame a mad elephant. He obtained enlightenment while sitting under an Asoka tree before a gathering of the gods, who thereupon acknowledged him as Mahavira and set him on a five-tiered throne. Here he cast off all his clothes, tore out his hair and gave away all possessions, retaining only a white robe given him by Sakra (Indra).

Mahavira's life of unexampled virtue was spent in meditation and showed, through various tales, his complete lack of self-regard, imperviousness to physical pain, and detachment from worldly concerns. As death approached, he spent his last seven days preaching to the rulers of the world, the chief teaching being absolute prohibition on killing, which led to the belief that the most virtuous life is spent sitting still and fasting. On the seventh day Mahavira ascended a diamond throne bathed in supernatural light, but his death was unseen. He was declared a Tirthankara, an omniscient being higher than a god, who spends some time as an ascetic and then as a teacher on earth and whose soul is liberated from samsara by possession of the five kinds of knowledge.

The universal cycle of Jains is seen as a

opposite
Vishnu in his boar avatar, Varaha, rising from the ocean depths with Prithivi, Earth, in the crook of his arm. On his right sits Brahma, bearing the Vedas, on his left sits Shiva. Twelfth-century Chauham style slate carving. Victoria & Albert Museum.

right
Ravana rallies the demons against Rama's army. The fortress-palace of Lanka was built for the demons by Visvakarma, the Hindu form of Tvashtri, occupied by Kubera, god of riches, and seized back by Kubera's half-brother Ravana. Sixteenth-century Moghul painting.

below
Vishnu enthroned in his heaven, Vaikuntha, with his consort Lakshmi, and surrounded by his ten avatars or earthly incarnations—the last is yet to come. As safeguard of man's aspirations, he inspires devotion rather than fear.

Eighteenth-century Jaipur painting. Victoria & Albert Museum.

opposite
The Horse Court from the fourteenth-century temple of Vishnu at Srirangam. Though the Aryan horse was replaced as Indra's mount by an elephant, in Hindu mythology the horse was to be Vishnu's last incarnation when he would accomplish the final destruction of this Mahayuga.

wheel that eternally revolves, bringing a waxing and waning of virtue. Each complete cycle produces forty-eight Tirthankaras, who cannot intercede on behalf of the faithful, for there is no ultimate god; their value to mankind is as objects of meditation, beings who have escaped from the wheel of life. Jain gods and demons are largely of Hindu inspiration, but while demons can work out their salvation, gods cannot obtain liberation without first becoming human beings.

above
The graceful Sarasvati, goddess of poetry and music. Once a river deity, she was associated with rites performed on her banks and became goddess of speech and inventor of Sanskrit. Mother of the Vedas, she executes what Brahma conceives. Relief from the Vimla Vashi temple.

opposite
The white marble Vimla Vashi temple at Dilwara, dedicated to the goddess Sarasvati, originally a wife of Vishnu, who repudiated her as too quarrelsome and gave her to Brahma. She is Brahma's chief consort though she cursed him to be worshipped only once a year. Eleventh century.

page 90
Radha and Krishna in the grove. In myth, by the power of illusion and ecstasy, Krishna satisfied equally all the gopis of his youth and the wives of his maturity. In love poetry and song a popular motif is his love for a favourite gopi, Radha. Eighteenth-century Nurpur painting. Victoria & Albert Museum.

page 91
Chola bronze of the sixteenth century illustrating an episode from Krishna's boyhood, when he subdued the snake demon Kaliya by dancing on his heads. Like the heroic figures of many mythologies, the infant Krishna could defend himself against all demon attacks.

above
Durga, fierce consort of Shiva and mighty demon-slayer. Born fully grown and beautiful, she used one of the gods' weapons on each of her ten hands to destroy the demon Mahisha, who threatened to dispossess the gods.

Chamba painting, eighteenth century. Victoria & Albert Museum.
opposite
Garuda, eagle king of the birds, charger of Vishnu and Lakshmi (here in incarnations of Krishna and Radha), and pursuer and devourer of evil men and

snakes. In his incarnation as Jatayu he helped Rama find the abducted Sita. Eighteenth-century painting.

above
Kama, god of love, riding a symbolic
elephant composed of womankind.
As is seen from the languishing of
nature after Shiva killed him, Kama
represents the creative spirit, but popular
mythology emphasises his frivolity.
Trichinopoly painting. Victoria & Albert
Museum.

opposite
Arjuna, hero of the epic *Mahabharata*,
standing on one leg (top left) while
performing penances to gain the favour
of the gods in the coming battle. The force
of his austerities made the heavens shake
and brought him Shiva's support.
Seventh-century rock carving at
Mahabalipuram.

above
North gate of the Buddhist stupa at
Sanchi. The sculptures, dating from the
first century BC, illustrate the Jataka tales,
myths of Buddha's previous lives on
earth, whose function was to fit Buddha
into a pattern familiar to Indian
believers.

opposite
Manjusri, the Buddhist god of wisdom
and grammatical knowledge. Tibetan
gilded bronze of the seventeenth century.
While Buddhism faded away in its land of
origin, it became the dominant religion
in many parts of Asia, each new
homeland adding a native mythology.

page 98
Buddha in meditation. Mara hoped to
distract him with a violent storm, but
Mucilinda, king of the Nagas (in
Hinduism too, serpents deriving great
spiritual strength from austerities), coiled
himself underneath Buddha and sheltered
him with his hood. Eleventh-century
sandstone, Bayon.

page 99
Sakra (Indra) commanding the transfer of
the unborn Vardhamana from the
womb of Devananda into that of Trisala.
Miraculous birth and portents of greatness
were welcomed by his parents, unlike
Buddha's. From a fifteenth-century
manuscript of the *Kalpasutra*, Jain
scriptures. Victoria & Albert Museum.

Greece

Greek mythology is among the best documented, through art and literature, of any in the world. For this reason, it is among the best known, and has become part of the common currency of Western civilisation. It was an integral part of the culture of the highest civilisation of the ancient world, and its images spread with the influence of the Greeks. A highly complex mythology, it has been subjected to any amount of analysis and critical interpretation, on psychological and sociological lines—both in modern times, and in the days of classical antiquity.

The chief ancient sources are 'Homer' (the *Iliad* is dated about 800 BC, the *Odyssey* considerably later); Hesiod's *Works and Days*, written in the eighth century, and his or his school's *Theogony*; Pindar's *Victory Odes* of the fifth century; written in the same century and using the same sources, the tragedies of Euripides, Aeschylus and Sophocles; and the mythical history given by Pausanias about AD 170. All these authors were already adapting the primitive material to express a current or personal world view, and the influence of the fifth-century philosophers seems to have given further impetus or licence to invent didactic or aetiological myths. Archaeology may help to unravel the 'true' primitive mythology, explaining the settlement of the various regions of ancient Greece (today's mainland, islands and Asia Minor) by Greek-speaking invaders from the north. Social anthropology may add interpretations explaining myths in terms of the form of societies they set up—according to the needs of a warrior, a pastoral or an agricultural people; or according to patriarchal or matriarchal succession (a notable feature of Greek myth is succession to the throne through the performance of feats of valour and/or violent usurpation and incest). Psychology may point out the universal values exemplified in the myths, and the chords of personal pride and guilt they strike in all hearers. For present purposes, we shall take at face value the interpretations made by the ancient Greeks themselves, who systematised a mass of local and particular mythology that had developed in communities isolated by geography to form a mythological prehistory leading up to the massive Dorian settlement of the Peloponnese, about 1000 BC, which was equated with the return of the Heraclids to

Mycenae. The divine and semi-divine genealogies they constructed not only formed patterns for a social structure and mores (the Olympians, though majestic and powerful certainly, were swayed by human passions), but formed a link between historical dynastic successors and the cosmic forces which at first created and ruled the world.

Though some accounts gave Ocean or Time as the beginning of everything, the most usual belief was that Chaos was the source of creation. From this infinite void came Erebus, darkness, and his sisters Gaea, earth, and Nyx, night. Erebus and Nyx gave birth to Hemera, day, and Aether, air. Nyx was also the mother of various inscrutable forces important in Greek myth: the three Moerae, Fates; the Keres, personifying violent death; Thanatos, natural death; Hypnos, sleep; Morpheus, dreams; Eris, strife; Tyche, fortune; and Nemesis, guardian of moral and natural order which brought retribution to transgressors.

Gaea's son and husband was Uranus, the heavens, and they founded the first dynasty of the gods. Their offspring included the sea, Pontus, and the mountains, followed by twelve Titans, the three one-eyed Cyclopes, and the three Hecatoncheires, hundred-handed giants. Uranus cast his children into the depths of Tartarus, a place of punishment for the wicked, until with the connivance of Gaea Cronus, time, castrated and supplanted his father. From the spilt blood were born the half-human half-serpent Giants, the three Erinnyes or Eumenides (Furies) and, according to some versions, Aphrodite.

Cronus, youngest of the Titans, founded the second dynasty of the gods, which presided over an age of perfection, the Golden Age, when men were naturally good, work and warfare unknown, and death a pleasant sleep with immortality beyond the grave. Among the more important Titans were Rhea, the sister-wife of Cronus by whom he fathered the Olympian gods Zeus, Hera, Poseidon, Hades, Demeter and Hestia. Oceanus and Tethys were the parents of three thousand sons and three thousand daughters, the Oceanid nymphs, as well as all the seas (including Proteus with his ever-changing disguises), and the springs and rivers of the world. Among these were Achelous with his ever-changing shapes as snake, bull, or

bull-faced man, and Styx, goddess of the river surrounding Hades, the world of the dead, by whom the gods swore their most solemn oaths. Hyperion, early sun-god, was father of Helios, sun, Selene, moon, and Eos, dawn. Dusk was represented by the Titans Coeus and Phoebe, whose daughters were Asteria, starlight, and Leto, mother by Zeus of the Olympian sun-god Apollo and moon-goddess Artemis. Another Titan, Iapetus, was the father of four founders of human culture, Atlas, who bore the heavens on his shoulders and guarded the entrance to the underworld in the far west, Menoetius, Prometheus and Epimetheus, whose wife was Pandora.

The progeny of the Titans were of greater importance than their parents in the succeeding Silver Age of the world, a period of increasing hardship and degeneracy, when men had to build houses and work, but were mentally weak and impious, long-lived though after death not immortals, but spirits inhabiting the underworld. In the Brazen Age which followed, men were stronger, but bent on mutual destruction; a time of strife and violence, when death meant annihilation. During these ages the third dynasty of the gods came to the fore. Their associations were partly cosmic, but even more moral and social.

Cronus was overthrown as ruler of the gods much as he had overthrown his own father. His actions determined by one of the recurrent prophecies or oracles (always fulfilled, in unexpected and tragic ways) that are a feature of Greek mythology, he attempted to avoid being dethroned by a son greater than himself by swallowing each of his children at birth. After five children had perished this way, Rhea went into hiding in Crete to give birth to the sixth, Zeus. He was tended by the goat Amalthea, who fed him milk and honey and then food from her horn of plenty, and the Curetes, warrior demi-gods whose clashing arms drowned the infant's cries. Meanwhile Rhea gave Cronus a stone to swallow. When he was grown, Zeus returned, overcame his father and forced him to vomit up the stone (later known at Delphi as the navel stone of the earth, or Omphalos) together with his brothers Poseidon and Hades and his sisters Demeter, Hestia, goddess of the hearth, and Hera. The Titans were driven to

Mount Othrys until after a ten-year battle, in which Zeus was helped by Gaea and her children the Cyclopes and Hecatoncheires, they were defeated and consigned to Tartarus, the lower depths of the underworld. Here as their warders the Hecatoncheires were virtual prisoners. Gaea thereupon shifted allegiance, and bore three giants, Antaeus, Tityus and Typhon, whose opposition Zeus eventually overcame by the thunderbolts made for him by the Cyclopes, smiths. The fire-breathing Typhon with his hundred snake heads he imprisoned under Mount Etna, whence its volcanic eruptions. Tityus, for attempting to rape Leto, was killed by her children Apollo and Artemis, and thrown by Zeus into Tartarus, where two vultures forever tore at his liver.

Together with his brothers and sisters and later other gods, Zeus occupied Mount Olympus in Thessaly, a mountain which reached up into the heavens, where they ate the food of immortality, ambrosia, and drank nectar. Though thought of mainly in human form, of great size and ideal beauty, the Olympian gods could change shape at will. Zeus in particular did so to pursue his amours, among goddesses and mortals: his progeny was vast, as befitted the chief of the gods and god of violent and imperious nature who manifested himself in the thunderstorm. And his position as chief of the gods could be asserted by making him the father of various deities previously existing in their own right.

Zeus first married Metis, wisdom or prudence, daughter of Oceanus; but, warned by Gaea that their issue would be stronger than he, he swallowed Metis. The child, Athena, born fully grown and armed, sprang from her father's forehead, cleft by the axe of Hephaestus. His next wife was the Titan Themis, justice. Her children included the Horae, hours or seasons, whose creation was a feature of the worsening conditions of the Silver Age and who guarded the entrance to Olympus; and, according to some versions, the Fates. Zeus' second Titan wife was Mnemosyne, memory, mother of the nine Muses; and by the Oceanid Eurynome he was the father of the three Graces, Charites.

Zeus' permanent consort, associated with his supreme power and called queen of heaven, was his sister Hera. On her he fathered the major Olympian gods Ares and Hephaestus, as well as Eileithya, goddess of childbirth, and Hebe, goddess of youth (and, before being supplanted by the Trojan prince Ganymede, cupbearer of the gods). Though respected and revered as queen of the gods and patroness

Core, 'the Maiden', Persephone in her role as carefree daughter of the fertility-goddess Demeter, whose eight-month reunion was the time of earth's abundance. Core symbolised the sprouting seeds. Bronze statuette, c. 480 BC. British Museum.

of marriage, Hera appears most often in myth as unforgiving pursuer of her rivals for Zeus' love and of their progeny. Among her divine rivals were Leto, mother of the twins Apollo and Artemis, and Demeter, whose daughter was Persephone. Some of the innumerable mortal women loved by Zeus gave birth to heroic demi-gods. Among them were Danae, to whom Zeus appeared as a shower of gold and who bore Perseus; Leda, whom he loved in the shape of a swan and who bore two eggs, one containing the children of Zeus, Pollux and Helen, the other the children of her husband Tyndareus, Castor and Clytemnestra; Alcmene, wife of Amphitryon, who bore him Heracles; and Europa, whom he abducted in the shape of a white bull and who bore him Minos, Rhadamanthus, and Sarpedon.

The exploits of such heroes form the bulk of Greek mythology, when they proved their valour either in communal enterprises such as the Theban wars (the 'Seven against Thebes') and the Trojan war, or in individual feats where with divine aid or the use of supernatural powers they overcame all odds, usually gaining thereby a wife or a kingdom. In all these exploits, however, Olympian parentage and Olympian help were of capital importance; and in these matters the Olympians rarely agreed, each supporting his or her own favourite, the choice resting usually on personal reasons rather than any ideas of justice. Thus for example in the Trojan war, Hera supported the Greeks because the Trojan Paris had passed her over in judging who was the fairest of the goddesses; while Aphrodite, who had won, supported Troy. Zeus supported the Trojans while Poseidon opposed them, sending a sea-monster to consume the king's daughter Hesione because they had refused to pay him for his help in constructing the walls of Troy.

When the Titans were overthrown the division of authority between the gods had been decided by lot. Zeus received dominion over the upper world, Hades over the lower world, and Poseidon over the sea, rivers and springs. Poseidon's wife Amphitrite was a Nereid, one of the beautiful sea-nymphs friendly to men. (Another famous Nereid was Thetis, mother of Achilles.) Among Poseidon's

The temple of Apollo at Corinth. Built about 540 BC and destroyed by fire during the Roman conquest of 146 BC, it was dedicated by the Corinthians at the height of their commercial power to the god whose cult most decisively shaped Greek society.

children by Amphitrite was Triton, half-fish and half-man; and among the countless other offspring of this violent, tempestuous and quarrelsome god were various monsters or parents of monsters and, most illustrious, the hero Theseus. Poseidon's gifts to man included the horse, which sprang forth when he struck the ground with his trident in a dispute with Athena over the city of Athens (Athena's gift, which won her the city, was the olive tree). Poseidon was the father of Pegasus, the winged horse, by Medusa, one of the three Gorgons, monsters whose gaze turned men to stone and who dwelt near the Hesperides, daughters of night, at the western extremities of Ocean.

Hades, who ruled the dark regions of the lower world, was an inexorable god, goading the unwilling into his realm with a pitchfork, and was hated by gods and men alike. Having been ferried by Charon across the river Acheron, the souls of the dead, accompanied by Hermes, were met by Hades' dog Cerberus, who guarded the gates of Hades so that they could never again emerge. After judgment, the soul was allocated to a place of torment in the lower underworld, Tartarus, or if virtuous given a place in the joyous Elysian Fields. The alternative reward, for heroes, was eternal life in the far off Isles of the Blessed, where the Golden Age was recreated. The possibility of a pleasant aspect to life after death was reflected in Hades' identification with Pluto, giver of wealth, food and corn.

The most famous Hades myth is in connection with Demeter, goddess of fertility, and her daughter by Zeus, Persephone. Zeus gave Hades permission to take Persephone as his bride, whereupon he snatched her while she was picking flowers and bore her off in his black chariot to his kingdom. Demeter's grief while searching for her daughter caused all nature to languish, but with the help of Helios, who saw everything, she traced Persephone. Eventually, seeing the barrenness of nature, Zeus relented and sent Hermes to fetch Persephone back. But she had eaten part of a pomegranate given her by Hades and therefore a compromise had to be reached: for eight months Persephone would be able to stay with her mother, and for the remaining four, the winter, she would return to Hades. While in Hades she was considered a fearsome, tragic queen; but on earth she remained the carefree girl picking wild flowers, known in Attica as Core, the daughter. During her search for Persephone on earth, Demeter was befriended by a mortal king and queen. Having accidentally killed their son Demophoon while attempting to confer immortality on him, she instructed their

other son Triptolemus in the arts of agriculture. He travelled the world in a chariot drawn by dragons and serpents, teaching men the arts of settled civilisation, agriculture, law, peace and marriage. The Eleusinian Mysteries, held in Demeter's honour at Eleusis and Athens, celebrated her as bringer of these benefits to mankind.

While the universe was divided between the brothers Zeus, Poseidon and Hades with their cosmic and fertility associations, Apollo, perhaps once the supreme god, had a capital importance in shaping the character of Greek society. The type of male beauty by which the Greeks set great store, god of youth and light, he was a benevolent pastoral god, patron of poetry and music, whose retinue on Mount Parnassus included the Muses, and whose playing of the lyre and flute entertained the gods on Olympus. He was also a god swift in retribution. Those who displeased him met sudden death from his darts (possibly the rays of the sun with which he was associated), such as the many sons of Niobe, who had vaunted her fecundity by comparison with Leto, who had borne only Apollo and Artemis. No suggestion of rivalry or criticism was tolerated.

But equally, he could intervene to prolong the life of his favourites, such as Admetus, whom he had helped to gain the hand of Alcestis by yoking a wild boar and a lion. He nurtured medicinal plants, and the use of herbs and potions was taught to his son Asclepius, god of medicine, whose mother was Coronis, daughter of the king of the Lapiths, the first primitive men to build with stone. The great enemies of the Lapiths were the Centaurs, wild creatures who had the body of a horse and the torso of a man, offspring of Ixion as part of Zeus' punishment for his attempted wooing of Hera (the other part of the punishment was to be chained to a wheel forever revolving over the flames of Tartarus). Asclepius was brought up by the one beneficent Centaur, Chiron, a skilled surgeon who also taught the arts of warfare to the heroes Heracles, Jason, Actaeon and Achilles.

Perhaps the magical skill of healing was part of Apollo's greatest gift, that of prophecy. By overcoming the serpent Python sent by Hera to destroy him at his birth on the island of Delos, he established the chief seat of his cult, at Delphi. Here, enveloped by fumes rising from a sacred cavern, the priestess Pythia delivered ill-understood judgments and prophecies, whose obscurity was an important motif in myth – and history. The Delphic oracle, and others throughout Greece, each with a priestess called a sibyl, were consulted

before any weighty enterprise, and especially over the foundation of cities and colonies. Apollo himself liked to build, and he helped in constructing the walls of Troy, whose side he took in the war. He loved the Trojan princess Cassandra, and conferred on her the gift of prophecy, but condemned her never to be believed when she rejected his love. Most of his loves, for young men or for women, were unsuccessful or tragic. His emblem the laurel was a nymph, Daphne, who changed into a tree to escape him.

Apollo's sister Artemis, the huntress armed with bow and arrow, shared his association with the countryside: she was guardian of flocks, of wild animals and of the young, human and animal. At Ephesus she was identified with an Asiatic fertility-goddess, leader of the Amazons, female warriors who founded many cities in Asia Minor. Artemis also shared Apollo's dual nature as benefactor and punisher. Though known as the virgin goddess, she had at least one lover, Orion, son of Poseidon, whom Apollo tricked her into killing. Thereafter her vengeance was swift on any who crossed her (such as the Greeks in the Trojan war) or violated her modesty, such as Actaeon, who saw her bathing, was changed into a stag and torn to pieces by dogs. Her companions were the nymphs, beautiful, long-lived but not immortal divinities associated with every aspect of nature – water, mountains, woods and trees – but not especially well known for their chastity. Their favours were sought by gods and mortals, and their frequent pursuers were the satyrs, half-men half-goats, associated with the fields and woods and known for their virility and for participation in Dionysiac orgies. The chief of the satyrs was Pan, son of Hermes. He was god of shepherds and goatherds and a famed musician.

Dionysus was the antithesis of Artemis, though also the victim of Hera's jealous fury. Hera caused his mother Semele, daughter of Cadmus of Thebes, to ask Zeus to appear before her as god of thunder. As a result the mortal mother was consumed by lightning, but Zeus saved the unborn child and sewed him into his thigh until ready for birth. He grew up tended by nymphs on Mount Nysa, but Hera drove him mad. He embarked on widespread travels throughout the Mediterranean, Asia and India, teaching civilisation and especially the cultivation of the vine. Fortunate were those who honoured him as god and respected his followers. Such was Midas, king of Phyrgia: though his own foolishness caused him to ask for all he touched to turn to gold, Dionysus mitigated the results by transferring the

pages 104–105
One of the temples overlooking the
harbour of the Greek city of Selinus in
south-west Sicily. Through asking the
Selinans to arrange a sacrifice to
Poseidon, Hamilcar of Carthage brought
about his own defeat in 480 BC. This
temple marks the return of Selinus to
Greek allegiance.

The temple of Aphaea on the island of
Aegina, built about 510 BC, when this
early mother-goddess was identified
with Artemis as protectress of flocks.
After the defeat of Aegina by Athens in
456 BC Aphaea was identified with the
other virgin goddess, Athena.

gold-producing gift to a river in which Midas was to bathe. Those who spurned Dionysus, on the other hand, were sent violently mad, such as Lycurgus, who killed his own son, or Pentheus, torn to pieces by his mother and sisters on Mount Cithaeron, or the women of Argos, until the city set up shrines to the god. His cult took the form of intoxicated orgies, led by his retinue of satyrs and wild dishevelled females entwined with snakes and clashing cymbals, known as Maenads. Orpheus, son of a Muse, who with his magic lyre could charm all nature, became a follower of Dionysus after returning from Hades unable to regain his bride Eurydice. He was finally torn to pieces by Maenads. His head and lyre floated to the island of Lesbos, still singing of Eurydice.

The relatively late cult of Dionysus, centred on Thebes, also contrasts with that of Athena, city-goddess of Athens and thus preserver of the state, from birth bearing arms to defend it and sitting on the right hand of her father Zeus in the council of the gods. As daughter of Metis, 'prudence', she was goddess of wisdom, to whom the owl was sacred, and her role in warfare was most often in giving counsel on military strategy. She thus developed into a goddess protective of peace, who invented the olive, the plough and the rake, taught men how to tame horses and oxen and how to build ships, and invented the flute and trumpet. She was patroness of potters and of the domestic arts, especially weaving. Arachne, a mortal who successfully challenged her in this field, was turned into a spider for her presumption, condemned to spin forever. But Athena's early aspect as goddess of war was never forgotten: she was depicted helmeted and with a shield known as the aegis, fringed with snakes and bearing in its centre a Gorgon's head (presented to her by Perseus). In this guise she supported the heroes Jason, Perseus, Bellerophon, Heracles, Diomedes, and especially Odysseus, and energetically entered the fray on the side of the Greeks in the Trojan war. From her father Zeus she inherited strength and valour, and the weapons of thunder and lightning, but together with Hera and Poseidon she sometimes plotted against him. One of her temples at her chief seat, Athens, was dedicated to Athena Nike ('victory'), but the chief temple, the Parthenon, celebrated her as 'the Virgin', a seemingly paradoxical title for her role as local mother-goddess.

Ares, god of war, had none of the ambiguous nature of other Olympians. His character was pure violence, though his prowess in battle hardly matched his belligerence, and he was hated by both parents and fellow gods, especially Zeus and Athena, who helped Diomedes wound him at Troy. He was also overcome by Heracles, and by Otus and Ephialtes, who kept him prisoner in a bronze jar in the course of their attack on the Olympians (they were only prevented by Apollo from crushing Olympus by piling on it Mount Ossa and Mount Pelion). His off-spring included personifications of fear and anger, and also Eros, god of love and especially of its sufferings.

Eros and Harmonia, wife of Cadmus, Ares fathered on Aphrodite, goddess of beauty who also loved Poseidon, Dionysus and Hermes, by whom she bore Hermaphroditus. Aphrodite was, however, married to Hephaestus, the lame smith-god, who with the help of Helios caught her with Ares by lowering a cobweb-fine metal net over their bed, to the amusement of the gods. Aphrodite also loved a mortal Anchises, by whom she bore Aeneas; and another mortal, the beautiful Adonis, whose love, after he was killed by a wild boar, she shared with Persephone (he was associated with the Near Eastern dying and rising vegetation-god).

As for Hephaestus, his cult must have been of later origin, since his skills were those of metal-working which the Greeks learnt at a relatively developed stage of their culture, and which brought them advanced weapons, armour and war-chariots. His mythology may betray an unsuccessful attempt to supplant Zeus, for he was said either to be the child of Hera alone, or to have been cast out of heaven by Zeus, the explanation of his lameness. At any rate the gods owed him many of their powerful weapons as well as their palaces. His son Erectheus, who was tended in babyhood in the form of a snake by Athena, and whose sight drove to madness the daughters of Cecrops, first king of Attica, grew up to invent the use of a chariot with four horses. Another creation of Hephaestus was Pandora, the first woman, whom he fashioned from clay on Zeus's orders, in order to plague mankind.

Hermes, messenger of the gods, may also have been a relatively late introduction, for the myth of his infancy shows an attempted, and foiled takeover of Apollo's role. He was born in Arcadia, the son of Zeus by one of the Pleiades, Maia, daughter of Atlas, and on the first day created a lyre to celebrate his birth and then stole the cattle of Apollo, using his favourite device, trickery (for which with magic arts he was admired) to avoid discovery. But the two were reconciled by Zeus, and Hermes presented Apollo with the lyre. Hermes remained, however, skilled in divination and in the magic arts, with the help of his rod, the caduceus, later given to Asclepius. He retained a cult as pastoral god in Arcadia and at Argos, seat of the house of Atreus. He was popular especially among the lower classes, as the energetic traveller with his winged sandals honoured at every crossroads, and as god of gymnastics, of fraud, commerce and above all of luck.

In Greek mythology the borderline between divine beings and men remains fluid. But Prometheus, son of the Titan Iapetus, was perhaps the first culture-hero, his name meaning forethought. He and his foolish brother Epimetheus were assigned by Zeus to allocate gifts and powers to men. Epimetheus took the task upon himself and failed to give men the protection from the elements enjoyed by animals. Alternatively Prometheus cheated Zeus by arranging that only the useless parts of an animal should be sacrificed to the gods as burnt offerings, so that Zeus hid fire. Furthermore he sent Epimetheus a wife, Pandora, whose curiosity led her to open the forbidden box containing the evils and disease that continue to plague mankind, which thus reduced the fertility of the earth. In any case, Prometheus stole fire from the gods and brought it to earth. This so angered Zeus that he sent a flood to drown mankind, with the excuse of quenching the uncontrollable fire. Prometheus was punished by being chained to a mountain where an eagle pecked out his liver every day (it renewed itself each night). He had time, however, to warn Epimetheus' son Deucalion and his wife Pyrrha of the impending flood and they were saved in the ark they built. When the flood subsided, Deucalion and Pyrrha emerged on Mount Parnassus and threw stones from which grew men and women, one of the men being Hellen, father of Dorus, Aeolus, and Xuthus and grand-father of Achaeus and Ion. Hellen was thus ancestor of the Greeks.

Mythology supplied each great city or kingdom with its own heroes to form a link between these ancestors and historical rulers. Thus Cecrops, an aboriginal being half-man and half-snake, founded Athens and installed there the worship of Athena and Zeus in preference to that of Poseidon, suppressing blood sacrifice. He was succeeded to the throne by Erechtheus, son of Hephaestus.

Theseus, a later Athenian hero, born in Argolis, distinguished himself in early youth by killing a number of monsters, including the tyrant wrestler Cercyon and Procrustes, and then restored his father Aegeus to the throne of Athens, usurped by his uncle, and rid him of his wicked wife the sorceress Medea. He then sought

above, right
Terracotta statuette of the early fourth century found at Locri, a Greek colony in the extreme south of Italy. With her tambourine, the figure is probably a Maenad, one of the followers of Dionysus, at times wild proselytisers of his cult throughout the Greek world. Museo Nazionale, Reggio.

opposite, top
Hermes, with winged sandals and travelling hat, the *petasus*, in his stern role as escorter of souls to Hades. He is entering a chariot with Aphrodite, by whom he was father of Hermaphroditus, drawn by Eros, her son by Ares, and Psyche. Terracotta plaque. Museo Nazionale, Taranto.

above
Dionysus riding a goat, one of the pastoral animals associated with this god of the vine and of ecstasy, who was brought up by nymphs on Mount Nysa in Thrace, and whose effeminacy or languor concealed an imperious demand for worship. Terracotta statuette. British Museum.

opposite, left
Boreas, the north wind. Like the other winds, and the stars, he was the son of Eos, goddess of the dawn, and Astraeus, son of the Titan Creus, identified with the force of the sea. Boreas was the trade wind for the island of Peparethus, which struck this coin. British Museum.

opposite, right
Syracusan dolphins surrounding a helmeted head, probably of Athena. The coin marks the defeat of the Athenian expedition against powerful Syracuse in 412 BC. Independent as the Sicilian rulers were, they liked to relate their power mythologically to mainland cults. British Museum.

to free Athens from paying tribute to king Minos of Crete. The tribute consisted of seven youths and seven girls a year, which were fed to the Minotaur, the bull-man monster offspring of Minos' wife Pasiphaea and a bull, which was housed in a labyrinth constructed by Daedalus. Theseus went to Crete as one of the seven youths and killed the Minotaur with the help of Minos' daughter Ariadne who, infatuated with him, gave him a thread by which to retrace his steps through the maze. On his return to Athens, Theseus forgot to hoist the prearranged signal of a white sail meaning success. His waiting father threw himself into the sea in despair, and Theseus took the throne. He later married the Amazon queen Antiope and had a son Hippolytus; and later still married Phaedra, Ariadne's sister, who loved and was spurned by Hippolytus. In spite, she accused him of attempted seduction, and had Poseidon punish him. When Hippolytus fell from his chariot and died, Phaedra killed herself. Theseus took part in the Calydonian boar hunt, was one of the Argonauts, and took part in the Trojan war and other exploits, apart from founding Athens as a great democratic city. But his end was tragic: Attica was invaded by Castor and Pollux, whose sister Helen Theseus had abducted, there was an insurrection, and Theseus sought refuge on the island of Scyros, where he was murdered.

Mycenae claimed Perseus, son of Zeus by Danae, whose father Acrisius, king of Argos, had been warned by an oracle of his overthrown by a grandson. Danae and the infant were therefore cast into the sea in a chest, but with Zeus' aid were washed up on the Aegean island of Seriphos, and sheltered by its king Polydectes. As Polydectes had designs on Danae, he ordered Perseus to fetch him the head of the Gorgon Medusa from Libya. With the help of Athena and Hermes, Perseus obtained the necessary equipment for the task: the helmet of Hades to make him invisible, a mirror so that he would not have to look directly at the Gorgons, a sickle, a bag to hold the head, and winged sandals to make his escape. On his return, having accomplished the task, he rescued Andromeda, daughter of the king of Ethiopia, from sacrifice to a sea-monster, and married her. He used the Gorgon's head to turn various opponents to stone, including Atlas, who became the north African mountain. On return to Greece, he accidentally killed his grandfather with a discus at funeral games held in Thessaly, and assumed the throne of Argos. He founded the Argolid cities of Persepolis and Mycenae, having exchanged thrones with the king of Tiryns.

Athena Promachos ('Defender of the City'), helmeted and with her hands raised to hold shield and spear, lost from this statuette. Though she took an active part in battles from birth onwards, her defensive role in Athens and Attica made her goddess of peace. British Museum.

Heracles, brandishing his club, brings Cerberus, the three-headed watchdog of Hades, to his taskmaster Eurystheus, who cowers in a cauldron. The fearsome monster, whose snakes indicate his infernal origin, was soon taken back to Hades. Vase from Caere. Louvre.

His grandchildren included Amphitryon, king of Tiryns; Eurystheus, king of Mycenae, who imposed the labours on Heracles; and Alcmene, mother by Zeus of Heracles.

Thebes claimed to have been founded by Cadmus, son of Agenor, king of Phoenicia and brother of Europa, abducted by Zeus in the shape of a bull. During his fruitless search for his sister, Cadmus had consulted the Delphic oracle, which told him to follow a cow and to found a city where it rested. It stopped at a spot in Boeotia, near a spring guarded by Ares' son in the form of a snake. With the help of Athena, Cadmus slew the snake and sowed its teeth, from which sprang up armed men, who immediately fought each other until reduced to the five strongest, the Sparti, ancestors of Theban aristocracy. They helped build the Cadmea, future citadel of Thebes. Cadmus civilised the Boeotians and taught them an alphabet, and he was privileged to marry the daughter of Ares and Aphrodite, Harmonia. The wedding was celebrated on Olympus, and Harmonia received a dress woven by Athena and a necklace made by Hephaestus – but the admired necklace was to cause a series of tragedies, and other misfortunes dogged the couple through their children, for they suffered from Hera's enmity. She caused the death of their daughter Semele before the birth of her son Dionysus; their grandson Pentheus was torn apart in a Dionysian orgy; and their grandson Actaeon was dismembered by his hounds. Ultimately Cadmus and Harmonia abandoned Thebes and conquered Illyria, which they ruled in the shape of great serpents.

Other Theban heroes included the twins Amphion and Zethus, twin sons of Antiope and Zeus. Exposed at birth, they grew up among shepherds, overthrew their stepfather Lycus and took command of Thebes, Amphion using his skill on the lyre to charm stones into building themselves up as fortifications. When his wife Niobe's boasts brought the death of their children, Amphion committed suicide. The story of Oedipus had some similar elements. Also exposed at birth on Mount Cithaeron because of a prediction that he would kill his father Laius, king of Thebes, Oedipus was brought up by the king of

Corinth, not knowing his true parentage. He learned of his destiny from the Theban oracle, and sought to evade it by fleeing Corinth. Instead, he unknowingly killed his father and, by solving the riddle of the Sphinx, sent by Hera to plague Thebes, rid the city of the monster and thus won the hand of its widowed queen, his mother Jocasta. Thebes fell on evil days, and by his own persistence Oedipus discovered that his own guilt was the cause. Jocasta hanged herself, Oedipus blinded himself, and was led by his daughter Antigone into exile at Colonnus in Attica, leaving his uncle Creon to rule Thebes.

The quarrels of Oedipus' sons Eteocles and Polyneices over the joint rule to which they succeeded gave rise to the wars of the Seven Against Thebes, seven great warriors from all over Greece ranged against Eteocles, and all doomed to die horribly except their leader Adrastus, king of Argos, who succumbed ten years later to grief over the bloody sequel of revenge in the war of Epigoni (descendants of the Seven).

Heracles, the most famous of all Greek heroes, and son of Zeus, was born at Thebes, though his mother Alcmene was the wife of Amphitryon king of Tiryns in Argolis. Myths connect him with both cities. On his birth, Hera sent snakes to attack him and his twin brother Iphicles, son of Amphitryon, but Heracles strangled them. His natural strength and skills were heightened by a number of illustrious teachers, but with his strength grew violent ways. His stepfather sent him to tend his flocks on Mount Cithaeron, and during this time he chose a life of heroism and glory, and killed a lion that had been destroying the flocks and freed Thebes from paying tribute to the king of Orchomenus in Boeotia. In gratitude Creon king of Thebes gave Heracles his daughter Megara as a bride, the wedding presents being weapons from the gods. With the death of Amphitryon, he returned to Tiryns, but soon was stricken with madness by Hera and killed his three children by Megara. He went into exile and was advised by the Delphic oracle to expiate his guilt by serving Eurystheus, king of Mycenae, for twelve years.

During these years he performed the famous twelve labours. He strangled the lion terrorising Nemea in Argolis. He overcame the Hydra or water-snake ravaging Lerna, near Argos, striking off eight of its heads and, with Iolaus' help, burning the necks so quickly they could not duplicate themselves; the ninth, immortal head he buried under a rock. After a year's chase he brought back alive to Mycenae the Arcadian stag sacred to Artemis. He

113

likewise caught the Erymanthian boar, which terrified Eurystheus. He cleaned in one day the stables of Augeas, which contained three thousand oxen and had not been cleaned for thirty years, by diverting two rivers. He rid Lake Stymphalis in Arcadia of its man-eating birds, frightening them with a rattle given by Athena and shooting them with arrows as they fled. He captured the white Cretan bull, a gift to Minos from Poseidon and father of the Minotaur, carrying it to Mycenae on his shoulders (it was later killed by Theseus). He tamed the man-eating mares of Diomedes, a Thracian king and son of Ares, by killing Diomedes and giving his flesh to the mares. He procured for Eurystheus' daughter the girdle of Hippolyte, symbol of power of the Amazon queen, but through Hera's machinations he killed Hippolyte. He captured the red oxen of Geryon, a winged three-bodied monster who lived in the far west, by killing their guards, the giant Eurytion and the two-headed dog Orthrus – like the lion and the Hydra, a son of Typhon – and then Geryon himself. He tracked down the golden apples kept by the Hesperides, daughters of Atlas, after long travels (for no one except Nereus, Old Man of the Sea, knew where they were) during which, among other feats, he freed Prometheus, who advised him to send Atlas for the apples; while Atlas was doing this, Heracles bore the weight of the heavens on his shoulders. The last labour, accom-

opposite
Bellerophon, tamer of Pegasus and grandson of Sisyphus, king of Corinth, was falsely accused of attempted seduction by the queen of Argos and given in punishment the task of killing the fire-breathing Chimaera, here receiving the death-blow. Bellerophon thus won half the kingdom of Lycia. Mid-fifth century BC. British Museum.

below
Atalanta hunting a lion with bow and arrow. After Meleager's death, Atalanta married Melanion, who won her by beating her in a foot-race—but only by dropping Aphrodite's tempting golden apples in her path. Both were later turned into lions. Halicarnassus mosaic. British Museum.

plished with the help of Athena and Hermes, was to bring Eurystheus Hades' three-headed dog Cerberus; this he did on Hades' conditions, with his bare hands, but the dog so frightened Eurystheus that Heracles soon took him back to the lower world.

After his period of service to Eurystheus, Heracles accomplished many other exploits, taking part in the Calydonian boar hunt and the Argonauts' expedition, as well as pursuing a private feud with the Trojans, in which he killed all the royal house except Priam, and another feud with Eurytus, a king in Thessaly, whose daughter Iole he wished to marry. His wife Deianeira, jealous of Iole, sent Heracles a robe which clung to his body and burnt it, so that Heracles, in trying to remove it, tore his own body to pieces.

Many of the heroes, including Heracles, Castor and Pollux, Orpheus, Peleus and Theseus, took part in the expedition to Colchis of Jason to fetch the golden ram's fleece held there by King Aeetes, son of Helios, under the guard of a serpent that never slept and fire-breathing bulls. Jason was given this task by his father's half-brother Pelias, who had usurped the throne of Iolcus in Thessaly. Sailing on the ship *Argo*, the heroes overcame various hazards on the voyage to Colchis, including Sirens and Harpies, and once in Colchis were faced with another series of 'impossible' tasks, all overcome with the magic aid of Medea, Aeetes' daughter, whom Jason

married after his triumphant return home.
When Jason later abandoned Medea for the
daughter of Creon of Corinth the sorceress
killed her two sons by Jason, killed Creon
and her rival–with a poisoned garment
that burned her to death. Jason perished
by his own hand.

Another great communal expedition
was the Calydonian boar hunt in Aetolia.
This was led by Meleager, son of Oeneus,
king of Calydon, and Althaea. Because
Oeneus had slighted Artemis, she had sent
a boar to ravage Calydon. The most
famous heroes assembled to hunt it, but the
first to draw blood was a woman, the
swift-footed huntress Atalanta. Though
Meleager delivered the death blow, he
presented the boar's skin as trophy to
Atalanta. When his uncles disputed this,
he killed them, and for this he was killed
by his own mother, who threw on the

fire a piece of wood which held the key
to Meleager's life and then hanged herself.

Greatest of all the wars, and most nearly
bordering on history, was that fought
between the Greeks and the Trojans,
whose heroes were taken as the ideals of
Greek warrior aristocracy. Again, heroes
from all over Greece assembled to support
a fellow king, Menelaus of Sparta, whose
wife Helen, daughter of Zeus and Leda,
had been abducted by Paris, son of the
aged Priam, king of Troy. The leader of
the Greek expedition was Agamemnon,
king of Mycenae and son of Atreus, ill-
fated descendant of Pelops the legendary
hero of the Peloponnesus (whose father
Tantalus was condemned to eternal hunger
and thirst within sight of food and drink
for having presented the flesh of Pelops
as a feast to the gods). The greatest Greek
warriors were Ajax of Salamis and

Three-bodied winged serpent-man,
probably Geryon, the son of Gaea's
monstrous offspring Typhon, who was
killed by Heracles in the course of his
tenth labour. Pediment decoration from
the Temple of Athena, c. 560 BC.
Acropolis Museum, Athens.

left
Medea, Jason's sorceress wife,
demonstrating to Jason's uncle,
Pelias, who had usurped the throne of
Aeolcus, how she rejuvenates a ram.
In trying the process himself, Pelias died.
Late sixth century. British Museum.

Achilles, son of Peleus, king of the Myrmidons (ant-men) in Thessaly, and the sea-goddess Thetis. Thetis had failed to confer immortality on her son by dipping him in the Styx, leaving a weak point at his heel where she had held him. He was a true model for warriors, for he had deliberately chosen a short life of glory, and he was to fall to an arrow of Paris in his heel; his generosity equalled his violent courage against enemies. On the Trojan side he was matched in valour by Hector, another of Priam's sons, who also perished. The siege of Troy lasted ten years, and was ended only by the trickery of the Greeks in presenting the Trojans with the gift of a huge wooden horse from which, once inside the walls, the Greeks debouched to lay waste Troy.

The Trojans were defeated but the gods who had taken their side in the war would not allow the Greeks to savour victory. Even their supporter Athena turned against them with the rape of Cassandra. The return of the heroes, especially that of Odysseus, persecuted by Poseidon, was delayed by a lengthy series of obstacles. Many returned to find their wives unfaithful and their thrones usurped, notably Agamemnon, murdered by his wife Clytemnestra, avenged by his children Orestes and Electra, whose guilt thus continued the curse on the house of Atreus. A marked feature of the wanderings and family quarrels ensuing from the Trojan war was the foundation of new colonies and kingdoms by the heroes.

above
Temple at Acragas (Agrigento) in Sicily and probably dedicated to Castor and Pollux, the heroes of Laconia. Known as the Dioscuri, 'sons of Zeus', their sisters were Helen and Clytemnestra, wife of Agamemnon. They were thus closely involved in the Trojan war.

opposite
Man, possibly a Lapith, with a Centaur.
Metal statuette, possibly early eighth
century BC. With the help of Theseus,
the Lapiths overcame the Centaurs and
won control of Thessaly in a fight begun
at the wedding of Perithous, their king,
and Hippodamia of Argos.
Metropolitan Museum of Arts.

above
Amazons with a fallen enemy. These
warlike haters of men made forays from
Cappadocia into mainland Greece to
avenge the abduction of Antiope by
Theseus and they sided with Troy.
Ionian silver chariot decoration from
Perugia. British Museum.

Ariadne, abandoned on the island of
Naxos by Theseus on the return voyage
from Crete after the slaying of the
Minotaur. Dionysus consoled her there
and she bore him Thoas, to become king
of Lemnos. Wall painting from
Herculaneum. British Museum.

The sacred site at Olympia. According to myth, the Games at Olympia were expanded by Pelops when he became powerful as king of Pisa in Elis. But since he won the kingdom and his bride Hippodamia through treachery and murder, his line was accursed.

opposite
Hermes with Paris, son of Priam king of
Troy. By forcing Paris to present the
golden apple to Athena, Hera, or
Aphrodite, the gods deliberately provoked
decimation of mortals through the
Trojan war: Aphrodite, whom he judged
fairest, offered him Helen, wife of
Menelaus of Sparta. Metropolitan
Museum of Arts.

above
Achilles receiving his armour from his
mother Thetis and from Hephaestus, the
divine smith and maker of the weapons
of the gods. Despite his mother's efforts
to give him divine protection, Achilles
accepted his destiny as a mortal.
Nearchos fragment, 560–50 BC.
National Museum, Athens.

right
The blinding of the Cyclops Polyphemus
by Odysseus. Trapped by the one-eyed
giant in a cave in Sicily, Odysseus
escaped after blinding him: one of the
many adventures on his way home from
Troy. This episode prolonged the
Odyssey by angering Poseidon. Eleusis
Museum.

Rome

Roman mythology has commonly been derided as a pale copy of the many cults assimilated during the expansion of Rome, the best known being the Greek-Roman equivalents. Such assimilation was perhaps inevitable in any situation where a relatively young and lately civilised society came into contact with and ultimately conquered civilisations of great antiquity which had elaborated complex mythologies over the centuries (and who, of course, attributed their former glory to the agency of their gods). The rapidity of Rome's expansion from a stage of clan or family structure where each group if not each individual had a particular set of beliefs, may itself have been a factor in Roman religious eclecticism. At any rate, while officially the doctrine was *cuius regio eius religio*, that subject peoples should accept the god of the conqueror, in practice the gods of the conquered were one by one brought to Rome. Though their unfamiliar social and personal aspect (mysteries, orgiastic celebrations, etc.) may have struck contemporary critics, the native Roman mythological modes did in fact colour each cult in its Roman form.

At the time when the civilisations the Romans were to call degenerate were at the height of their culture, settlers in Italy were still barbarians. During the third millenium Bronze Age Terramarrans from eastern Europe displaced the Neolithic Ligures, who had come from North Africa via Spain to settle in the Genoa region. These were superseded in turn by iron-working peoples from Hungary known as Villanovans, in the eleventh century BC. From these elements were built up the Latins, who according to tradition founded Rome in 753 BC.

Not until the ninth century with the arrival of the Etruscans, probably from Asia Minor, did a literate, civilised people enter the scene. Though primarily agricultural, their urban civilisation fostered fine metallurgy and pottery. As their writing has still not been deciphered, little can be known with certainty about their beliefs, but divination seems to have been an important factor, with the will of superior, nameless gods imparted through thunder, lightning, etc. The inferior deities, six male and six female, known to the Romans as Dei Consentes (advisers to Jupiter), were assimilated by the Etruscans themselves to Greek deities when they had formed trade links with Corinth and then Attica. The Etruscans subjugated the native peoples and used them as slaves. Their expansion partly depended on their superior armoury, and among other things they were said to have introduced the chariot into Italy. Naturally the gods of this successful people seemed worthy of respect, and some aspects of them were to be incorporated in Roman beliefs.

Rome owed its foundation and cohesion to the Etruscan menace to the north, for it originated as a collection of villages in a defensive position on the Tiber. The Romans thereby made the Tiber the southernmost limit of Etruscan rule until 616 when the Tarquins, Etruscan tyrants, became kings in Rome. Early Roman mythology certainly reflects the cosmological concerns of a pastoral people (and indeed, with Jupiter, the chief god, represented by a stone or flint, shows clear survivals from Neolithic times). But it strikes one chiefly as a political mythology. Jupiter, god of the storm and of lightning, the Smiter, was worshipped (above all in spring and autumn, opening and closing of the season for both war and agriculture) as the supporter of the Romans in battle with the Sabines. The Sabines, a neighbouring tribe, had been invited by the Romans to a feast so that the Romans could seize their women and make them their wives. According to the myth, women had hitherto shunned Rome because of the rough ways of its men, but exogamous marriage patterns are clearly indicated, and the myth must relate to the time when the Romans abandoned their rough pastoral traditions and became settled agriculturists. In the ensuing battle the Sabine women intervened, and peace was established between the two tribes. This was but one alliance. Jupiter became supreme god of the forty-seven cities of the Latin Confederation.

Jupiter was worshipped in a triad with two other gods, whose attributes were similar. Mars was the god of war and of agriculture. He seems to have been closely associated with the elective kings, whose leadership laid the foundations of Rome's greatness. The spears of Mars were kept in the Regia, the house of the kings of Rome in the Forum. The arms of Quirinus, originally a Sabine war-god, also had ritual significance, and he was later identified with Romulus, the deified founder of Rome. Romulus was said to be the son of Mars and Rhea Silvia. Together with his twin brother Remus, the infant Romulus was cast adrift by his great-uncle Amulius in a basket. But they were rescued by wolves, who suckled them and brought them up to be hardy shepherds, who banded together with others to found a city on the hill where they had been exposed. In a later quarrel Romulus killed Remus and became first king. As the city grew in strength, pitched battles occurred with the Etruscans, and in the course of one Romulus vanished into a cloud and became the god Quirinus.

Romulus was succeeded as king by Numa, Rome's legendary lawgiver, who established its rites, introduced a calendar, and brought Jupiter down to earth to show men how to ward off lightning and thunder. His wife Egeria, a water-nymph, advised him. His wisdom, or craftiness, protected Rome. Having learnt that the city would prosper so long as a shield that had fallen from heaven remained in Rome, he had eleven duplicates made to lessen the chance of its loss. He it was who introduced the worship of Minerva. Her name was Etruscan in origin, derived from Menrva, goddess of the morning and evening half-light, but identified by the Etruscans with Athena. In fact she may have come to Rome via the Italians to the south. She was an armed goddess who presided over intellectual activity and was patroness of the fine arts and crafts, medicine and other professions, and all schools. She was worshipped on the Capitol in a triad with Jupiter and Juno. Originally goddess of the moon and thus fount of the calendar, so important in Roman ritual, Juno became protectress of women, especially in childbirth, and above all Juno Moneta, 'the warner', guardian of the Capitol. Her sacred geese gave timely warning of the Gauls' attack on Rome in 390 BC, and she again saved Rome from the invasion of Pyrrhus in 275 BC at the battle of Beneventum.

Minerva. Though helmeted and wearing the aegis which she borrowed from her Greek counterpart Athena, she was seen in Rome primarily as the goddess of wisdom (whose symbol, the owl, she holds in her hand) and as patron of crafts and intellectual pursuits.

Beyond Jupiter, Mars and Quirinus, there were only two major deities in early Rome. Janus, the god of entry, was represented by an actual gate in the Forum and later as a man with two faces back to back, for gates face both ways; his cult may be connected with the fact that Etruscan deities were commonly given shrines at gates. A similar though less important deity was Terminus, god of the boundary stone, guardian of property and of peace between neighbours. The other major deity was the state version of the domestic gods Lares, spirits of the ancestors who guarded the household, and Penates, who guarded the family's store-cupboard near the hearth. This major deity, Vesta, represented the fire in the hearth, focus of the family and of the state. As in the family it was tended by the unmarried daughters, so in the state the sacred fire was constantly kept alight by the Vestal Virgins. They had to maintain the fire and their chastity for a period of thirty years' service, the penalty for failure being public beating, and the positions were filled by honoured members of important families throughout Roman history. Such was the importance of fire that Servius Tullius, who was king 578–34, claimed parentage of a slave girl of his predecessor Tarquinius Priscus and the Lar of the royal hearth.

This is one of the few myths attaching to the numerous deities of the various activities and objects of everyday life in an agricultural society gradually being transformed into an urban civilisation. *Numen* or divine power was imagined in almost everything, and many of the gods are mere names for use in propitiation by rather materialistic, legalistic ritual, bordering on magic. Significantly, Fortuna with her wheel was a powerful oracular mother-goddess whose ways were unknown to men. Among other gods that had to be propitiated but attracted little native mythology were Saturn, god of sowing, elements of whose festival, the Saturnalia, have carried over into Christmas festivities; Februs, god of the dead, later identified with the Etruscan Dis and Greek Pluto who presided over the restless spirits of the dead, *Manes*; Faunus and Fauna, rural deities of the earth; Flora, goddess of flowers; Pomona, goddess of fruit trees; her husband Vertumnus,

The Forum in Rome. A market, it was surrounded by shops, temples and public buildings and was the hub of communal life and the exchange of ideas, though the name means the place *outside*, since it was built on marshland between the hills of the original settlement.

129

the seasons; Carmenta, who determined the fortunes of children at birth; and Febris, fever.

Greek mythology entered Rome from two directions. From the south, where Greek colonies had been established since the eighth century, came Minerva, and three mortals whose merits had brought them divine immortality: Heracles (known in Latin as Hercules), and Castor and Pollox, who fought with the Romans against the Latins and Tarquins at the battle of Lake Regillus in 496 BC and thus won hegemony in Latium for the new Republic (traditionally founded 509 BC). All three gods protected trade, and were worshipped inside the City.

From the Etruscan Dei Consentes, already identified with Greek gods, and their assimilation to Roman deities came the wholesale adoption of Greek mythology. And the tendency to anthropomorphisation was accelerated by the adoption of the Etruscan custom of temple building and representation of gods. It should be noted, however, that these gods were not totally accepted until the Second Punic War (218–201 BC), for until then they were worshipped only outside the City. The parallels made were as follows: Zeus, Jupiter; Poseidon, Neptune; Ares, Mars – with the later addition of a female counterpart, Bellona; Hephaestus, Vulcan – formerly god of furnaces; Hermes, Mercury, god of peaceful trade; Hera, Juno; Athena, Minerva; Artemis, Diana; Aphrodite, Venus – formerly goddess of spring, from whom Julius Caesar claimed descent; Hestia, Vesta; Demeter, Ceres. The last of the new deities, who had no counterpart in the early Roman pantheon, was in many ways the most influential: Apollo, worshipped chiefly in his oracular role.

The native Roman tendency to quasi-magical ritual was reinforced by Etruscan reliance on augury (which was to lead to superstitition and ultimately to cynicism, with the educated turning to philosophy rather than religion). Apollo's cult had a highly political flavour through his shrine at the Greek colony of Cumae. Here the Sibyl, prophetess of Asian origin and, some claimed, descendant of a Trojan princess endowed by Apollo, gave forth oracular statements. The Sibyl of Cumae had approached Tarquinius Superbus (534–10 BC) offering to sell him nine prophetical books for half his fortune. When he refused, she threw three, then another three books into the fire. Finally he agreed to pay the original price for the remaining three, and these were preserved in the temple of Jupiter on the Capitol and consulted in times of national emergency. The first recorded occasion was in 493, when

the oracle commanded construction of a temple to Demeter, Iacchos and Persephone, under their Roman names Ceres, Liber and Libera. Thus the Eleusinian mysteries were introduced to Rome. Hermes and Poseidon also entered the Roman pantheon at the behest of the Sibyl, as did Aesculapius, the Greek Asclepius.

After the Roman defeat at Lake Trasimene in 217 BC, expiation seemed to be called for in order to win the Punic War. Along with a growth in what we might consider the grotesque – sacrifice through gladiatorial games for entertainment, emphasis on prodigies, etc. – were two trends affecting mythology proper. The first was the introduction of Greek ritual for both Greek and Roman gods – the birth of Graeco-Roman religion. The second was the direct importation of eastern cults. The Sibylline Books ordained the worship of Cybele, the Great Mother of Asia Minor and thus a link with the supposed Trojan ancestors of Rome – but also goddess of Hannibal's homeland. Her introduction with honour in 204 duly caused Hannibal to leave Italy for ever the following year. Along with Cybele came Attis, the shepherd-god who had castrated himself out of mad passion for Cybele, and her priests, the Galli (Phrygian Corybantes), self-castrated, orgiastic celebrants of the cult. The barriers to eastern cults were down. Bacchanalia in honour of Bacchus, the Roman form of Dionysus, also took root, notwithstanding Senatorial proscriptions once the Carthaginian menace had receded. They were followed by Syrian deities with similarly wild cults, notably Adonis and various fertility-goddesses; and from the same quarter, later on, the unconquered sun-god Sol Invictus. From Syria also came notions of immortality derived from astronomy, and soothsayers who introduced astrology.

From Egypt after the fall of Antony and Cleopatra came the Graeco-Egyptian state religion of the Ptolemies. This made use of the dominant Osirian cult of late Egypt which, conveniently, featured non-theriomorphic gods – but in the triad with Isis and Harpokrates was incorporated the debased hybrid cult in which the sacred bull Apis, a fertility-god, was joined to Osiris in Serapis. Though looking rather like Pluto, his fertility and solar aspects were increasingly stressed. The artificiality of the cult did not lessen its appeal, and after a century in Rome the Temple of Isis was built in AD 38 by Caligula. The image of mother and child was to have a profound effect on early Christian iconography.

The last important eastern introduction

besides Christianity was of the Persian god Mithras, who entered Rome via the satrapies of Asia Minor in the first century AD, and by the end of the third was being hailed by Diocletian as imperial protector. His mostly male worshippers found in Mithras not just a fertility cult in which the hero slays a bull, but an ethos revealed in mysteries and based on Persian dualism that supported both moral and military discipline. Mithras too was solarised, for his celebratory feast was shared with the sun-god Sol, the god of Constantine before his conversion to Christianity and proclamation of the Edict of Milan in 313. Though Christianity was henceforth the established religion of the Empire, it was not till the end of the century that toleration was withdrawn from the cults of the Vestal Virgins and of the Great Mother, and paganism systematically suppressed.

Even the most ancient cults still had life in them till then, and this was partly the result of the deliberate fostering of native Roman mythology by Augustus and the poets of the first century AD. It was a largely artificial mythology, a glorified history whose chief inventor and populariser was Virgil. It made Aeneas chief of the Trojan heroes who were supposed to have founded Rome. Under eastern influence, the divinity of emperors was proclaimed, but not convincingly, and worship in their lifetime was accorded only to their Genius, or protective spirit. Augustus called himself only a son of god, and his prototype in myth was the hero Aeneas, bringer of settled peace to Rome.

According to Virgil, Aeneas was the son of Anchises, a Trojan nobleman, and Venus. He was married to Creusa, daughter of Priam, who bore him Ascanius, also known as Iulus. After the fall of Troy he escaped, carrying Anchises on his back and accompanied by Ascanius and Creusa. On Mount Ida he rallied the remaining Trojans and sailed with them to Crete and thence, on Apollo's instructions, to Sicily. En route his ship was driven to Carthage, recently founded by its queen Dido. Venus and Juno roused mutual passion in them, but at Jupiter's command, Aeneas abandoned Dido to pursue his destiny. Despite Dido's suicide, Aeneas was commended for his resolve – with the implication that Antony should thus have renounced Cleopatra.

Apollo as god of the sun, with Mithraic radiate crown, driving his quadriga across the heavens. Though Apollo was not identified with any native Roman god, the solar role is a Roman addition to the Greek god of light, grace and poetry.

left
The Apollo of Veii. Etruscan terracotta
statue of about 500 BC, the end of the
period of Etruscan domination in Rome.
Perhaps because he had come to Rome
through Etruria, the Roman Apollo was
chiefly influential through the oracular
Sybil of Cumae.

On the advice of the Sibyl of Cumae, Aeneas penetrated the underworld to seek guidance from his father, by now dead. Anchises gave him foreknowledge of their great Roman descendants and of their deeds of glory and told him how to establish himself in Italy. Aeneas sailed to Latium, at the mouth of the Tiber, which was ruled by Latinus, descendant of Saturn and son of Faunus. Latinus welcomed Aeneas and proposed that his daughter Lavinia should marry him. But Turnus, king of the Rutulians, already sought her hand and attacked the Trojans. His attack was joined by the people of Latium, stirred up by Juno, who opened the two gates of the temple of Janus, thus signifying war, and by Etruscans under the monstrous Mezentius. After lengthy and bloody battles, in which Aeneas was joined by other Etruscans, the enemy was defeated and Aeneas married Lavinia and founded the Roman people.

left
An augur examining the entrails of a victim. This, together with the interpretation of lightning, was the special Etruscan contribution to the Roman art of divination, which relied heavily on the behaviour of birds—hence the wings. Etruscan mirror back.

The portico columns of the temple of Castor and Pollux built in AD 6 on the site of their first temple in the Roman Forum, built 484 BC. The Dioscuri were patrons of sailors, and thus of traders. A weights and measures office was attached to the temple.

134

Head of a young Faun or Satyr. Minor deities, they shared some of the connection of their leader, Pan, with the primitive forces of nature. Most commonly they were seen garlanded with vines, as followers of Bacchus. Museo Nazionale, Rome.

opposite, top
Pan, protector of herdsmen and famed musician, in Greek myth son of Hermes and a nymph. In Rome he was identified with the rural deity Faunus, a prophetic god and grandson of Saturn. Mosaic pavement from Gennazano. Museo Nazionale, Rome.

left
The three Graces, figures borrowed from Greek mythology. Daughters of Jupiter by an Oceanid, their names were Aglaia 'Brilliance', Thalia 'Bringer of flowers' and Euphrosyne 'Joy'. Their joyous dance with the nymphs marked the advent of spring.

below
Three musicians from an Etruscan tomb fresco in Tarquinia. Their grace and serene expressions seem to belie the oft-repeated observation that Etruscan rèligion was gloomy, a hopeless struggle to understand the will of the gods through divination. The painting illustrates the olive, traditionally brought to Italy by the Etruscans, together with the vine.

left
Serapis, a bearded god resembling Pluto, and in his Graeco-Roman manifestation quite unlike the Egyptian gods from whom he was compounded, Osiris and the bull Apis. Bringer of fertility (whose symbol is his crown), and riches. Bust excavated in London. Guildhall Museum, London

opposite
Neptune Triumphant, with his consort Salacia, who seem to be fearsome deities neither to their ocean subjects nor to the fishermen. The improbable quadriga is a reminder of Neptune's beneficent role as creator of the first horse. Louvre.

opposite
The Anatolian god Men, one of many hybrid eastern cults adopted in the Roman Empire. Armed like Mithras, with his Phyrigian cap and his foot on the slain bull, he bears the Roman emblems of Bacchus, the thyrsis, a staff tipped with a pine cone, and another pine cone.

right
Augustus, first Emperor of Rome, who by restoration and building of temples and public monuments and by enlightened patronage of the arts fostered a renewal of traditional Roman beliefs. Virgil identified him with Aeneas. Cameo by Dioscorides. British Museum.

below
Virgil seated between the Muse of Tragedy, Melpomene, on the right, and the Muse of Epic Poetry, Calliope. Through his lofty mythological account of Rome's origins in the *Aeneid* he caught the imagination of contemporaries. Mosaic from Sousse, Tunisia.

opposite

Bacchus, god of wine, dressed in grapes and accompanied by his emblem, the panther, to whom he offers the dregs of his wine. The writhing snakes were characteristic companions of his wild followers, the Bacchantes. He stands in a fertile vineyard beneath Mount Vesuvius.

An astrological globe. Contact with Asia Minor and through it with Persia added another superstitious practice to those already established in Rome. As early as 139 BC, an unsuccessful attempt was made to expel the Syrian soothsayers, known as Chaldeans, from Rome.

left
Thank-offerings of the kind dedicated to Minerva medica, patron of physicians, or later to Aesculapius, god of medicine and son of Apollo. In the literal-minded Roman way of contractual dealings with the gods, each offering clearly indicates the part cured.

right
Father Tiber, god of the river. It is thought that to appease Tiber's wrath over the building of bridges at Rome, sacrifices were cast into his waters each May. The supreme priests of Rome were called pontiffs, 'bridge-makers'. Fresco from Pompeii. Louvre.

below
Nereids with a sea-monster. Charming daughters of the sea-god Nereus in Greek myth, these nymphs liked to disport themselves on the ocean surface, and to give help and comfort to sailors, who dedicated seats to their worship along the coastlines. Mosaic from Lambaesis, Algeria.

The Celts

The exact origin of the Celts is still uncertain, and since they were without a written language for centuries as their culture developed, we rely on archaeological evidence to recreate their early life and development. A warlike, vigorous people, they dominated much of Europe before the Roman hegemony spread north and west. By about 500 BC they controlled the areas we now know as southern Germany, Austria, Switzerland, and Hungary. By 400 BC they had claimed parts of Spain, southern Italy, the Balkans, and had spread through northern Europe to the British Isles.

The Greeks knew them as the Keltoi, the Romans as the Galli, Gauls, and both had reason to respect a people whose warriors sacked Rome in 390 BC and plundered the shrine at Delphi around 280 BC. But by the end of the third century BC the Celts were in decline, partly because they had over-extended themselves in their far-flung campaigns of conquest, leaving no centre of culture or military strength on which to found an empire. They thus became a fairly easy prey for the Roman legions in the first century BC as Caesar's armies swept north and east to take Gaul and then Britain.

Although the early Celts had developed their own language and dialects, they had no written language until the fifth century AD. Five centuries of Roman occupation all but extinguished the language, but it survived, together with its cognates, in Ireland, Wales, parts of Scotland, and in Brittany. Despite succeeding occupations by the Romans, Anglo-Saxons, Vikings, and Normans, the Celts preserved a powerful oral tradition. Writers of the second century AD testified that the Gauls were extremely eloquent, and one can understand they put great store by eloquence. Indeed, the power and prestige of a leader very much depended on his ability to impress by the spoken word. At the very least he could also keep his hold on his followers by boasting of past glorious deeds in which he or his ancestors had taken part.

Apart from the influence of their warrior-kings and chieftains, the Gauls developed a system of educating the young in the oral traditions of the people by means of druids, who also officiated in religious rites which included sacrifice. Other conservers of the oral traditions were the filid or seers, who were teachers and counsellors, and the bards. Both the filid and the bards combined in their repertoire the invention and elaboration of poems and folktales. The line between Celtic legend, myth and folktale is necessarily an uncertain one. However, in terms of function they need not be sharply distinguished, since a warlike, restless, marauding people with no settled empire or centre of culture was peculiarly dependent on the mythological elements in its own history to give it a sense of continuity and identity. The myths and stories were first written down by monastic scribes in the seventh century.

Two of the most dominant and persistent themes in the mythology, closely linked, are those of a journey to the otherworld, and the belief in a life after death. The Celts regarded death without fear, since it was merely a passage from this life to another, happy land where men and women lived together in eternal bliss. The bards and storytellers continually referred to *Tir inna Beo*, 'the land of the living',

where infirmity and old age were unknown. Music issued from the very ground, brightly coloured birds sang in the trees, and magic vessels provided food and drink inexhaustibly. This paradise had no particular spatial location – it existed anywhere and everywhere: under the sea, beneath the earth, at the end of a cave, and in distant lands. And even though it was a land of peace and harmony, the favourite pastime of a heroic people – fighting – nevertheless existed, for fighting kept the Celts happy (and conferred status besides).

The second principal strand of this major theme, the voyage to the happy otherworld, also reflects the basic characteristics of the Celts. In the writings handed on by the monastic scribes of the seventh century, no theme occurs so frequently, or with such enthusiasm and imagination, as the voyage to the otherworld. A profusion of colours, magical and fantastic landscapes, islands with fabled shores and all manner of escapades for the voyager compete for attention. Some authorities on Celtic art see a connection between the rich inventive forms of Celtic ornamentation and the unrestrained fantasies of the Celtic afterlife. In Celtic mythology, as in Celtic art, there is none of the rigidity or discipline of classical restraint. Instead there is a fluid, polymorphic world where ambiguity and paradox sit easily together.

The transmission of so much of pagan Celtic myth by Christian scribes inevitably brought a censoring element, but church policy and the vigour of the Celtic oral tradition made it to some extent inevitable that Christianity should be grafted on to, rather than supplant local pagan traditions.

In much the same way, in an earlier era, the Celtic gods had survived the attempt

opposite
Bronze mask with features stylised in a typically Celtic manner. Though the Celts seem to have conceived their gods in human form, few identifiable representations have been found, possibly because of the value placed on secret knowledge. From Garancières-en-Beauce. Musée de Chartres.

right
Severed head, a detail from the man-eating monster of Noves, near the mouth of the Rhone. Ligurians seem to have introduced a head cult in this area that spread among the Celts, who took heads as battle trophies and thought them magically endowed. Musée Calvet, Avignon.

147

of Caesar to Romanise them. He claimed that the Gauls worshipped Mercury, Apollo, Mars, Jupiter and Minerva, but these efforts to place Celtic deities under the Roman classification were bound to be unsuccessful, since Celtic gods had many different names and most had local forms.

Local variations in Celtic mythology, as between, say, Gaul and areas later known as Wales and Ireland, make general discussions somewhat difficult, for reasons of space. But scholars agree that the richest source materials for tracing the Celtic myths can be drawn from Ireland, for it was here that the Celts enjoyed unusual freedom from interference or domination to pursue their own traditions and culture in the richest, most formative period.

Even in Ireland, however, invasion from without was a dominant theme of the early myths. One of the principal sources is the *Book of Invasions*, a twelfth-century compilation which recounts successive invasions of Ireland throughout its history. The account does not include any native myth of the world's creation, though this may have been a deliberate omission by Christian scribes. However, native Celtic tradition did speak of a common ancestor for the Celtic peoples called Donn, 'the brown, or dark one', whose abode had been *Tech Duinn*, a small rocky island off the south-west coast of Ireland. Lord of the otherworld and god of the dead, Donn welcomed all his descendants to come to his home after death.

Several conquests of Ireland are recorded in the Book of Invasions, resulting in successive dynasties. The first was led by Partholon, perhaps from Spain. It cleared plains and created lakes, introducing agriculture, cattle-raising, gold-working, brewing and the first cauldron, and instituting cults and laws. The people of Partholon kept down their enemies the Fomori, hideous demons with supernatural powers, but after three centuries were wiped out by epidemic. The next invaders, the people of Nemed, continued to civilise Ireland but had to pay heavy tribute to the Fomori and ultimately fled Ireland. They were followed by the Fir Bolg, said to have been farmers from Greece, the Fir Gaileoin, and the Fir Domnann – who may correspond to the

Celto-Ligurian janiform or two-faced head from late La Tène sanctuary at Roquepertuse. The Celto-Ligurian League harassed the Greeks of Massalia (Marseilles) from about 400 BC. In relieving it in 125 BC the Romans began their conquest of the Celts. Musée Borély, Marseilles.

148

Belgae, the Gauls or Gaels, and the Dumnonii.

Most notable for their exploits and the special place they occupy in the Celtic heritage were their successors, the Tuatha De Danann, 'the tribes of the goddess Danu', or 'the divine peoples' according to some accounts. Their origins are obscure, but they arrived from 'the northern islands of the world' and vanquished their rivals in the Battles of Moytura, the most famous in Irish mythology. Of their leaders, Dagda and Nuada deserve special mention for their qualities and deeds. Dagda (literally, 'the Good God' but also known as 'the Mighty One of Great Knowledge') was famous for two particular attributes – his cauldron and his mighty club. A true father figure for the Celts, his appearance was coarse and he was held to have a fabulous appetite. Hence the vast cauldron which alone could do justice to his needs but which could feed his people besides.

In one of the battles of Moytura, where Dagda's people suffered reverses, the enemy Fomori filled Dagda's cauldron with a stupendous stew of boiled goats, sheep, swine, meal and fat. One account holds that the stew was so vast it had to be poured into a huge hole in the ground. As king and leader, Dagda was ordered to eat it on pain of being killed. The tale records that having swallowed all of the stew, using the vast ladle from his cauldron, Dagda proceeded to scrape the remainder with his fingers to round off a gargantuan meal. This has been interpreted as a fertility rite; and Dagda also summoned the four seasons of the year. As for his great club, it was so heavy it had to be borne on wheels, it slew nine men at a stroke, and when he dragged it behind him, Dagda left a track as deep as a boundary ditch between two tribal provinces.

Nuada, the other great leader of the Tuatha De, wielded a fabulous sword from which none could escape. His exploits in battle were heroic, but in one of the battles of Moytura, waged against the Fir Bolg, mortal enemies of Nuada's people, Nuada lost an arm and was carried from the field. Since the loss of a limb was incompatible with kingship, Nuada relinquished his leadership, but the choice of successor was an unhappy one. Bres, 'the beautiful one', was a descendant of the other great enemies of the Tuatha De, the Fomori, and before long the country was in thrall to them. But eventually a worthy successor to Nuada presented himself, and Bres was replaced by one of the most colourful characters in Celtic myth. This was Lugh, a bold, adventurous young challenger, reputed to be master of all the arts, in-

cluding the art of war. His talents included those of craftsman, huntsman, smith, poet, inventor, and – most important of all – sorceror. In the most famous battle of Moytura, fought against the Fomori, Lugh used his magical powers to restore to life all his followers slain in battle. The Fomori were routed and banished forever.

In time, however, the Tuatha De were themselves overcome and defeated by a new wave of invaders. The victors were the Sons of Mil, said to have arrived from Spain. They landed in the south-west of Ireland and defeated the Tuatha De in a series of battles, probably representing the conversion of Ireland to Christianity. According to one account, the Tuatha De were not entirely vanquished, but reached a bargain in which the Sons of Mil took the land of Ireland and the Tuatha De, using their magical powers, occupied the underworld. There they vanished from sight but continued as the 'Divine Peoples' of Celtic myth, their presence marked only by the 'fairy mounds' which folklore and custom still recognise in the countryside of Ireland.

Celtic lore is rich in tales of a trio of

Bronze relief of a horned deity with upraised arms from a wagon burial at Waldalgesheim, Germany. Late fourth century BC. Such burials were accorded to Hallstatt chieftains (the first true Celts), and subsequently to the warrior aristocracy of the Celts. Rheinisches Landesmuseum, Bonn.

goddesses concerned with battle and death with marked warlike propensities. Sometimes they appeared singly as goddesses of war, but the familiar representation is as a trio: Morrigan 'the Great Queen', Macha, and Badb. Badb, the essential goddess of war, sometimes took the form of a raven or a crow; Morrigan was a fearsome, even cruel deity; Macha a more attractive figure, who appears and re-appears in many legends. This trio of goddesses was known throughout the Celtic world, from southern Europe to Ireland, and although they did not engage directly in battle, their magical powers were used to defeat the enemy in numerous ways. Thus for example in the famous saga of the hero Cuchulainn, Macha, goddess of the Ulster capital, afflicted the knights of Ulster with a paralysing weakness, while Medb, Queen of Connaught, together with the two Munsters and Leinster, raided Ulster to obtain the brown bull of Cooley (Cuailnge). Ulster was defended single-handed by Cuchulainn, with the support of the goddess Morrigan and his father Lugh. Cuchulainn was eventually disarmed spiritually and physically: three witches disguised as crows made him violate taboos, and he lost his magic lance. But he died as a hero, on his feet, strapped to a stone pillar, as the blood drained from him.

Apart from these goddesses of war, there were other Amazonian figures who led armies into battle. Often, they were also endowed with legendary sexual prowess. This is in tune with the general character of the Celtic tales, with their admixture of robustness, carousal, and sensuousness, and little room for romantic love. The Celts included the cult of the mother-goddess in their rites, as archaeological evidence testifies. Indeed, the Tuatha De were the descendants of the goddess Danu, and in some local instances, the ruler of the otherworld was a goddess, rather than a god, just as some folktales represented the otherworld as 'the Land of Women'. Danu may be connected with Bridget, daughter of Dagda, who was patroness of Kildare and of learning, culture and skills. She was known as Brigantia in northern England, and survived as St Bride in Christianity.

In the diverse, immensely flexible Celtic tradition, myths of anthropomorphic gods and goddesses of war, of the cultivated fields, of fortified places, of fertilising rivers, and of sacred trees, mingle with animal myths, such as the famous saga of two great bulls fighting to the death; a legendary boar; and supernatural creatures such as the ram-headed serpent, the 'divine horse', and magic birds.

above
The god Cernunnos, known throughout the Celtic lands, from the interior of the silver-plated Gundestrup bowl. In his left hand he bears a ram-headed serpent. The diverse forms of the animals about him and his own antlers suggest the magical form-changing aspect of Celtic myth.

opposite
Deity from the exterior of the Gundestrup bowl, bearing two stags. Stags' antlers may have been symbolic of annual renewal, and the bowl or cauldron was a potent symbol of fertility and abundance, as seen in the myth of Dagda's cauldron. National Museum, Copenhagen.

left
Bull (the horns are now missing) with a warrior about to plunge his sword into its neck. Bulls feature in both continental Celtic and Irish mythology, as objects of marauding raids and as fertility symbols—perhaps both in the Brown Bull of Cooley. From the base of the Gundestrup bowl.

151

left
Free-standing stone pillar, originally surmounted by a head, found at Pfalzfeld in the Rhineland. The relief carving, suggesting that the stone may have been a focal point in cult, is of the 'La Tène' culture (c. 500 BC, to the arrival of the Romans in Central Europe)

opposite, left
Fighting animals as a decorative motif in Christian art. The style on this panel from the North Cross, Ahenny Co. Tipperary, is typically Celtic, as is the sense of a world filled with animals mirroring and helping in the struggles of human life.

opposite, right
Entrance to the side chamber on the north of the Bronze Age tumulus of New Grange, in Co. Meath. Inside can be seen two large stone basins, perhaps representing the cauldron of abundance which was an attribute of Dagda as lord of life and death.

opposite, bottom
Pair of bronze wine-flagons embellished with fanciful animals chasing a duck. Fourth century BC, from the Moselle valley (Basse-Yutz). As early as 500 BC the influence of Greek colonies penetrated far north among the Celts, with the export of wine.

left
The dying hero Cuchulainn, bound to a pillar-stone, with Babd Catha, Babd the goddess of battle in her raven form, perched on his shoulder. As he died, his falling sword cut off the hand of the enemy about to take his head as a trophy. Modern statue, General Post Office, Dublin.

opposite
Page from the Book of Kells, a Gospel Book produced by the monks of Ireland around AD 800. The way in which Celtic art forms decorate Christian scripture is an apt illustration of the incomplete overthrow of the Tuatha De Danann by the Sons of Mil. Trinity College, Dublin

below
Man's head forming the handle of a bowl from Ireland found in a Viking tomb in Miklebostad, Norway. It is suggestive of the Celtic head cult, and of the custom of nailing the defeated enemy's head or death mask to the warrior's doorpost. Bergen Museum.

below, right
The 'Paps (nipples) of Anu', the mother-goddess often confused with Danu. As a goddess of plenty she was especially associated with fertile Munster, the ancient kingdom of south-east Ireland. After their fall, the Tuatha De occupied the underworld.

right
Megalithic tomb or passage grave cemetery at Loughcrew, Co. Meath. The grave sites of former inhabitants may have inspired much of Ireland's mythological history, and certainly aroused fear: they were said to be the haunts of female spirits or hags.

left, above
Standing stones in alignment at Cloghane, Co. Kerry. Such stones may have served to mark boundaries, and in some ritual function. Boundaries, such as those marked by the club of Dagda, easily gained a supernatural aura where possession of land was central to society.

left, centre
Dolmen at Kilclooney, Co. Donegal. With their single horizontal slab of rock, dolmens were known in folklore as 'beds of Dermot and Grania', referring to the legend of Dermot's elopement with the beautiful Grania, the betrothed of Finn—a Tristram and Iseult prototype story.

left, below
Benbulben, the mountain in Co. Sligo where Dermot (probably identifiable with Donn, lord of the otherworld) was killed by his foster-brother in the guise of a magic boar, when Finn (the god Lugh) through resentment failed to use his healing powers to save him.

opposite, left
The Turoe Stone in Co. Galway, a granite block probably used for ritual purposes in the third century BC. The restless, irregular curves of the La Tène style decoration seem to convey in abstract form the teeming world of Celtic imagination.

opposite, right
Dun Anghusa, a great fort on Inishmore, Aran Islands, said to have been built by the Fir Bolg, whom the Tuatha De Danann had restricted to Connaught, or to the offshore islands, after the first Battle of Moytura.

opposite, bottom
Grianan Ailigh, a prehistoric stone fort in Co. Donegal just west of Derry. It was the seat of the dynasty of the northern Uí Néill, founded about AD 400, which held sway till the eighth century and finally fell to Brian Boru in 1002. It is a large example of the typical Celtic ring-fort.

Scandinavia

The origins of Scandinavian mythology lie well back in the Bronze Age, which lasted for more than a thousand years, from about 1600 to 500 BC. The myths tell of great kings and heroes whose outstanding characteristics were bravery in battle, strong loyalties to their kinsfolk, respect for their women, and pride in laws which they believed to be handed down by the gods they worshipped. These were fierce gods, who demanded heavy sacrifices but who rewarded the faithful with good crops and favourable weather, drawing on their command of the sun, the sky and the elements. The mythology of Scandinavia presents a rich, complex, often a confusing texture, in which major themes and deities intermix with local cults established and preserved by the special characteristics of sea-girt lands and islands stretching from the sub-arctic regions to the northern shelf of Europe.

The creation myths of these people of the north, as they were known in the earliest periods, told of an earth formed from a great emptiness known as Ginnungagap. This surrounding void concealed an inner reality where potential life existed, and when the frozen wastes of the north lands came into contact with the fiery regions of the south, the fires melted the ice, which yielded the giant Ymir, ancestor of the giants which occur in the earliest myths. Ymir was nourished by another mythical creature, a cow, which licked the ice blocks until other beings were formed. In one account man and woman were formed from the left armpit of the giant Ymir, whilst his two feet gave forth a race of frost giants. Ymir was eventually killed by the descendants of Buri, who was also the offspring of the primeval cow, and Ymir's body was used by the slayers to form the world—his flesh providing the soil, his bones the mountains and rocks, his blood the sea and his hair the vegetation of the earth.

The details and the origins of these creation myths are uncertain, since they come to us from oral traditions of an adventurous people whose seafaring exploits are more familiar in the historical period of the Vikings, who invaded and pillaged territory stretching from Iceland and Greenland in the far north, to Britain, the Low Countries and France, and as far south as Sicily and Constantinople, via the Volga. The chief written sources for the earliest myths are those of the Icelandic poet and writer Snorri Sturluson, who set down his *Prose Edda* about AD 1220. Another main source is a manuscript discovered in an Icelandic farmhouse in the seventeenth century, the *Poetic Edda*. Together, the Eddas allow us to reconstruct the tales and poems about gods and heroes, elves and giants of the mountains, dwarfs, monsters and fiery dragons—contests of strength and wit, some comic, some tragic: all culminating in the destruction of the world of gods and of men in a final disaster of Ragnarok, where the gods went down fighting, overwhelmed by fire and water.

One of the earliest, recurring myths of Scandinavia, portrayed in many rock carvings, tells of the wheeled wagon or chariot of the sun travelling across the heavens. The sun is represented as a disk and the wagon is drawn sometimes by horned beasts, sometimes by horses. The sun disk is sometimes portrayed with a ship, perhaps symbolising the journey of the sun below the earth when it sinks beneath the sea and night falls. Whatever the explanation, the sun disk and the sacred ship appear together in the earliest rock carvings and also in later ornamentation and artefacts, indicating the seafaring preoccupations of these Bronze Age ancestors of the Vikings.

Another primary symbolic instrument was the axe, wielded by the earliest deities and by the heroes and giants in their battles with lesser men. The axe, together with the spear, was thought to have divine or mystical powers, and both weapons were the constant companions of a warlike race whose deities ruled the sky and sent down thunder, lightning, or gave the life-giving rain to earth and the crops.

The greatest figure in the early myths was undoubtedly Odin, god of battle and of death. Odin (the Woden of the Anglo-Saxons, whose name is preserved in the word Wednesday) lived in Valhalla, home of all true warriors who died heroic deaths on the field of battle. The kingdom of the gods was Asgard, scene of numberless heroic battles and deeds. So many myths and legendary deeds have been woven around the name of Odin that it is difficult to disentangle one from the other, but the main outlines of the dominant myths have survived through the centuries of oral tradition and the transcriptions of Christian scribes after the pagan period.

Self-sacrifice for Odin was a fierce cult among the warriors, who paid homage to their great god in battle. In their fights with the giants, monsters, dragons and serpents, the warriors were protected not merely by Odin's mighty spear Gungnir, which had the power to determine victory by the direction it took over the battlefield, but also by Odin's supernatural powers, which gave the warriors immunity even when they fought without armour. Odin was a fierce but also a generous god, giving treasure and rewards, often in the form of rings, to his faithful followers. Among his many possessions, the god also had two ravens which he used to bring tidings from distant lands and extend his dominion. The sight of a raven was taken to be a good omen of Odin's protection, giving magical powers for the field of battle.

Among the other emissaries of Odin were the valkyries, or warrior maidens, fearsome creatures who hovered near the battlefields, ready to drink the blood and devour the corpses of the vanquished. Through time, the valkyries became less bloodthirsty, appearing as princesses in armour, on horseback, ready to escort warriors back to the halls of Valhalla, to feed them and quench their thirst with horns of mead. Brynhild was perhaps the most famous of the valkyries, and her story is recounted in the legend of Sigurd the Volsung. Brynhild defied Odin's commands and gave victory in battle to one of the warrior kings whom Odin had condemned to death. To punish her, Odin placed Brynhild within a wall of fire where she slept under a spell cast by the god, until Sigurd, on his magical horse Grani, rode through the flames to rescue her.

Elsewhere in the early myths the valkyries appear as contenders for Odin's powers, riding into battle together, often befriending young heroes or giving them swords and urging them to great deeds.

The three major gods worshipped in pagan Sweden: one-eyed Odin on the left beside a tree, perhaps the World Tree; Thor with his hammer in the centre; and on the right, the fertility-deity Freyr, flanked by a small goddess, Freyja. Tapestry, c. 1100, from Skog church, Hälsingland.

At other times they joined battle themselves, flinging mighty spears against Odin's warriors. Valhalla was in no sense a peaceful or harmonious place, therefore. Feuds were rife and Odin had rivals. A vengeful god who demanded many sacrifices–including women–Odin ruled by fear as well as by his prowess in battle. The customary form of sacrifice demanded in the cult of Odin was that of immolation, often self-immolation in the case of women who had lost their husbands in battle. When Brynhild learned that her rescuer Sigurd had been killed in battle, she had herself burned to death on a great funeral pyre so that she might join him in the other world and at the same time acknowledge the ultimate power of Odin.

Worshippers of Odin were expected not merely to meet death fearlessly, but to welcome it in the service of the god, and it is said of Ragnar Lodbrok, one of Odin's warriors, that he met his death in a snakepit with the words: 'Laughing, I die.' The terrible hold exercised by Odin over his followers came not merely from his prowess in battle, but from his supernatural abilities to take various forms, including that of an eagle which could lie as though asleep, but whose spirit could suddenly assume other forms, such as a wild beast, a dragon, or a fish, and journey instantly to distant parts. He had gained these powers by hanging on the World Tree, Yggdrasil, core of the universe, which had a serpent at its foot and at its top an eagle which, together with the god Heimdall, guarded Asgard. After nine days of this self-immolation, and having lost an

eye in return for a drink from the spring of knowledge guarded by the giant Mimir beneath the Tree, Odin had learnt to understand the magic runes.

Odin was not an omnipotent god, however, as the death of Balder, reputed to be one of his sons, confirms. Balder had been rendered immune to wounding by his mother, Frigg, who had taken pledges from all trees, plants and metals, so that weapons made from them could cause her son no harm. Balder's well-known immunity provided useful sport for the gods, since they could hurl their weapons at him knowing that they could not harm him. But Frigg had overlooked one small plant which grows not on the ground, but in the oak tree–mistletoe. One day Balder's brother Hoder hurled a spear tipped with a dart from the mistletoe. Balder fell dead.

Odin had foreseen the death in his dreams, but he was powerless to bring Balder back to life. His failure was much more than a personal one, for the death of Balder signalled the doom of the gods and the destruction of the kingdom of Asgard. Moreover, the death of Balder was not an accident, but had been engineered by Loki, a trickster god who had a major part in the Scandinavian myths. Loki was renowned for stirring up trouble in Valhalla. He played the main role in the death of Balder by providing Hoder, Balder's brother, with the mistletoe dart which brought the death of the hero. Loki hated Balder and wanted his death, but as a cunning trickster he concealed his hatred and always took care to keep in the good counsels of Odin,

acting as an emissary for various errands in the god's service. For his various exploits Loki was well served by his ability to assume different forms, from a horse, to a falcon or a fly.

Balder's death and other acts of treachery were among several evil omens which foretold the doom of the gods. One omen was a mighty winter, bitterly cold, which lasted for three years, with no summertime to relieve the world by providing harvests. At the same time a vast serpent emerged from the waves, blowing poison and causing floods to envelop the earth. As the waves advanced, a ship appeared, steered by the trickster Loki and carrying a crew of giants. Odin led his warriors to a huge plain to fight the last great battle, but the defeat of the gods was already ordained. Odin was not killed by any weapon, but was swallowed by an ancient enemy of the gods, a giant wolf. Odin's son Vigar seized the wolf and wrenched its jaws apart, setting his foot on the lower jaw in a shoe which had been in the making since the beginning of time. But although Odin was avenged, the kingdom of Asgard was brought to an end and the earth sank beneath the waves. Only the World Tree survived, sheltering a couple who would one day repopulate a renewed, purified earth, a regeneration heralded by a new sun and the return of Balder.

As the cult of Odin waned in Scandinavia, Thor, the Germanic thunder-god, began to replace Odin in many parts. A huge, red-headed figure with a beard, blazing eyes, and a vast appetite, Thor travelled across the sky in a chariot drawn by goats. His chief weapon was his mighty hammer, Mjollnir, but with his great gloves he could shatter rocks to hurl at his enemies. His main adversary was the World Serpent, one of the terrible children of Loki, which lay in the depths of the sea, curled about the earth across the oceans.

Of the many stories of Thor's encounters with the World Serpent, the best known tells of Thor's visit to the sea-giant Hymir to propose a fishing trip. Since Thor had disguised himself as a youth, Hymir sent his visitor to catch bait. Thor cut off the head of an ox and when they set off to fish, Thor took the oars and rowed to the region of the World Serpent. The serpent took the bait of the ox-head and Thor hauled with all his strength to bring in his huge catch, even pressing his feet through the bottom of the boat. Just as Thor raised his hammer to strike the head of the serpent, his companion in the boat, the frightened giant, cut the line–and the serpent vanished beneath the sea. Other versions of Thor's encounter with the World Serpent relate that Thor killed the monster, and give Thor the title Sole Slayer of the Serpent.

Thor made many journeys to the land of the giants, sometimes in the company of the ubiquitous Loki of other myths, sometimes travelling alone across the skies in his chariot. At all times he carried his famous hammer, a symbol which appears everywhere in the art and ornaments of early Scandinavia, though sometimes in the form of an axe. Most of the myths record that it had a short handle, broken in one of the battles of the gods. But despite his wanderings and fierce appearance, the cult of Thor was closely linked with the safety of the community, with ties of family and of men's possessions and home life. One ancient myth tells of Thor's marriage with Sif of the golden hair, symbolising a divine marriage between the god of the sky who could create and command thunderstorms, and the goddess of the earth. When Thor rode to earth he brought rain to make the fields fertile and to germinate the crops.

Thor and Odin were two of the principal cults of the north lands, but in a region where mountains, fjords and lakes divided up the regions into many separate communities, there were naturally other cults, some localised, others more widespread as a seafaring people carried myths, legends and hero tales to distant parts. In some regions goddesses thrived together with their husbands or brother gods. Freyr was a fertility-deity, usually modelled in a phallic form, who ruled with his twin sister Freyja, and they may represent a cult of deities of the dead older than that associated with Odin and his magic. Many myths tell of battles between their family, the Vanir, and Odin's, the Aesir. In some regions, however, Freyr was worshipped alongside Odin and Thor. Freyr was closely associated with the sun, and his ardent wooing of the beautiful maiden Gerd, despite many obstacles in the path of their love, is again taken to represent the wooing of the earth by the sky, bringing rich harvests to the world of men.

These recurring themes suggest the preoccupations of a people living under stern, sometimes savage climatic conditions, where harvests were always at the mercy of the seasons and play of the elements. The seasons could be capricious, and if an early winter or a cold spring brought havoc to annual crops, men were forced to seek sustenance from the sea, either as fishermen or as warriors setting out to unknown destinations to pillage and plunder. In such a world of uncertainty, symbolised by the capricious Loki, gods and heroes were courageous, even terrifying, and necessarily larger than life, commanding the elements with one hand, despatching monsters of the deep with the other.

opposite
Viking warriors brandishing axes. Thor's hammer was sometimes represented as the war-axe used by his followers. Though they worshipped him as upholder of law, they were ruthless pillagers abroad. Stone at Lindisfarne Priory, Northumberland, sacked by Vikings in AD 875.

below
Bronze Age rock carving, showing two ships, four men and a small animal, probably a horse, together with a sun disk in the form of a ring, one of the symbols of the sky-god Odin and the form often taken by gifts he gave as rewards for faithful service.

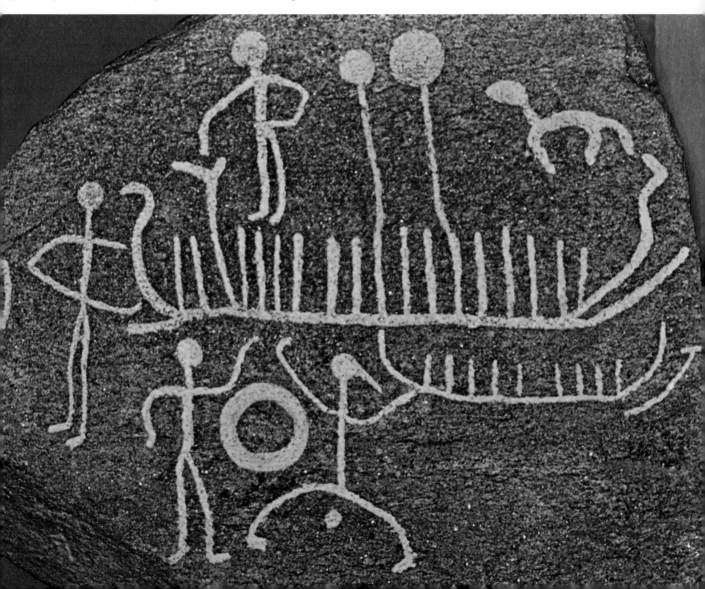

Ritual objects of the mesolithic period in Denmark, earlier than 2000 BC. Carved in amber, they often took the form of the animals, such as bear, that they worshipped. Hunting cults gave way to earth and then to sky and warrior deities. National Museum, Copenhagen.

pages 164–5
Bronze gold-plated sun disk drawn on a
chariot by a horse. Such chariots were
associated both with Odin, who as god
of the dead also traversed the sky on his
eight-legged horse Sleipnir, and with
Thor, whose sky-chariot was drawn by
goats. Found in Zealand. National
Museum, Copenhagen.

below
Reconstruction of a huge ceremonial
shield from the Sutton Hoo ship burial.
The eagle was both Odin's magic form
and the guardian of the World Tree and
enemy of the Serpent. It presided over
sacrifice and battle. British Museum.

right
Detail from the Sutton Hoo shield. In
Anglo-Saxon England the dragon, with
its sharp teeth, three pairs of wings and
forked tail, corresponded to the serpent
elsewhere in the north. Breathing fire and
sometimes flying over houses, it guarded
the treasure in gravemounds.

left
The carved whalebone Franks Casket, probably late seventh-century Northumbrian and decorated with pagan and Christian scenes. On the front right is Weland the Smith, a supernatural trickster. The panels are surrounded by runes, keys to Odin's magic power. British Museum.

opposite, lower right
Bronze figure of the phallic god of fertility, Freyr. With that of his twin sister Freyja, a development of the primitive earth mother, his cult probably antedated those of the sky gods. Found at Rallinge, Södermanland. National Historical Museum, Stockholm.

below
Purse lid from the seventh-century ship burial at Sutton Hoo, Suffolk, England. The pagan Anglo-Saxons shared many beliefs with the Scandinavians. The god flanked by animals is a typical Odin representation, and the eagle was one of his forms. British Museum.

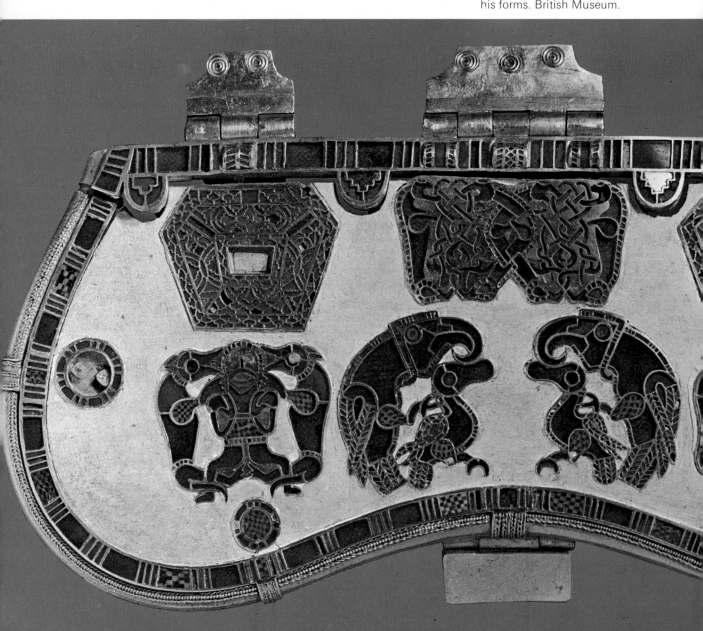

Hinged gold clasp decorated with cloisonné and filigree work, from the Sutton Hoo ship burial. The motif at the ends is linked boars with crested backs and tusks, the boar being a symbol of Freyja of the Vanir, goddess of fertility and of the dead.

left
A ship outlined in stones at Gnisvere, one of many found on the Baltic island of Gotland. Ships were associated with worship of the Vanir, fertility gods of earth and sea descended from Njord, probably deriving from ancient gods of the underworld several centuries BC.

below
Helmet with a boar crest. Such helmets were treasured by Swedish kings as emblems of Freyja's golden boar, known as the Swine of Battle, but also seemingly connected with divination. From seventh-century Anglo-Saxon burial mound at Benty Grange, Derbyshire.

bottom
Gold collar of the Migration Period, third to sixth centuries AD, when Celts and Germans moved north and west, bringing the cult of Odin of which such royal collars were symbolic. From Möne, Sweden. National Historical Museum, Stockholm.

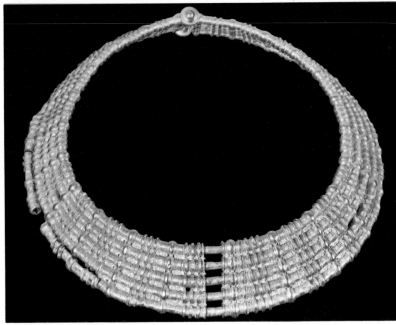

opposite
Head of a snarling monster carved in
wood, from the Oseberg ship burial, in
southern Norway. There were four other
such ceremonial or symbolic heads in the
burial. Typifying the monsters of darkness
were the dragon and serpent, ever ready
to swallow up men and gods.

below
Ceremonial axe-head recovered from the
grave of a man at Mammen, Denmark.
The face with its blazing eyes on the haft
end represents Thor, while the writhing
serpent with its typically interlaced form
on the blade represents his chief
adversary, the World Serpent.

bottom
End of the carved wooden wagon from
the late ninth-century ship burial at
Oseberg. It was probably connected with
the fertility cult, and the carved figures of
snakes and monsters are associated with
the powers of the earth. University
Historical Museum, Oslo.

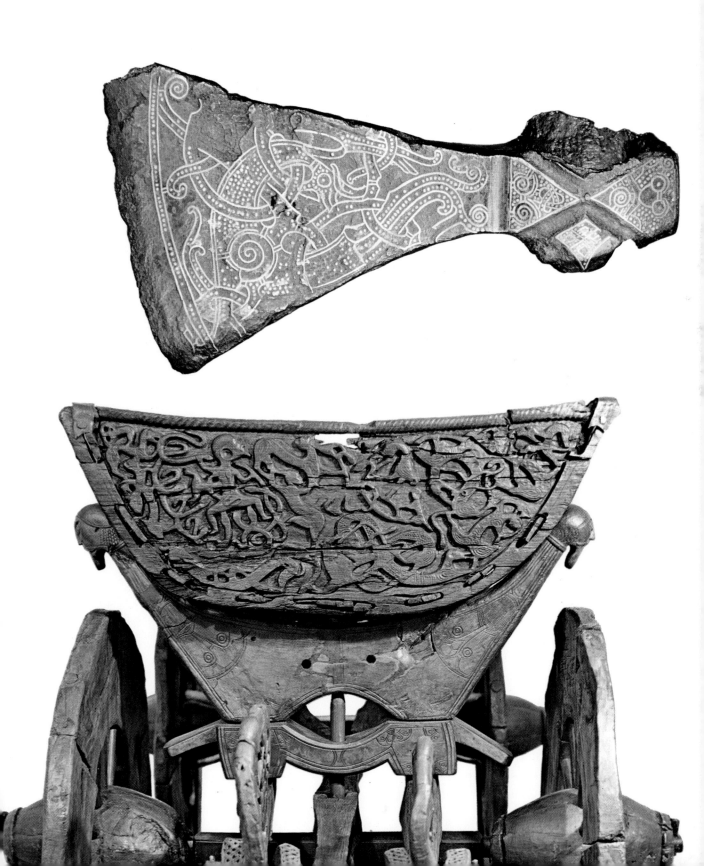

Viking spearhead with inlaid
ornamentation representing suns, and
probably for ritual use. Like the axe, the
spear was believed to have mystical
power. Odin's spear Gungnir, thrown
over the heads of the enemy, determined
the course of the battle.

opposite
Part of the tenth-century Gosforth Cross,
from Cumberland, which combines
Christian symbolism with scenes of the
pagan gods' struggle against evil. The
figures may represent Loki and his wife,
who saved him from poison, the
vengeance of the gods after the death of
Balder.

above
Warrior wearing belt and the horned
helmet typical of sixth-century champions
of Odin in Sweden. These warriors were
believed to have the protection of Odin's
supernatural powers, with no need for
armour. Gilded bronze buckle from
Finglesham, Kent. Institute of
Archaeology, Oxford.

left
The Thingvellir in Iceland, seen from the site of the Althing, a law assembly of Icelandic chieftains held once a year and opened on Thursday, day of Thor, the fount of human laws. The modern Icelandic parliament bears the same name

below
Silver amulet worn to bring the protection of Thor. It combines his eyes and beard, here formed in the shape of his hammer, with the beaked eagle head taken over from Odin. Tenth century, from Odeshög, Ostergotland. National Historical Museum, Stockholm.

above
Gold bracteate from Risely, Kent. Between serpent-like monsters is a figure typical of representations of Odin, though here he has the staring eyes and beard of Thor. The shaking of Thor's beard caused storms and his gaze was lightning. Institute of Archaeology, Oxford.

China

China is a vast land, with considerable variations of geography, climate and population. The northern zone, stretching as far as the Mongolian steppes and the zone south of the Yangtse river, which includes subtropical areas, flank the great Yellow river basin, now a temperate zone but formerly warmer, which saw the rise of the first Chinese civilisations known to the archaeological record. In the mesolithic period hunter-fisher communities built farming villages for shifting occupation near the confluence of the rivers Huangho, Fenho and Weishui, and practised some form of fertility cult. This culture, known as Yangshao, gave way to the Lungshan, spreading east to the lower reaches of the Yellow river and south to the Yangtse, and founding permanent settlements on the basis of improved agriculture. Lungshan society seems to have been relatively complex, with social stratification indicated in the archaeological evidence of burials, which also attests the early forms of the Chinese ancestor cult.

Lungshan gave way to Shang, a dynasty traditionally founded in 1766 BC, which established its capital at Anyang in 1384 BC and lasted about 700 years. Shang seems to have been founded by the most powerful of various warring fortified villages, and saw the introduction of horse chariots, and the elaboration of techniques of bronze-working and writing. The chief examples of writing so far found occur on the shoulder blades used for oracular prediction, a system that survived with little change into the historical period. From these oracle bones the names of twelve Shang emperors of Chinese tradition have been confirmed as historically correct, and their ostentatious burials, complete with wholesale human and animal sacrifice, show that the mystical veneration accorded Chinese rulers was also of early origin. Many aspects of Shang cosmology also survived. A state recognisable to modern eyes as China was to emerge at the end of the Chou dynasty (c. 1030–221 BC), successor to the Shang, with unification under the Ch'in, and the foundation of the Han (202 BC–AD 220).

Three factors important in Chinese myth had thus emerged by the earliest stages of China's three thousand years of written history: oracular prediction, ancestor worship, and veneration of the emperors. The early patterns of Chinese belief were to prove their strength in relation to the three major philosophies that were China's official religions, and were to shape the mythologies that grew up round them. This to some extent accounts for the parallel forms in the different systems of the gods, their hierarchies, groupings and bureaucracies, patterned on earthly models. Taoism, founded by Lao Tzu (trad. 604–517 BC – probably a little later), taught that the universe is governed by Tao, the Way: cosmic energy compounded of the yin, representing the negative, female principle, and yang, representing the positive, male principle of life. All creation, including man, is a product of these forces; and man can understand the universe through understanding his own nature. Clearly mythology had an important ethical role in such a system. Taoist belief fostered mysticism and magic practices as a means of affecting the cosmic forces; and Lao Tzu himself became the subject of myth, including virgin birth after a seventy-year gestation, already a hoary sage.

The ethics of Confucius (551–479 BC) were more firmly based on social reality: his purpose was to uphold the aristocracy as natural leaders through self-discipline, clear thought and moral example. The benefits of education for advance under paternalist rule were exemplified in the Han recension of the Shu Ching, 'Book of History', which justifies subservience to the state under the guidance of Confucian scholars and well illustrates the interaction of history and myth in Chinese thought.

Buddhism, which came to China about 300 BC, integrated itself into the Chinese pattern. Though figures of the Buddhist pantheon were officially subordinate to the native gods, and fell into typically Chinese groupings (for example the Five Buddhas, modelled on the Great Emperors of the Five Peaks and associated with the five elements of Taoism), the converse process also took place when, for example, the deified Lao Tzu was grouped in a triad with P'an-ku and Yu-huang, the August of Jade – which paralleled the Three Jewels of Buddhism.

Since the Chinese imagined a cosmos centred on man, and China, with ancestors providing links and intercession between men on earth and the gods (with past rulers performing a similar function for the state), mythologised history was of capital importance for state cohesion. And if a dynasty failed, it was because Heaven had withdrawn support from it. The most important text for this traditional history is the Confucian Shu Ching, though it survives, like other important source material, only in a form as reconstructed by Han scholars. The originals were burnt on the advice of Li Szu in 213 BC, in an effort to prevent comparison of the current Ch'in dynasty under the novel rule of Shih Huang Ti, first unifier of China, with the imagined Golden Age of past dynasties, though these had in fact led to constant internal dissension. According to the Shu Ching, the first rulers were the Three Sovereigns Fu-hsi, Shen-nung and YenTi; followed by the Five Emperors, Huang Ti (the Yellow Emperor), Chuan Hsiun, K'un, Yao, and Shun. These eight rulers together created the universe and introduced civilised ways to China. They were followed by the Hsia and Shang or Yin dynasties, leading into the Chou dynasty under which the history was written.

Creation myths survive only in late forms, and seem not to have concerned the Chinese overmuch. They account for the ordering of primeval chaos and the establishment of balance between heaven and earth necessary for cosmic harmony and good government. According to one version, Chaos, represented by the Emperor of the Centre, Hun-tun, sometimes in the form of a sack, was pierced by lightning, represented by the emperors of the Northern and Southern seas, Hu and Shu, and so allowed the world to be born. Hun-tun had various forms according to the dynasty in which the myth originated, with the founder of each dynasty exiling the wicked personification of chaos so as to establish good order. The alternative and most common account of creation speaks of a cosmic egg, Chaos, which separated into the yin principle, heavy Earth, and the yang principle, light, pure Sky. Between the two parts was P'an-ku, a dwarf, who daily for eighteen thousand years grew ten feet, his body gradually pushing apart earth and sky. On his death, the cardinal mountains, the heavenly bodies, thunder, lightning, rain, rivers and seas, the soil of the earth, and precious metals were derived from his body.

Embroidered funeral surcoat depicting a
crane, symbol of happiness, with peaches,
symbols of long life, encircled by the
pa pao, the Taoist Eight Precious Things.
The bats beneath symbolise the god of
happiness. Nineteenth century.
Victoria & Albert Museum.

There are various accounts, too, for the creation of men and women. They were the children of Fu-hsi, first of the Three Sovereigns, and his sister Nu-kua; or they were modelled in yellow earth by Nu-kua, until she became impatient and created some by spattering mud from a rope (the modelled men were nobles, the random spatterings the common people); or they were modelled in clay by P'an-ku, since he felt the need for intelligent beings capable of directing life in his creation – but he damaged some and they became cripples; or men simply developed from the fleas on P'an-ku's body.

As for the universe itself, though formed of a cosmic egg, its lower half, the earth, was square, and lay immobile beneath the inverted round bowl of the sky, which rotated, creating constant stellar motion about its axis, the Pole Star. This structure was often likened to the ancient Chinese chariot, square with an umbrella canopy. The central pole, corresponding to P'an-ku's body, or the four or eight pillars around the periphery which replaced this support, at once separated and linked heaven and earth. Ease of communication caused confusion between men and gods, so the emperor Chuan Hu had the link broken: Ch'ung, governor of the south, was to preside over heaven and bring order among the gods, while Li, governor of fire, was to establish good rule among men.

There are variants to this myth, but all affirm that man, meaning the ruler of China, must establish order, indeed a bureaucracy, in heaven and earth so that the universe can function harmoniously. Dynastic stability or instability was reflected even in the heavenly bodies. Thus normally there were ten suns each day, one by one drawn in a chariot by dragons from a hollow mulberry tree in the east to the jo-tree in the west. But at the fall of a dynasty more than one sun appeared in the sky at once, for new emperors, like the sun, began their careers in the hollow mulberry tree. When Shun, last of the Five Emperors, was about to take the throne from Yao, ten suns appeared at once and threatened to burn up the world. Yi the Good Archer was given a magic bow by Shun and shot down nine of the suns, thus saving the world and justifying Shun's rule. When Yi obtained the elixir of immortality from Hsi Wang Mu and became identified with the sun, his wife Heng-o stole it and fled to the watery moon, yin, already inhabited by a hare, where she became the celestial toad.

The sun is made of fire and is yang, like the earth. The central pole and four pillars supporting the heavens above the square earth were represented by the five cardinal mountains. The emperor had to tour the four cardinal points in order to take possession of his realm, but the most important were the eastern and western. T'ai Shan, the mountain of the east (a real mountain), was the starting point of the suns' daily journey and the location of the afterworld, so that the mountain determined men's destiny and the hour of their death. The east was ruled by Mu Kung, sovereign of yang and god of the Immortals. The emperor was thought to follow the course of the sun, so sacrifice by the emperor on the slopes of T'ai Shan was an important part of the assumption of power. Since metallic ores were found in mountains, T'ai Shan also saw sacrifices connected with the magical power of fire associated with smiths and the forging of dynastic swords, symbols of supreme power. The importance of imperial security sometimes justified human victims for such sacrifices.

In the far west was K'un Lun, stretching immensely high into the air and equally deep into the earth. It was the source of winds and of the Yellow river and on the slopes of its nine stages dwelt the Lord of the Sky, seen as a warrior in armour or as a silkworm chrysalis whose magic one-legged bird, the shang yang, was the portent of rain. On K'un Lun was situated the Western Paradise, whose Royal Mother was the goddess Hsi Wang Mu, in early Chinese belief a fearsome tiger- and leopard-woman of wild aspect who brought plague; but under Taoist influence becoming a benevolent figure living in a golden palace by a Lake of Gems where a magic peach tree provided the food of immortality. These peaches were once stolen by the monkey-fairy Sun Hou-tzu, who had already defied Yen-lo Wang, chief of the ten kings of the dead, and stolen the pills of immortality from Lao Chun (the deified form of Lao Tzu) and wished to prove his right to the title Governor of Heaven. All the gods and goddesses were pitted against his defiance, in which he was aided by the draughts of immortality and magic powers. Finally Buddha imprisoned him in a mountain, but he was released by Kuan Yin, goddess of mercy and of the north star, the Chinese form of the Bodhisattva Avalokitesvara and identified with the Taoist Tou Mu. Sun then accompanied T'ang Seng on a pilgrimage to bring to China the true teachings of Buddha from the Western Paradise (i.e. India). On their successful return Sun was rewarded by Mi-lo Fo, otherwise known as Maitreya or the laughing Buddha.

Since K'un Lun was also the source of the Yellow river (and by extension of all rivers), it was the home of the wrathful Ho Po, Count of the River, whose support could be gained by human sacrifice or rich tribute thrown into the waters. The rivers flowed into the four seas that lapped each side of the square earth. Most important of these was the (real) Eastern Sea, into which the river of the heavens, the Milky Way, also emptied. In the Eastern Sea were the P'eng-lai islands, originally five floating paradises on which grew the plant of immortality, but later anchored with giant tortoises on the orders of the Celestial Emperor, and guarded by Yu-ch'iang, god of the northern ocean wind in the shape of a human-headed, serpent-footed bird, and sea-god in the form of a huge kun whale which created storms, blackening the sky, when it changed into the vast p'eng bird. The other winds were released from a sack by the Count of the Wind, Feng Po or Fei Lien, bringer of drought and usually seen as a bird-dragon. The realm of the Count of Dragons was the home of a giant who caused the loss of two of the island paradises of the Eastern Sea. But another fiery dragon was beneficent: it took the place of the hole rent in the sky during an attempted usurpation by the monster Kung Kung. This dragon's waking, sleeping and breathing determined night and day, the season, rainfall and wind. There were five types of dragon: heavenly and imperial, who respectively guarded gods and emperors; spiritual, who controlled wind and rain; earthly, which deepened rivers and seas; and guardians of hidden treasure.

The first dragon was said to have appeared to the first of the Three Sovereigns Fu-hsi who, like the other mythical early rulers, restored heavenly order by combating the floods that threatened the world after Kung Kung had impaled Mount Pu Chou on his horn and thus made the world asymmetrical, tilting to the north-west. Fu-hsi and his consort Nu-kua, both serpent-bodied and usually entwined, represent yin and yang, and restored order with set-square and compasses. Fu-hsi also introduced men to fishing, animal husbandry and silkworm-breeding. He was succeeded by ox-headed Shen-nung, who invented ploughing and slash-and-burn techniques.

Li T'ieh-kuai, one of the Taoist Eight Immortals, who through merit had been granted immortality by eating the peaches of the Western Paradise. He could revive the dead with the medicines in his gourd. Porcelain, nineteenth century. Wellcome Medical Museum.

Ma-ku, a fairy sorceress who lived in the second century AD and reclaimed from the sea a large coastal area in Kiangsu, converting it into a mulberry orchard. The introduction of sericulture was attributed to Fu-hsi. Painting by Hsiang Kun. British Museum.

The first of the Five Emperors, the Yellow Emperor Huang Ti, defended this agricultural civilisation against his rebellious minister Ch'ih-yu, inventor of war and weapons, by inventing in his turn the chariot wheel (and the potter's wheel), the compass, ships and armour. Huang Ti's descendant K'un (also the name of the third of the Five Emperors) helped the fourth Emperor Yao by taking the advice of a tortoise and a horned owl to steal the magic Swelling Earth of Huang Ti, and with it succeeded in confining the waters with dams. Huang Ti, enraged at the theft, sent Chu-jung, Fire, to kill K'un, but from his body, three years later, emerged Yu, as a winged and horned dragon.

Yu sought and obtained Huang Ti's permission to use the Swelling Earth, and so became the dam-builder of Shun, the fifth Emperor. By blocking up 233,559 springs Yu contained the most damaging floods, and he further channelled the waters by building ditches with the tail of the Winged Dragon and cutting watercourses through mountains, by taking the form of a bear. He also became a smith and, having mapped out the universe, inscribed the precious information on nine cauldrons. Possession of these cauldrons was to become symbolic of the right to rule, and as dynasties weakened, the cauldrons grew lighter. Yu himself claimed the throne as founder of the Hsia dynasty, and was succeeded by his son Ch'i, born of the rock into which Yu's wife turned herself when she accidentally saw Yu in the form of a bear. Riding two dragons to visit heaven, Ch'i brought back knowledge of music to mankind.

The Hsia dynasty, dated c. 200–1520 BC, further codified the pattern of rule in China and forms the link between the world of culture-heroes and its historically attested

successor, the Shang. The pattern thus set was also transferred to a heavenly empire. The supreme ruler of heaven was the August Personage of Jade, Yu-ti, whose wife was a form of Hsi Wang Mu, goddess of the Western Paradise, and who was the personal god of the emperor of China. The palace of the supreme sovereign, like all homes, was guarded by innumerable specialist gods. Among the most important were the kitchen-god, who received offerings twice a month and a special feast of honey at the New Year to seal his lips, for then he visited Heaven as spy on the family to report on them; and the Men Shen, door-guardians, who warded off the demon spirits, usually associated with violent deaths, who lurked, sometimes in the shape of animals or beautiful girls, ready to seize any opportunity.

Just as on earth there was a hierarchical bureaucracy, so in heaven, Yu-ti deputed the maintenance of harmony to Shang Ti, god of the sky, who became identified with the Taoist August of Jade Yu-huang. He received sacrifice through his doorkeeper the Transcendent Dignitary and further deputed control of natural phenomena to subordinate gods under the direction of the Great Emperor of the Eastern Peak, head of a ministry with upwards of seventy-five departments which judged men and animals, allotting roles and length of life in various reincarnations. The government of heaven was paralleled by the god of the soil and his subordinates, the Ch'eng-huang, administrators in each district, responsible for wall and moat, for ensuring protection of crops from floods, drought and wild animals, and protecting people from wrongful seizure by Yen-lo (Buddhist Yama), king of the dead. They conducted preliminary judgment on souls just like a mortal district administrator. This divine administration persisted until the twentieth century, having first been evolved in simpler form under the Shang, when Shang Ti was supreme deity, three millenia before.

The Four Kings of Hell, who guarded the register of judgments. They parallel the Buddhist Four Diamond Kings of Heaven, who lost their lives in defence of the Shang dynasty, and lived on Mount Sumeru, or K'un Lun. British Museum.

right
Tigers were linked with K'un Lun, location of the Western Paradise. The White Tiger of the West, associated with metals, was the king of beasts, just as sovereignty was linked with metallurgy in dynastic mythology. Painting by Chen Chu-chung. British Museum.

below
The ox was a stellar deity, but according to popular mythology he brought men a message from heaven that they should be able to eat three times a day—instead of saying every three days, and so was forced to remain on earth to help man. Ming jade. Victoria & Albert Museum.

opposite
Horse in unglazed pottery of the T'ang dynasty, tenth century AD. Horses had an important military role in the defence of the empire, and they were also used to defend tombs against demon attack. K'un took the form of a white horse to dam the waters of chaos.

此是關聖帝君神像夜讀春秋
側立周倉手持偃月刀軍民人
供之

Ploughing a ricefield with the aid of an ox,
an art taught mankind by the ox-headed
emperor Shen-nung. The rice grains were
filled by Kuan Yin squeezing her breasts.
Screen made of jade, said to be the
bone-marrow of P'an-ku. Reign of
K'ang Hsi. Seattle Art Museum.

Jade screen depicting silk-weaving. Presiding over it was the Heavenly Weaver Girl, the constellation Lyra, whose husband the Celestial Cowherd, Aquila, was separated from her by the Milky Way. They met once a year, crossing by a magpie bridge. Seattle Art Museum.

193

left
A judge of hell. There were ten law-courts, each equipped to deal with a particular type of transgressor. Before being passed to the tenth judge for assignment to a suitable new incarnation, each soul had to pay for crimes till then unexpiated. Late Ming pottery statue.

opposite, top
Spring fishing festival in a South China village, akin to the yearly fishermen's offerings to Ho Po, Count of the Yellow river. These fertility rites coincided with marriage festivals in prehistoric times. Famille verte dish. Reign of Ch'ien Lung. Victoria & Albert Museum.

opposite, bottom
The Assembly of the Immortals in the Western Paradise for the feast of Hsi Wang Mu, by the Lake of Gems, or Green Jade Lake, in the gardens of her palace. The feast ended with peaches of immortality, produced every six thousand years. Late Ming painting. British Museum.

opposite
Dragons were water-spirits of the clouds in heaven as well as the seas on earth. This one is associated with the moon, where beneath a Cassia tree the hare pounds the elixir of immortality for Heng-o. Eighteenth-century emperor's robe. Victoria & Albert Museum.

below
The *ch'i-lin*, emblem of the upright judge Kao-yao, who punished the wicked but spared the innocent. Its appearance was a sign that the emperor's judgments had achieved ideal balance in support of cosmic order. Early nineteenth century. Victoria & Albert Museum.

opposite
One of the two Men Shen or door
guardians, images painted on paper and
pasted to the doors of all dwellings to
protect them against the onslaught of
demons as part of the New Year
celebrations. They were deified T'ang
generals. Painting from Soochow,
nineteenth century.

above
The Temple of the Lamas in Peking.
Buddhism first reached China about
300 BC and both achieved a native form
and exerted influence on Taoism,
especially through the idea of
reincarnation. The Tibetan form was
favoured by the Manchus because of its
magical aspect.

Japan

The essential core of Japanese mythology was built up by people who probably came from the Asian steppes via Korea in remote prehistory, and settled in the islands, driving the aborigines, the hairy Ainu, to the northern mountains. They found themselves in a mountainous land broken up by swift rivers, a land of volcanoes but of fertile soil and temperate climate, where nature seemed abundant and beautiful, and round which the sea, too, was prodigal in its blessings. They lived in tribes or clans, each following its own god; but a common feature of their beliefs seems to have been appreciation of the land which supported them. A persistent characteristic of Japanese thought is the belief that the divine *kami* (literally, more highly placed), is immanent in all nature, from exceptional men and animals, to mountains, trees, flowers—the very pebbles. Despite volcanoes, earthquakes and storms, the beneficence of nature seems to have dominated in Japanese thought, and in the mythology there is no theme of cosmic disaster, nor any thread of guilt and tragedy.

Nor does any real morality attach to the gods the early Japanese worshipped: all displayed a variety of mood and character, and none was either omniscient or omnipotent. Their spheres of interest were defined, but dichotomy between good and evil, spiritual and physical, seems to have been virtually non-existent. Such ideas were to be imported later, with the introduction of Buddhism, when the early cult was first called Shinto. The rites of Shinto were chiefly concerned with purification through ablution, exorcism, and abstention from contact with the impure. By and large, however, it was a cult of glorification rather than of propitiation.

The spheres of interest already mentioned owed their origin to the particular nature-gods worshipped by the various clans or tribes into which Japanese society was divided. Our knowledge of early Japanese mythology derives chiefly from texts written at Nara in the early eighth century AD. In systematising oral tradition, these compilations gave primacy to the sun cult practised by the Yamato tribes in central Honshu, and derived the genealogy of the royal house from the sun-goddess, while the earth cult centred on Izumo, on the west coast of Honshu facing Korea, where the state was actually founded, was

given a secondary role. One of the results of this effort to establish a divine lineage was anthropomorphisation of the gods.

No attempt can be made in this essay to describe all the gods of Japan: deriving as they did from every facet of nature, large and small, their number in the early period, according to tradition, was eight million. And the pantheon was far from static: through time deities were added as emperors, warriors, heroes and religious leaders were deified. Furthermore in AD 538 Buddhism in its Chinese form was introduced via Korea. A Japanese Buddhist pantheon developed, and was especially important in the seventh century, when Buddhism was supported by the regent Shotoku Daishi (593–621). Shinto adapted itself to this, with the development in the early ninth century of Ryobu or double-aspect Shinto, which declared the Shinto deities to be aspects of the Buddhist. The most influential figure in this was the Buddhist priest Kobo Daishi (774–834), founder of the Shingon sect. This allowed Shinto to continue as the official national religion, from which derived the most important mythology for social cohesion, leaving Buddhism as a more personal faith. Nevertheless, Buddhism had an important political effect in fostering the ideal of chivalry, *bushido*, glorified in history by the *samurai* with their Zen ethic—many of them becoming the heroes of mythology; and an important effect in mythology with the introduction of themes of generosity, patience and protection of animals—based on Buddhist notions of reincarnation.

Meanwhile, the creation myths of Shinto continued to be invoked by emperors as justification for their rule. According to these, creation was the work of the seventh generation of gods that had arisen from the primeval oily ocean, the male called Izanagi and the female Izanami. They descended from heaven on the rainbow bridge, and Izanagi formed the first island from ocean drops falling from his sword or lance. Here they learned to make love by watching wagtails and set up a pillar round which they performed a marriage rite (clear indication of a primitive cult of fertility and phallicism also evidenced in other practices). The offspring of this marriage were islands—but owing to a misdemeanour of Izanami during the rite, the first islands were misshapen and disowned, set adrift in the sea.

After re-enactment of the marriage ceremony, this time with Izanami correctly subservient, the remainder of the islands of the world (Japan), and the gods of sea, winds, trees, etc. were produced. The last to be born was the god of fire, who so burnt his mother that after producing more gods from her vomit and excrement, she died in agony. She descended to the gloomy underworld, Yomi, which had two entrances, a long winding road leading down in Izumo province, and another leading from the sea shore into the abyss where all the waters of the earth collect. In his grief, Izanagi first cut off the head of the fire-baby; from the blood sprang eight more gods, and a further eight, mountains, from the body. Then Izanagi descended to Yomi to seek his wife. But she had already tasted the food of hell and could not follow him back to earth. By insisting, and seeing her already putrefied body, Izanagi humiliated Izanami, who pursued him with the help of the female demons of hell, eight thunder-gods and the soldiers of hell; shouting at each other, they pronounced the first form of divorce. Thus the patterns of marriage, procreation, death and divorce were established.

On his return to earth, Izanagi, polluted by hell, performed the first rites of purification. Bathing in a river in Kyushu, Izanagi first created gods of evils, and then gods to keep these evils in check. Then he bathed in the sea, creating sea-deities. Finally, washing his left eye, he created Amaterasu, goddess of the sun; washing his right eye, he created Tsuki-yomi, god of the moon; and from his nose he created Susanoo, god of storms, whose name means Impetuous Male. To these three great deities Izanagi assigned overlordship of the universe. Amaterasu received a five-strand jewelled necklace as ruler over heaven; the moon was to rule the kingdom of the night (but soon faded from mythology); and to Susanoo was assigned the ocean. Susanoo, however, refused, for he wished to descend to hell to be with his mother. Before departing, he ascended to heaven in order to take leave of his sister Amaterasu.

As Susanoo approached, storms and earthquakes so shook the mountains that Amaterasu suspected an attack and took her stand at the entrance to heaven, an Amazonian figure armed with 1,500

arrows. The redoubtable brother and sister agreed to exchange pledges and so create offspring. Susanoo gave Amaterasu his sword, which she broke into three and chewed, then breathing forth three goddesses; Susanoo likewise chewed her five-strand necklace and breathed forth five gods. Amaterasu declared that these too were her children, since they came from her necklace; and the eight gods descended from the sun were later claimed as ancestors of the imperial family and the seven noblest families of Japan.

The uneasy relationship between Susanoo and Amaterasu continued with Susanoo polluting and devastating her fields and temples, for which she forgave him, and finally throwing his flayed horse through the roof of the sacred house where she was weaving silk for ritual use. Mortified and frightened at this, Amaterasu hid herself away in a cave. Her refusal to emerge (corresponding to winter) cast

the earth in darkness and left the field free for the gods of evil. The other gods sought to entice the sun-goddess out of her cave, and finally succeeded by setting cocks to crow and getting the goddess of mirth to perform an obscene dance outside the cave entrance. The gods' laughter at this spectacle aroused Amaterasu's curiosity, and on peeking out she saw a mirror, the first to be made, which the gods had hung in the branches of a tree. When the goddess had fully emerged to investigate this marvel, they blocked the entrance to the cave and so re-established day and night. The mirror, with its magical associations, and the necklace of the Amaterasu myths formed part of the imperial regalia of Japan.

The sword, also part of the regalia, was found by Susanoo and presented to Amaterasu when, expelled from heaven, he came down to Izumo province, and killed the eight-headed serpent or dragon

about to devour a maiden. The sword was retrieved from the dragon's tail. Having married the girl, Susanoo established himself at Suga as god of fertility as well as storms. Their son was the god Okuninushi, god of medicine and magic and lord of Izumo, who was the subject of a myth cycle during which he descended to the underworld, bound Susanoo and stole his weapons, and with the help of a dwarf, Sikuna-bikona, built the non-celestial world. His descendants at Izumo maintained control of secret religious matters after Amaterasu sent her grandson Ninigi down to earth to take charge of public, political affairs, i.e. to establish the imperial dynasty of Yamato.

This arrangement was preceded by another attempt by Amaterasu to create order on earth. She sent the moon-god (or in some versions Susanoo), to enter the service of the food-goddess Ukemochi. But the god, disliking the way she spewed

above
Child and protectress, possibly Kintaro and his mother, a Yama-uba. These mountain-spirits were often ugly and terrifying, but Kintaro's wild upbringing in the mountains gave him strength to avenge his *samurai* father. Print by Kunisada. Victoria & Albert Museum.

opposite
The Dragon King of the Sea, Ryujin, bearing in his hands one of the Tide Jewels. His daughter married Prince Fire Fade, and their son was father of Jimmu Tenno, first emperor of Japan. The Tide Jewels ensured the mastery of the line. Victoria & Albert Museum.

forth her blessings, killed Ukemochi. Amaterasu's anger at hearing of this accounts for the fact that sun and moon sit back to back and never look each other in the face. Further messengers, finding that the body of Ukemochi had given birth to rice, millet, corn, beans, an ox, horse and silkworms, brought these treasures back to Amaterasu, who discovered and taught their use.

Ninigi's sons established links with the powers of the sea. Known as the princes Fire Fade, an expert hunter, and Fire Flash, an expert fisherman, they one day exchanged roles. Fire Fade lost his brother's hook and, in retrieving it from the depths of the sea, met and married the daughter of the Dragon King of the Sea. For his return journey to Japan to bring back his brother's hook, he was given the magic sea jewels controlling the tides, through which he obtained ascendancy over his brother. When his wife was about to bear their child, she told him to leave her in seclusion, but he disobeyed and saw her giving birth in the shape of a dragon. Thereupon she fled back to the sea, leaving a human baby boy behind. She sent her sister to look after the baby, and on reaching manhood he married this aunt, their offspring being Jimmu Tenno, who became first emperor of Japan in 660 BC. The difficulties encountered by his successors in tribal conflicts, the struggle against the Ainu and war with Korea are reflected in numerous myths, featuring among others Yamatodake, heroic prince of the third century AD, who overcame his adversaries by trickery and magic as much as valour; his son the emperor Chuai, who died quelling an insurrection in Kyushu; his widow the empress Jingo, who conquered Korea with the aid of the sea jewels controlling the tides; and her son, the emperor Ojin, later deified as Hachiman, god of war, and later still identified with the Buddhist Kwannon, goddess of mercy.

With the Korean tribute came also Buddhism. It was fully established at Nara in the late sixth century, Nara becoming capital in 710. In 794, the Fujiwara clan, who had seized power and established civilian, Shinto rule, moved the capital to Kyoto and married into the imperial family. With their decline, after some three centuries, two feuding warrior clans came to the fore: the Taira, whose great hero Kiyomori entered myth as the protégé of the sea-goddess Benten and whose clan was to fall at the hands of heroes whose lives he had earlier spared; and the Minamoto, supported by Hachiman. Their great heroes were Yoshitomo and his brother Tametomo, who sank a Taira ship with a single arrow; and Yoshitomo's sons Yoritomo and Yoshitsune, with his mighty retainer Benkei. These heroes ensured Minamoto victory at the great sea battle of Dannoura, when the Taira committed mass suicide and the imperial sword was lost in the depths of the ocean. Yoritomo established the shogunate at Kamakura, to be succeeded by the Ashikaga shogunate at Kyoto and then at Yedo, ultimately by the Tokugawa. The shogunate was to exercise real political power in Japan until 1868, with a feudal substructure of *daimyos*, lords, supported by the warrior *samurai*; but by its nature it was a prey to clan rivalry – which threw up heroes inhabiting the borderland between myth and legend.

The heroes of this long period of confusion include Kintaro, son of a mountain-spirit or Yama-uba and a warrior wrongfully banished from court, who by prodigious strength and wisdom vindicated his father and entered the service of the Minamoto hero Yorimitsu. Yorimitsu was a great opponent of the blood-sucking oni, Buddhist devils adept at escaping through charms and trickery; the male oni abducted and raped women, while the female liked to seduce priests. They corresponded to the Shinto tengu, malicious bird-men inhabiting mountain trees, who were said to be offspring of Susanoo and were powerful swordsmen. They had affinities too with the kappa, water-spirits possibly of Ainu origin, who ate blood and cucumbers; they were parasitical creatures attacking through rape and buggery. Trickery could overcome them, for they were renowned for their politeness. Since the source of their strength was the pool of water lying in a hollow on their heads, the trick was to greet them politely: in returning the bow, the kappa would lose its strength. It was not considered undignified for the mightiest hero to overcome an adversary through cunning or magic. By such methods Tawara Toda slew the giant centipede threatening the realm of the dragon king. Though often malicious, the tengu sided with the Minamoto heroes Yositsune and Benkei, son of a tengu and a *samurai*'s daughter; both heroes were taught the arts of war by tengu. Despite the superhuman help they were able to give Yoshitsune's older brother Yoritomo in his fight against the Taira, both perished as a result of the first shogun's jealousy – possibly by suicide, considered a noble end for a warrior.

Popular tales, as opposed to the mythology of state and social institutions, include many animal heroes. These tales are based partly on the Shinto notion that all creatures are *kami*, from dragons to the tiniest insects, and partly stem from

Buddhist ideas of reincarnation, often illustrating animal gratitude. A marked feature of these Japanese folktales is that animals take human form rather than vice versa, sometimes to marry their human benefactors. Thus a pair of mandarin ducks, renowned for their marital fidelity, took human form to save from execution the servants who had kept them from being parted; and a cat belonging to an old couple turned herself into a geisha girl, Okesa, in order to support them. Other famous grateful animals include the sparrow whose tongue was cut by a washerwoman in punishment for pecking at her rice. Her neighbours, an old couple who had been kind to the sparrow, found and looked after it. When they were offered the choice of two boxes, they chose the smaller and it opened to reveal endless riches. Similarly a grateful dog provided its mistress with a supply of silk that made her fortune; and a grateful bee rallied its fellows to win a battle.

Other animals, however, are usually malicious, and these include badgers, one of whom turned itself into the shape of a man's wife and offered him his real wife in soup; or cats, who with supernatural powers victimised whole villages; one, who demanded human sacrifice, was overcome only by an equally monstrous dog. Indeed the purely animal stories normally illustrate malice, trickery and vengeance. In this respect they are similar to the very common ghost stories of Japan. Really folktales, they dwell on ghostly returns to scenes of disaster and violent death, including drowning and execution, in order to visit retribution on the living for treachery, abandonment or divorce, and they haunt them until satisfied, or until an incomplete action is resolved.

left
Fujin, god of the winds in his Ryobu. Shinto form, bearing a sack of winds. The wind-gods were among the earliest deities and helped in creation by filling the void between heaven and earth and clearing the primeval mists. Statue in Ninna-ji Temple, Kyoto.

far left
Raiden, one of the eight thunder-gods, demons in hell who pursued Izanagi, caught in the bath of the goddess of mirth, Uzume, whose dance enticed Amaterasu out of her cave and so ensured the return of the fertilising sun in the spring. Victoria & Albert Museum.

below, left
Yorimitsu, otherwise known as Raiko, hero of the Minamoto clan, whose feud with the Taira in the twelfth century was the background of many semi-divine heroes. Here he battles with a bull and a demon in human form. Print by Kuniyoshi. Victoria & Albert Museum.

below
Kishijoten, goddess of luck, who lent her characteristics as patron of riches to her Buddhist counterpart Benten, sea-goddess of eloquence and music, patron of geishas, who figures in the Tawara Toda and Kiyomori myths. Statue in Joruri-ji Temple, Kyoto.

Jo and Uba, spirits of the pine tree. Pine trees symbolise fidelity in marriage, and there are many myths of devoted lovers being turned into pine trees. They, the tortoises and the storks are also symbolic of old age. Print by Shunsen. Victoria & Albert Museum.

opposite

Warrior stunned by an apparition of the fox-goddess. The fox is among the oldest creatures of Japanese superstition, usually evil; but in myth Inari, god or goddess of rice, takes the form of a fox or sends fox messengers. Print by Kuniyoshi. Victoria & Albert Museum.

below

The priest Kuya-Shonin invoking Buddha. He founded the Rokuharamitsu-ji Temple in Kyoto in 963, so dispelling an epidemic. Myths of miracle-working surround many Japanese religious leaders, such as En No Shokaku, Kobo Daishi, Nichiren and Mito Komon.

above, right

Zocho, guardian of the south, one of the four guardians or Shi Tenno who protect the world from demon attacks. Evil spirits played little part in Japanese mythology until the advent of Buddhism, and even then were mostly mischievous rather than wholly evil. Kofuku-ji Temple, Nara.

right

Tadanobu, retainer of the Minamoto hero Yoshitsune. He is seen in the form of a fox-man. A fox, seeking vengeance on Yoshitsune for making its mother's skin into a drum, entered Tadonobu's body. Painting by Baikoku. Victoria & Albert Museum.

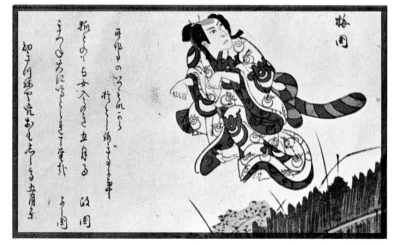

坂田金時
土蜘退治之圖

211

above
Print by Kuniyoshi showing figures
haunted by a giant spectral cat and by a
ghost in human form. Ghosts are legion
in Japan, where spirits inhabit every kind
of object, and are a popular subject for
artists, notably Hokusai. Victoria & Albert
Museum.

right
A kappa riding one of its favourite foods,
the cucumber. These water creatures
could be placated by men, and taught
them the art of setting bones. Their
intelligence may derive from monkey
origin. Painting by Hokuga. Victoria &
Albert Museum.

above, right
A spectral cat haunting a young man.
Cats were known to terrorise whole
villages. They often took the place of
foxes as malevolent creatures on
Shikoku, after foxes had been banished
from the island by Kobo Daishi. Print by
Kunisada. Victoria & Albert Museum.

right
Treasure ship sailing with the seven gods
of luck. They are Hotei; Jurojin, longevity;
Fukurokuju, longevity and wisdom;
Bishamon, missionary zeal and sometimes
wealth; Daikoku, wealth and patron of
farmers; Ebisu, patron of fishermen; and
the goddess Benten. Victoria & Albert
Museum.

left
Kirin. This mythical animal, often
portrayed in Japanese art, derived from
the Chinese *ch'i-lin*, a creature of good
omen which symbolised just rule and
punished the wicked with its single horn.
Painting by Royen. Victoria & Albert
Museum.

below
The Minamoto hero Yorimitsu,
accompanied as usual by his four
retainers or henchmen, killing a giant.
The hero pitted against a monstrously
large opponent is common, and some of
the heroes of Japanese myth were as
short as one inch. Print by Kuniyoshi.
Victoria & Albert Museum.

above
Yorimitsu being harried by the Earth
Spider and its monstrous forces—his
companions unaware of the menace.
Heroes too could summon up magic
powers; and trickery, such as
intoxicating the adversary, did not
diminish their valour. Print by
Kuniyoshi. Victoria & Albert Museum.

left
Yegara-no-Heida killing the giant serpent
Uwabami, who could swallow a man on
horseback whole. Serpents and dragons
represented dark forces beneath the
earth and the sea, and were also
connected with Susanoo as god of
thunder. Print by Shuntei. Victoria &
Albert Museum.

opposite, left
Jurojin, god of longevity, seated on his
animal, the stag. He is also represented
with other animals symbolising contented
old age, the crane and the tortoise.
Fastened to his staff is a scroll containing
the wisdom of the world. Victoria &
Albert Museum.

above
Sequel to the famous tale of the tongue-cut
sparrow: the wicked washerwoman, hearing of the
good fortune of her kindly old neighbours, also
visited the sparrow, but on being offered the two
boxes chose the larger, which contained devils that
devoured her. British Museum.

right
The old man who could make cherry trees bloom in
and out of season, by scattering ashes of wood
from a cherry tree inhabited by the *kami* of his dog,
whose gratitude for good treatment brought him
fortune and his jealous neighbour disaster.
British Museum.

Fujin, god of the wind. Detail of a print by Kunisada. Japanese mythology knows a number of wind-gods, usually in male and female couples: gods who took part in Izanagi's creation; gods of farmers and fishermen; and a terrible god of the whirlwind. Victoria & Albert Museum.

The North American India

The North American Indians, of Mongoloid stock, migrated into the continent from Siberia over a land link now broken by the Bering Strait. They came over a long period in small family groups, perhaps some ten thousand years ago, and fanned out to south and east. Gradually these hardy people adapted themselves and their culture to the regions where they became established, which varied from arctic to subtropical, desert lands where life was precarious to prairies abundantly stocked with game. The scattered groups reached stages of civilisation ranging from late palaeolithic hunting groups to advanced town-dwellers with elaborate social divisions. Once evolved, these cultures seem to have changed little over the centuries, until the advent of Europeans in the sixteenth century. The Indians, of course, resisted these changes (though the Plains tribes took readily to horses, introduced about 1750, and to guns), and in resolutely defending their land and way of life, most perished.

Since none of them had writing until the advent of the Europeans, the kernel of their culture, much of it in the form of mythology, was transmitted from generation to generation by members of the tribe with specially trained memories who excelled in the art of storytelling. These were allied with shamans whose trances allowed them to make contact with the spirit world of nature, on which they were so dependent, and of their ancestors, who were given offerings in return for protection (often in dreams ancestors would point the way to prosperity). Various artefacts also helped to fix traditions, such as bark paintings illustrating myths of tribal heroes, or the mnemonic Wampum belts of the Iroquois.

The details of the beliefs varied according to local conditions and activities, but some common themes run through all the mythologies. Three great deities form the dominant pattern: the power above, the earth mother, and the trickster. Regulating the seasons, and thus the spirits of animals and plants, were sun, moon, and the morning and evening stars–the twins. Some of the more advanced cultures produced elaborate creation myths to replace or supplement the primitive legends of the Great Mother in her world under the earth.

Among the Eskimo in former times, the simple ice-hunting communities of less than a hundred would shift with the seasons and the state of the ice, hunting walrus and whale in the sea during summer and in the winter fishing through holes in the ice for seals and fish. At such holes they might come into contact with the mysterious spirits of the ocean or with ghosts. Many perished in the harsh conditions, including old and young abandoned of necessity, and their spirits could be evoked by shamans or in dreams. At times of rejoicing over successful hunting ancestors would be included in the feasting, and later, at the end of winter, they might reveal the presence of caches of food deposited then but whose whereabouts had been forgotten. Ancestors or shamans might also indicate prospects for hunting (subconsciously based on astronomical or meteorological observation). The dead were identified with the dancing lights of the aurora borealis; in north-west Greenland the Pleiades were a pack of hunting dogs who had chased Nanook the Bear right up into the sky, while the Great Bear was seen as a giant caribou and Orion was described as three giant steps cut in the snow linking heaven and earth.

Other indicators for hunting were seen in bird flights and song, and the spirits of the hunters' prey, such as bear and fish, could be charmed into capture. The Old Woman who lived in the sea was important in controlling food supply. Known in the central areas as Sedna, this earth mother figure had been the child of giants. When her abnormal hunger led her to start eating her sleeping parents, they took her out to sea and cut off her fingers, which became whales, walrus, seals and fish. They then cast her into the depths, where she remained, determining the movements of her numberless offspring and causing storms at sea.

The tribes living along the north-west coast, from Alaska to Oregon, were primitive by the normal yardsticks, in that they practised no agriculture, living entirely on wild products and hunting. But such was the abundance of fish, seal, sea birds, caribou, deer and bears that hunting supported a high standard of living. Secure in their fiord valleys, it even allowed them the luxury in the off-season of prestige raids against rival tribes in their huge dug-out canoes.

The Haida, living on islands and relatively safe from attack, lived in villages where the houses sheltered whole families of up to fifty, decorated with fine wood and stone carving, often of the family' totem, for example a bear, salmon o beaver, which would be connected in heroic legend to some ancestor of the clan.

In the winter, with the products of th summer's fishing and hunting stored away the chief activities were tribal warfare and the retelling of myths and legends arising from hunting and martial adventure, in which force and cunning associated with supernatural powers were the weapon used by figures forever shifting from human to animal form and back. One o the most important characters was th trickster and creator Raven, on whom centred innumerable myths, in which he brought gifts to men by devious means or gulled them for the sheer delight o amazing them with his versatility. In typical story he was reborn as the grand son of a fisherman who kept the moon inside ten boxes nesting inside each other By clamouring for the moon as a play thing, he persuaded his grandfather to le him have the moon, whereupon he threw it up into the sky, where it stayed forever Another tale of an animal nursling con cerned a woodworm who was stealing away the oil supply of a south Alaska tribe, the Tlingit. Tribes were punished by the animal spirits if they killed other than for their food needs, for example b volcanoes.

Sometimes heroes with supernatural powers could protect against the menace of hostile nature, but these heroes had an ambiguous nature; one, for example having fulfilled his mission and retired to the spirit world, caused earthquakes when he wanted to pass a message to the medicine-man. While on earth he had caused the advancing forest to withdraw up th mountains, and had split the mountain so that rivers could pass peaceably instead of falling in destructive waterfalls. Yet another hero, Stoneribs, son of Volcano Woman, assumed in turn the skin of halibut dropped on the sea shore by a

The Flyer, painted in 1585 by the Virginian colonist John White, a friend of Sir Francis Drake who made the first authentic pictorial records of the New World, depicting the Indians' customs and ceremonies. British Museum.

The flyer.

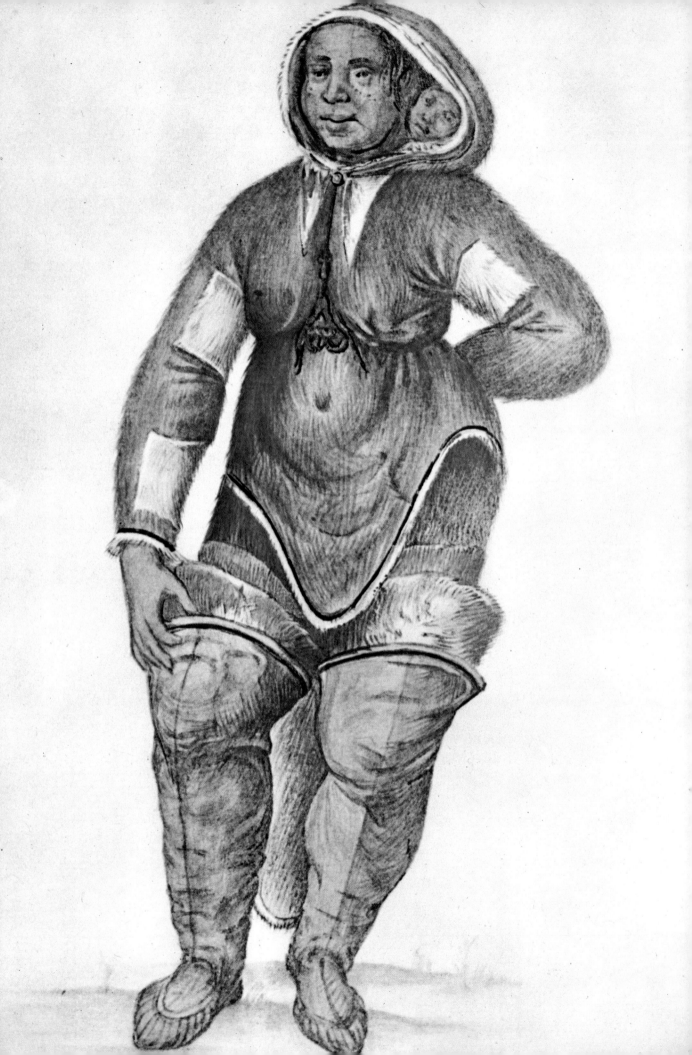

agle, and that of Qagwaai, a monster killer-whale. When, by changing shape and size, he had punished and escaped from the various sea-monsters that had been persecuting fishing tribes along the coast, the halibut skin was retrieved by the eagle and Stoneribs returned to his village a hero.

Among the most famous Haida myths illustrating the relationship between hunter and prey, that of Bear Mother relates how Rhpisunt, daughter of the Wolf clan chief, was abducted while gathering berries in the forest for having reviled bears. In the bears' mountain village she was ushered into a room festooned with bearskin coats and dominated by a huge man, the Bear Chief, and his wife, a monstrous creature with blazing eyes whose breasts were living and moving human heads. Through the advice of an old Mouse Woman, Rhpisunt pacified the bears and was married to the chief's son, bearing him two fine cubs. Eventually Rhpisunt's three brothers discovered her whereabouts, killed her husband, and brought her back to their village with her sons, who took off their bear coats and were revealed as handsome boys, skilled in hunting with the help of their dead father. They became intermediaries between the Wolf clan and their protectors the Bear People, whom they rejoined (as bears) on their mother's death.

In the great northern forests of present-day Canada, the Cree were a shifting population of hunters closely dependent on their forest environment with its moderately good stocks of game, which supplied them with food and clothing for bitterly cold winters and hot summers. Their mythology centred on the spirits of their prey, on winds, sun and stars important for hunters, and on an animal earth-spirit. The link with the spirit world was through ancestors, the 'old people', who lived in camps under the earth, and whose offerings of food were never to be accepted by a shaman who wished to return alive. As other tribes in the area, such as the Algonkian, developed agriculture, a mythology of fertility evolved, featuring goddesses and the moon and planets, and rainbows, clouds and thunderstorms (controlled by the Great Spirit).

Creation myths among both tribes,

Eskimo woman and child, showing the thick fur clothing and boots that enabled this hardy people to survive relatively unchanged in an area along the entire northern fringe of the continent, too harsh for the white man. Watercolour by John White. British Museum.

however, centred on the trickster. Among the Cree, beavers he was trying to trap used magic to flood all the land. But the trickster, helped by Wolf and his own magic, made moss grow to cover the waters and make a new world. Among the Algonkian, Gluskap made the beneficent aspects of nature from the body of his mother, earth, while his evil brother Malsum made the hostile, poisonous features of the natural world. Ultimately Gluskap killed Malsum with a magic weapon and he became a wolf. But Gluskap himself could surprise those who sought benefits from him, and when a man wanted to be taller and more handsome than all other men and so become a ruler, he turned him into a pine tree.

Further south, among the Iroquois and related tribes (to which Hiawatha actually belonged: Longfellow wrongly associated him with Algonkian), settled agriculture based on maize cultivation by the womenfolk supplemented hunting of deer, moose, beaver, squirrel and fox, as well as river and lake fishing, for which light birch bark canoes were used. Though warfare was common and cruelly practised, with scalp-collecting and ritual burning to test the courage of the vanquished, about a century before the arrival of Europeans social development had reached a level where a peace treaty could be drawn up between the five major warring tribes, who became the Iroquois federation.

Contrasts of war and peace may have fostered belief in a dualist struggle between good luck and bad, light and dark. Factors determining the outcome included the heavenly bodies, directions, seasons, and other spirits of nature, who were to be appeased by offerings of corn and food animals, often made by dancers wearing 'False Face' masks, which could ward off evil spirits. As usual, the spirits of ancestors took part in the lives of their descendants. Those of warriors inhabited the sky, and others lived in underworld villages where food was plenteous, and there was no sickness or warfare. This was the province too of the Mother of Animals; and other female deities protected crops. All were presided over by a supreme spirit, guardian of time and destiny, called the Great Manitou.

The mother of the earth fell through a hole in the sky from the land of her people beyond the sky into an endless lake. With her fell a cosmic tree with magical earth clinging to its roots. Two swans prevented the girl drowning and, advised by the Great Turtle, master of all animals, Otter, Beaver, Muskrat and Toad all dived into the lake to try to recover some of the earth on the tree's roots. All died in the

attempt, but Toad managed to bring up a mouthful of earth, which grew into an island for the woman, and went on growing to become the world. Great and Little Turtles then created sun and moon by collecting lightning in the heavens, and made holes for their passage through the sky. A recurrent quarrel between them over precedence led to the waxing and waning of the moon. Thunder and rain created a rainbow, pathway to heaven which first the deer and then the other animals ran along to become stars. The Woman herself bore twins personifying good and evil, the evil one killing his mother at birth. Each good creation was matched by an impediment to man, and so the topography, flora and fauna of the world were shaped, culminating in the evil brother's creation of the Rocky Mountains.

Heng, the thunder-spirit, was thought of as herald of spring rains, his lesser offspring as destructive powers. Thunder once saved a girl who had been abducted by one of the Serpent People in the guise of a handsome young man. She bore one of the thunder-spirits a son who possessed thunder power in his bow and arrow. For making lightning on earth this boy was banished to heaven where he could not strike men. In a similar accord between man and nature-spirits, an Eagle Mother released a hunter from captivity and in return his descendants never harmed eagles and made them offerings from all deer killed.

In the great central plains of America lived tribes well known in the legends and history of the European settlers, such as the Comanche, Pawnee, Sioux, Dakota, Arikara and Mandan. Natural conditions created an inevitable reliance on the herds of buffalo, deer and antelope that roamed the rich prairie land. Their seasonal migration was followed by the Indians, who in summer lived in portable skin tipis (teepees), and in winter returned to permanent earth houses in riverside settlements where agriculture was practised, especially by the women. The summer hunting parties were relatively small to permit easier trapping of buffalo, and this promoted the formation of sacred societies, each identified with a particular aspect of the Indians' life—such as buffalo themselves, dogs (who were the spirit messengers between the Arikara people and their gods), or warriors prepared to meet cruel death unflinchingly—an important test of any Indian hunter.

The spirits of the sky—thunder, lightning, the rainbow and the heavenly bodies, who affected not only the weather but also the prowess of warriors and the migration paths of their prey—could be propitiated by offerings of human pain, and warriors would torture themselves in the Sun Dance ceremonies. The great communal festivals usually took place in summer and the participants often wore special costumes, masks and body painting to simulate animals or the other spirits that imbued all life.

The particular spirits varied from tribe to tribe. Thus the Pawnee, who seem to have derived some of their beliefs from Central America, were especially interested in sky-spirits, and their ceremonies were based on elaborate myths built around astronomical observation. They attached importance to four stars especially: the North Star, beneficent creator; the Morning Star, their protector; the South Star, underworld leader of hostile forces; and the Evening Star, which heralded darkness and opposed the creative powers of the Morning Star (his daughter, however, when laid low by magic arrows, was a source of blessings). They believed that the world would eventually be destroyed, and that heavenly portents would announce the cataclysm. Such myths, and the ceremonies attached to them, were handed down the generations in so-called medicine-bundles, containing protective relics of ancestors or signs of divine favour.

Perhaps the most typical focus of attention among the Plains Indians was on earth-spirits such as the earth mother, who sheltered the all-important buffalo spirits. Buffalo were both desired and feared, for their absence could mean starvation and their presence the trampling down of a village. The Arikara people told how one of their ancestral heroes, with the help of magic and a Buffalo-girl, made the Buffalo People stop hunting human beings and turn wholly into animals. The Mandan, in their Lone Man creation myth enacted at the Okipa ceremony, had a complex story featuring the demiurge who took the form of a buffalo to beget a culture-hero who, with the help of other animals (and the usual trickery and magic) built a great canoe to save the Mandan people from a flood. The Arikara creation myth is similar to that of the Iroquois, except that the world was peopled from beneath the earth: first a race of giants begotten by spiders (inspired by dinosaur bones), which the great sky-spirit wiped out by flood; then people born of seeds of maize, planted by animals and released by the heavenly Corn Mother, with the help of Badger, Mole, Mouse, Owl and Kingfisher. At first these people fought, but they were taught the arts of peace and agriculture by the sky-spirit and the Corn Mother, and how to appease the gods of the eight directions by offerings of tobacco smoke.

In the great deserts of the south-west lived the Apache, Papago and Navajo tribes. In historical times they lived hard lives with poor game and poor soil fertility, but the Navajo particularly had carefully preserved myths dating from times of less desiccation and prosperous maize cultivation. The myths were recorded in traditional chants and sand-paintings, whose power could bring health and prosperity.

Their creation story, known as the emergence myth, tells of a First Man, First Woman and a trickster-creator in the form of Coyote. These beings inhabited four worlds in turn. In each their lack of success taught them the way to keep the powers of heaven and earth in check. The fourth world was destroyed by flood, and in fleeing it, they emerged on to an island in the midst of a lake. Coyote was forced to cast away the children of the water-monster Tieholtsodi, the waters subsided, and the fifth and present world was revealed. It was discovered that the sun and moon could be set in their courses only by the death of a Navajo each day and the death of another each night, with descent into the Fourth World. The tribes were distributed along with seeds brought from the Fourth World by Coyote; but humans claimed the credit for their prosperity, and so were punished by plagues and monsters sent by First Man and Woman. These were eventually conquered in a cycle of heroic labours by twin sons of their daughter Estanatlehi and the Sun. Estanatlehi repopulated the earth by creating from maize flour and dust from her breasts a man and woman to found each of the eight Navajo clans; she then retired to become goddess of the Sunsetland, whence she sent all benefits to the Navajo, countered only by the evils sent from the east by First Man and Woman: sickness, wars and white men.

Another famous story, embodied in the Beauty Chant, told how a girl, Glispa, had brought back supernatural healing powers from the underworld inhabited by the Snake People near the Lake of Emergence. She had been abducted by a Snake Man who was alternately a frightening old man and a young man dazzlingly handsome like the rainbow, and returned after two years to teach her brother a powerful shamanistic ceremony.

The tribes inhabiting the south-eastern corner of North America seem to have had among the highest cultures of all the Indians, if we are to judge by archaeological evidence of the earthen mounds they built as ceremonial centres of tribal life, often in the shape of sacred animals. This indicates a sophisticated, stratified society. The tribes included Cherokee, Choctaw,

Creek and Natchez. Unfortunately their very strength led to their systematic dispersal by European settlers, and little of the mythology survives. The creator-trickster was a Rabbit, who stole fire from the Sky People for the benefit of man. He seems to have had a rival in the form of a boy whose grandmother was or brought maize to earth, and who was magically protected by rattlesnakes and jaybirds. The Mound Builders also had a flood myth, possibly explaining the origin of social divisions and featuring, like many stories of the area, a confused journey (possibly to visit sun, moon and stars) in which women undergo various cruelties and a hero is born.

In the south-west lived the Indians of the Hohokan, Hopi and Zuñi tribes. In the comparative isolation and peace of the mesas, they developed a complex society designed to cope communally with a harsh environment. They built adobe pueblos to defend themselves against raids by other tribes in the south-west and the Plains displaced by drought from about the twelfth century. There developed the most organised culture and elaborate mythology of all North America, in which the divine and the political were closely intertwined. It was a matriarchal society, though participants in the religious ceremonies held in underground kivas were mostly men, who wore masks representing the kachinas, the nature-spirits. These attached to all nature and their role in a creation myth similar to that of the desert tribes determined all important events in the lives and activities of the Pueblo Indians. The main difference, appropriate to a matriarchal society, was that the successive worlds were seen as the four wombs of Earth Mother, consort of Sky Father. From the innermost emerged the pathfinder, One Alone, who cleared a way for the heavenly twins who were to teach culture and complete creation.

opposite
Carved wooden half-figure wearing a mask from Point Barrow, Alaska. Such large figures were rarely carved by the Eskimo, whose itinerant life in pursuit of whale, seal and fish discouraged unnecessary burdens. Even their weak relatives sometimes had to be jettisoned.

page 226
Mask surrounded by feathers from Anvik, Alaska. It represents a woman, perhaps one of the spirits whose help could indicate the movements of shoals and herds. The all-important and equivocal controller of sea creatures was the Woman of the Sea.

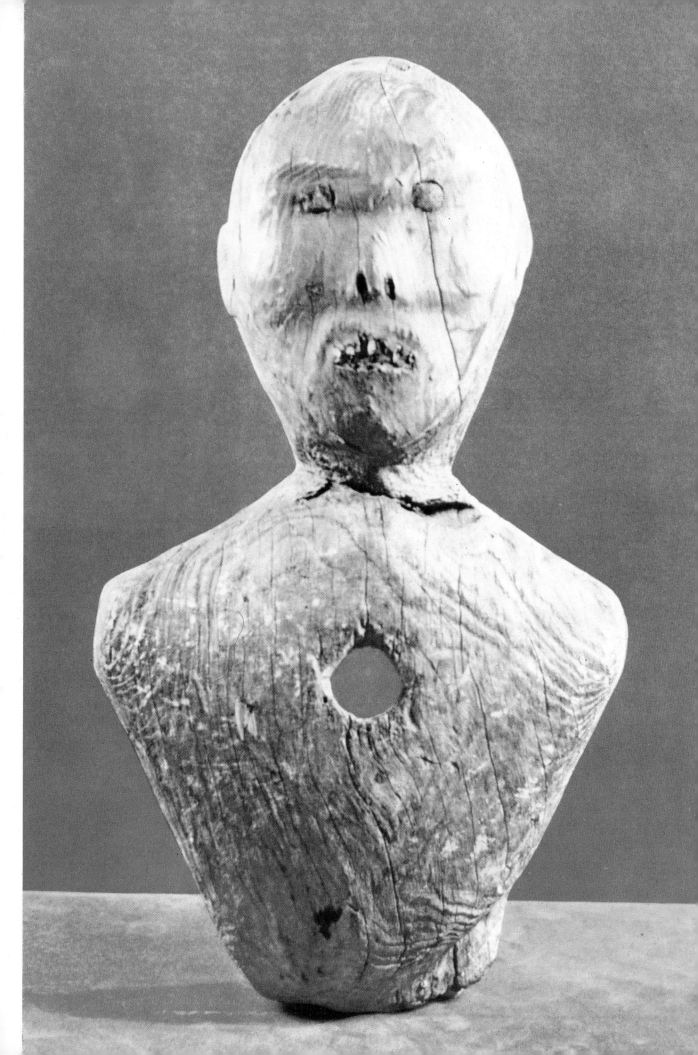

page 227
Carved and painted wooden headdress decorated with ermine and representing the 'Mystery of the Sea', worn in ritual enactment of myths among the north-west coast Indians. Such carvings were elaborated on the huge totem poles, doorposts indicating a family's clan.

below
Painted wooden mask with a fringe of human hair. Hair taken from an enemy's scalp could be purified and used thus by the victor to give him additional strength and protection. The north-west coast Indians gained prestige and slaves through tribal warfare.

opposite
Box drum of the Haida Indians of the north-west coast. The design represents a bear, both quarry and protector in local mythology. The Bear Mother story, where bears wear their coats only in public, aptly illustrates the thin line drawn between man and animal.

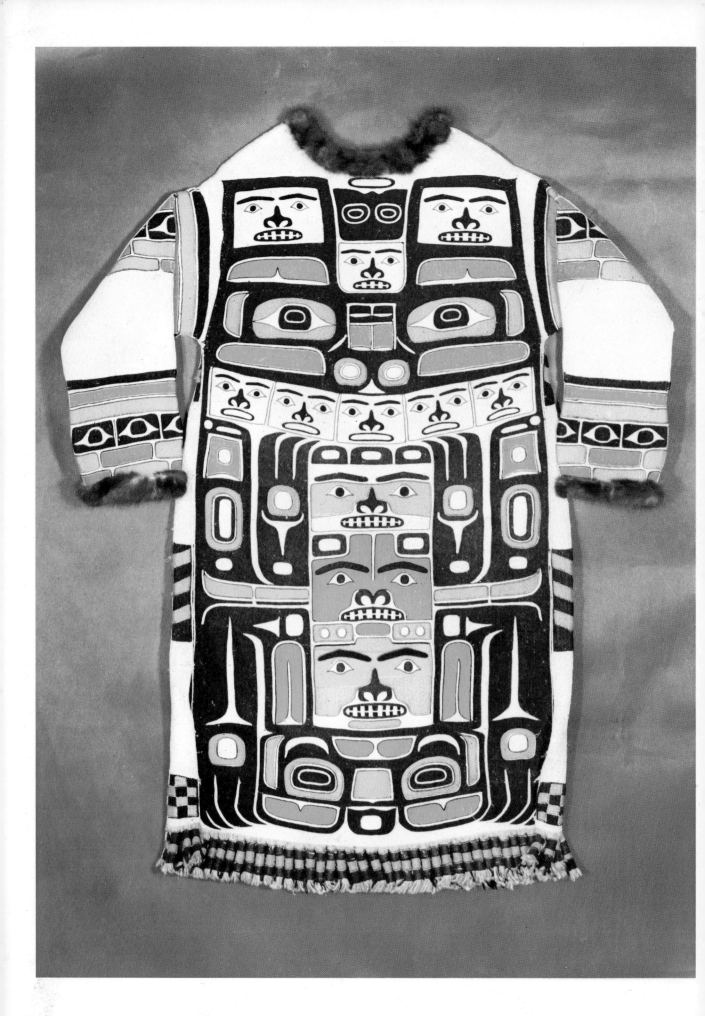

opposite
Man's shirt with a brown bear design.
Display of a totem animal allowed
strangers to find fellow clansmen to
befriend them, and so promoted mobility
and the spread and consistency of
mythological tradition throughout the
north-west coast area.

right
The Thunderbird. Haida Indian carving.
Ominous-looking, with the extra head on
its belly, it was an eagle strong enough to
pick up a whale in its talons. Its
wing-beats made the thunderclaps and
its beak the lightning. Elsewhere
thunder was the bringer of fertility.
British Museum.

page 232
A 'Speaker Mask', one of the grotesque
False Face masks worn at Iroquois
ceremonies in order to drive away the evil
False Face spirits from the tribe. The
Iroquois believed in a perpetual struggle
between creative and destructive forces.
Seneca Indian.

page 233, top
Snowshoe dance of the Chippewa
Indians of the northern forests. It was
performed after the first snow of winter
in order to thank the Great Spirit for
sending conditions that made tracking
and pursuit of game easier. Hunting was
central to Cree mythology.

page 233, bottom
Plains Indians performing the Buffalo
Dance, which was continued by
tribesmen, each wearing his personal
buffalo head, to the point of exhaustion—
for pain was pleasing to the sky powers
affecting buffalo—with new dancers
constantly recruited until the buffalo
came.

opposite
Plains Indian artefacts. Left, a quillwork
tobacco pouch with thunderbird design.
Right, drums decorated with thunderbird,
tipi and shaman in a trance; and sun
surrounded by symbols of stars. Top
right, Apache basket with the four
mystical directions.

below
An Apache beadwork collar, as worn in
religious ceremonies. The design
features the four sacred directions,
mirrored among the Navajo by the four
clans of the nation, who lived in four
houses at the corners of the earth,
protected by Bear, Puma and Wildcat.

below
A sand-painting design, reproduced in textile, of one of the chants of the south-western desert tribes. While the general form, especially the symmetry and recurring theme of fours, was traditional, healing chants were varied to suit individual cases.

opposite, top
Sand-painting from the Hail Chant. In the centre, surrounded by four rainbow bars, are sun (top) and moon (bottom), and male and female winds. In each cardinal direction are Storm People, the male bearing lightning and hailstones, the female light rays and clouds.

opposite, bottom
Thunder People bearing lightning and wearing masks of yellow evening light with the white stripe of dawn at the forehead. They flank a stalk of maize, for thunder presaged fertilising rains. Sand painting from the Hail Chant. South-western desert Indians.

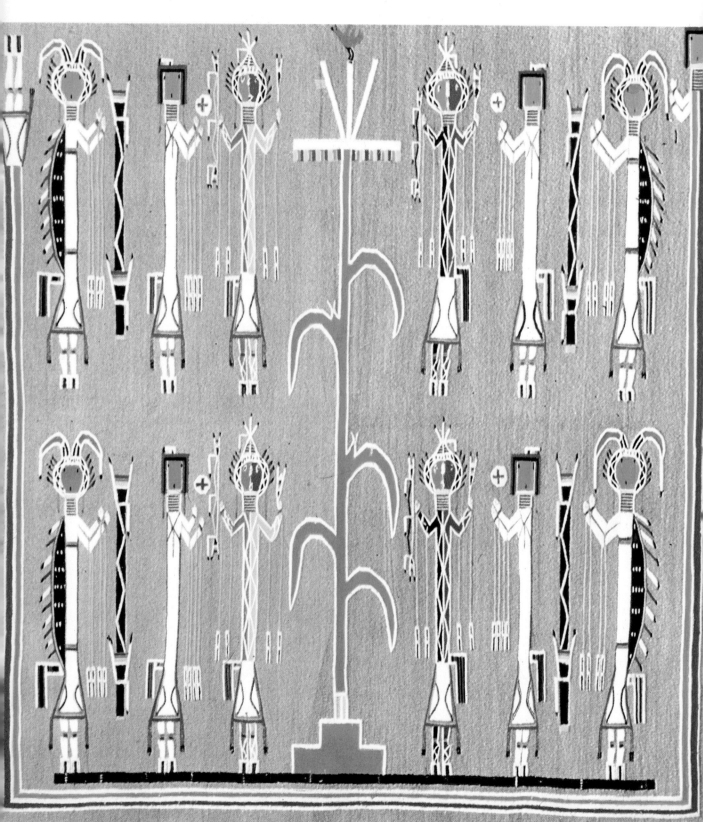

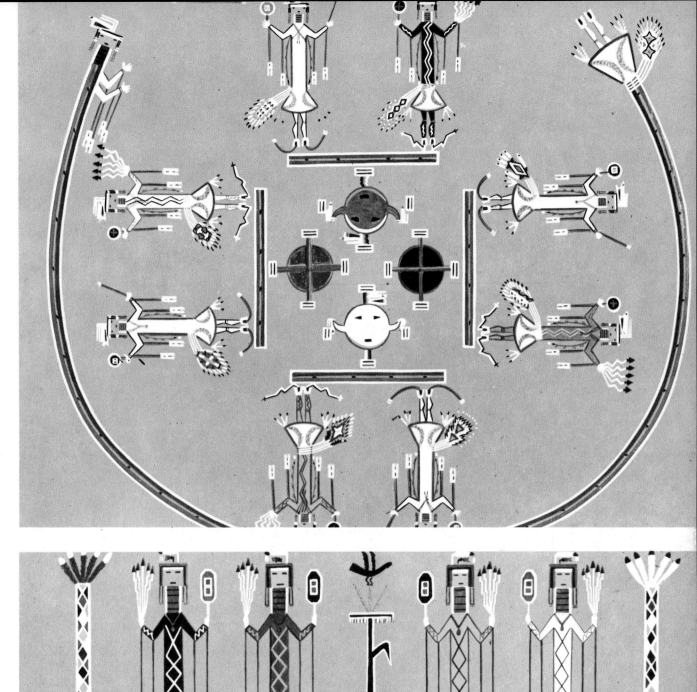

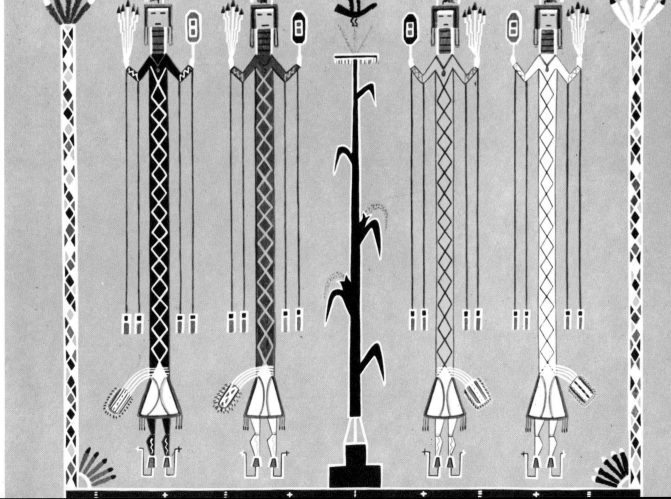

above
Stone pipe in the shape of a crouching figure, perhaps a shaman in a trance. While in the Central Plains tobacco was associated with the stars, in its native south-east it was linked with sexual happiness and so smoked at councils to promote tribal friendship. Moundville, Alabama.

page 240, top
Jar in the shape of a death's head with an incised decorative motif representing body-painting, which shows evidence of Mexican influence. Like many Indian tribes, the Natchez had a ghost story about heads with no bodies, known as the Rolling Heads.

opposite
Indians of the south-east as depicted in watercolours of 1585 by John White. Left, a medicine-man or shaman, a powerful figure among all tribes, since he made a direct link with the spirit world; right, a Florida woman and a warrior in ceremonial paint. British Museum.

page 240, bottom
Gorget, or good luck charm worn as a pendant on the chest, from Spiro Mound, Oklahoma. Made of incised shell, it clearly displays Central American influence. South-eastern myths were early confused with an overlay of outside influences.

page 241
Kachina dolls of lightning, corn, and snow and hail, 'souvenirs' of a ceremony. Kachinas, nature-spirits among the Pueblo Indians, were innumerable, for they were associated with every facet of life. Their parts were played by masked dancers at festivals.

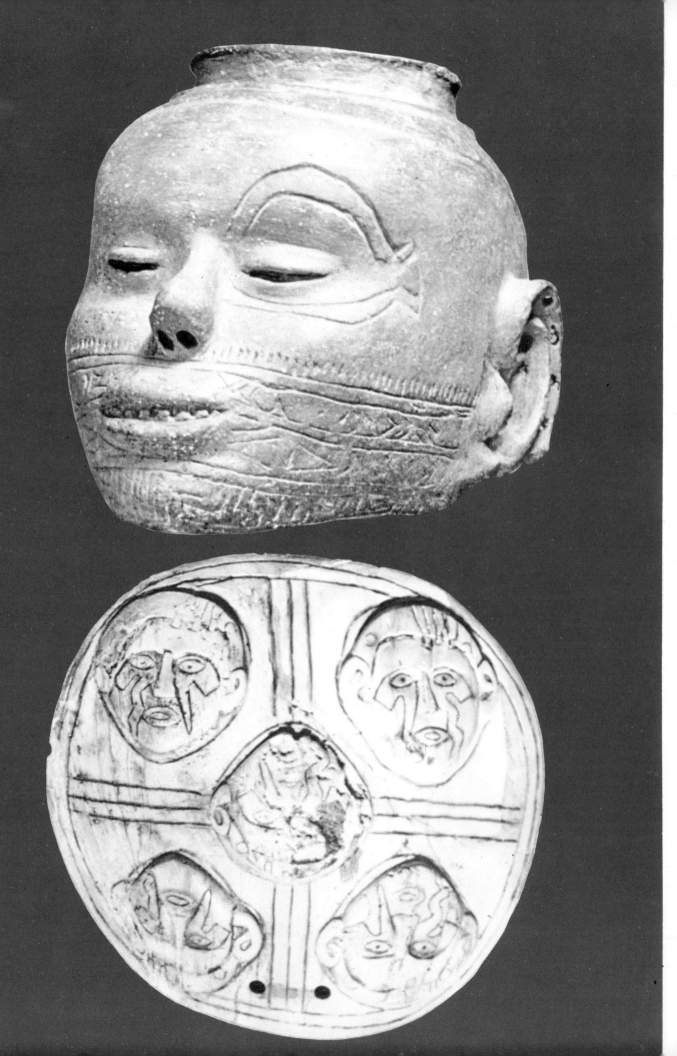

above
Karwan and Mana, the sprouting maize kachina spirits, who took part in the distribution of maize seedlings ceremonially sprouted in the kivas. Beliefs about kachinas were highly formalised, and they were held to spend only half the year with the people.

right
Late nineteenth-century water jar of Pueblo design. The red arrow directed straight into the buffalo's heart was intended to affect the hunt by sympathetic magic. Despite advanced social organisation, the ancient Pueblo Indians had neither potter's wheel nor kiln.

opposite
A Smoki ceremonial in a kiva. Kivas were underground meeting places for ritual organisation of tribal affairs by a council of religious and clan leaders. They were situated beneath courtyards flanking the central plaza of the Pueblo town.

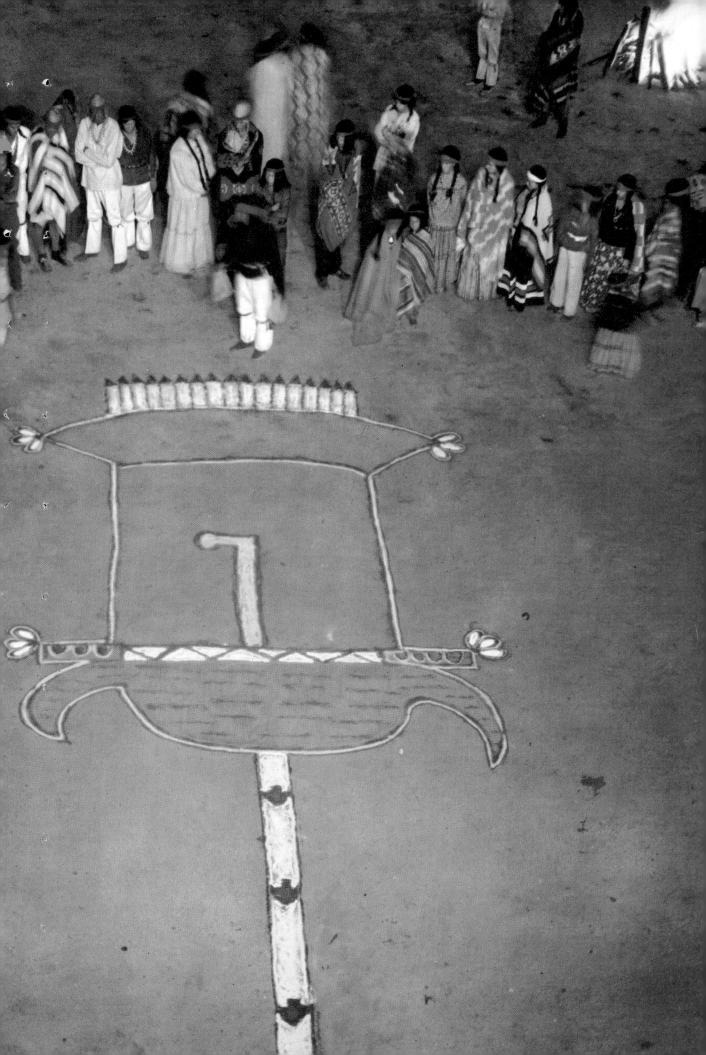

Developed cultures existed in Mexico and Central America as early as 800 BC, and the peoples inhabiting the area had glyph writing in the first century BC which they used to record their beliefs. Many of their manuscripts, known as Codices or magic books, their wall-paintings and friezes and their inscribed steles were destroyed by successive cultures and especially by the Spanish conquistadores, and on those that have survived the glyph writing has only recently been deciphered. Our knowledge of their beliefs has therefore been coloured by the Spanish friar chroniclers, who recorded, and sometimes censored, what beliefs they could glean from the conquered peoples in the sixteenth and seventeenth centuries. Plainly, however, the esoteric knowledge would not have been divulged to the conquerors; and besides, the Aztecs, who had quite recently achieved dominance in Mexico, had assimilated but distorted the ancient beliefs by their emphasis on sacrifice seemingly for cruelty's sake. It is this Aztec culture–or barbarism–that most people associate exclusively and wrongly with the area.

Two main cultural streams can be discerned, Nahua and Maya; and within each are two religious and mythological currents: a peasant pantheism based on superstition, and a cult of priestly mysteries of philosophical character. In the north, little is known of the Olmec culture on the Mexican Gulf, though it may have been connected with the settlement of about 800 BC at Tlatilco in the Mexico valley and thus with similar settlements in Peru. It is thought to be the source of some Nahua beliefs. After the destruction of the great Olmec centre at La Venta, Veracruz, in the fifth century BC the Zapotec culture carried on as its heir, spreading from Monte Albán near Oaxaca, to Mitla, then to Teotihuacán, and then to Tula, north of Mexico City. Zapotec culture reached its peak about AD 300 with the building of Teotihuacán, by which time the general shape of Mexican mythology had been established.

It was ultimately supplanted by the Toltecs (master craftsmen), who made the centre of their empire at Tula or Teotihuacán, near whose stepped pyramids topped with temples they built palaces in the sixth to ninth centuries. These were decorated with friezes which are one of our sources for Nahua mythology. The other major sources are two 'secret books' of the Aztecs, warlike conquerors of the Toltecs' divided successors. Coming from the north, they consolidated their power with the construction of their capital Tenochtitlán in 1325, only to fall two centuries later to the Spaniards. These Aztec documents are known as the *Codex Borgia,* which describes the Aztec calendar, and the *Codex Fejervary-Mayer,* which relates the gods to the calendar.

In the south was the ancient Maya culture, whose origins reached back to about 500 BC, but whose so-called classic period lasted from the fourth to the tenth centuries AD. This was established in the Central American isthmus, for example at Copán in Honduras, and in Mexico in Yucatán and Chiapas. Our knowledge of their myths comes chiefly from the Dresden, Paris and Tro-Cortesianus Codices, as well as steles and wall-friezes. The Mayas put up a strong resistance to the Spaniards until 1546 in Yucatán, and the related Itzás (who also had connections with the Toltecs, and conquered much of Yucatán in the tenth century) survived in Guatemala until the seventeenth century. The Toltecs were not the only northerners to make contact with Maya culture: their predecessors the Zapotecs, as well as the Huastecs north of Yucatán, had mingled culturally with the Maya at a formative period, and the result in mythology is a clear parallelism of gods and of outlook. Both Nahua and Maya had the notion of an elect, that as a people they were able to speak for the gods, and that because of their insight into creation they could make cosmic forces work for the benefit of mankind.

Concepts of the cosmos, of time and of cyclic creation are central to understanding of these mythologies. The Maya sacred books speak clearly of a creator existing outside space and time, who affirmed his godhead in descending into a 'second time' and creating the material universe. It was a monotheistic conception, with the supreme deity Hunab-ku (the Nahua god-goddess Ometeotl or Tloque Nahuaque) a free agent, and the lesser gods who governed the universe, the heavenly bodies, etc., subject to the laws of time and matter. These limited deities were aspects or manifestations of the supreme god. As is well known, the study of astronomy in Mexico and Central America was highly advanced, and the famous calendars marked not only days, months and years, but in the Maya calendar a great cyclic pattern of roughly three million years, with subdivisions of 158,000, 8,000, 400 and 20 years. In addition, for both Mayas and Aztecs there were divisions of 52 days and 52 years associated with revival of the sun and renewal of fire. At the close of each great cycle creation reached its fulfilment and a new creation began. The supreme god was the hub of the great cycle, while lesser gods were attached to each of the subdivisions, which themselves were cyclic, and so revolved like heavenly bodies at different speeds.

Corresponding to this temporal pattern was a spatial pattern associated with Kukulcan or Quetzalcoatl, symbolised by the four-armed quincunx, with high priest guardians (*balam* or jaguars) at the four points of the compass, each of which was associated with a particular colour, tree and bird symbolising fertile life. At the intersection of the four arms was a green tree, fountain of all life. The arms were also symbolised by four crocodiles floating on the primeval waters to support the world. In the centre was a thirteen-rung ladder leading up to heaven, and a nine-rung ladder leading down to hell. On the highest rung of the heavenly ladder was the supreme god, who incorporated a balance of opposing forces, while on the lower rungs strife, division and imbalance were represented by the lesser gods and aspects of the universe as men know it. The ladder to hell, increasingly cold and wild, was the path taken by men on their journey to rebirth, just as darkness precedes the dawn.

Before rebirth, according to the Nahua, men spent four years in Tlalocan, the heaven of Tlaloc the rain-god, where food was plentiful and they played childlike games and sang. A higher heaven, for those initiated into the wisdom of the god-king Quetzalcoatl, was the land of the fleshless,

A Maya dignitary of the seventh century AD. Both Maya and Nahua society had two hierarchies: a ruling intellectual nobility and a priestly caste of the sun. Beneath priests of Kukulcan (Quetzalcoatl) were noble judges of others' merits such as this figure, known as *Halach uinic.*

Four colossal figures which were once supports for the entrance to the temple of the Lord of the House of Dawn, or Quetzalcoatl as the morning star, at Tula, on the eastern border of the Mexican plateau, reputed capital of Quetzalcoatl as king of the Toltecs. Eighth to twelfth centuries AD.

opposite
Part of the stone of Tizoc, Aztec ruler from 1481. The carvings on its rim show Tizoc's deeds, this panel depicting warriors leading by the hair captives such as those whose hearts would be offered to Huitzilopochtli in the central depression of the stone.

Tlillan-Tlapallan, whose praises were sung by the poets. And beyond this heaven was the House of the Sun, Tonatiuhican, for those who had achieved full spiritual enlightenment and had earned eternal happiness with freedom from the material. The wicked were consigned to a land of darkness, inertia and boredom at the centre of the earth, presided over by Mictlantecuhtli.

Nahua tradition speaks of a female earthmonster swimming in the primordial waters, devouring everything with her numberless mouths. She was split in two, heaven and earth, by the gods Quetzalcoatl and Tezcatlipoca in the form of serpents symbolising time. Her body produced all the benefits of nature, but she continued to demand blood sacrifice and human hearts to eat.

In Mexican mythology, the principle of life descends from heaven, and in shedding its blood or in dying and mingling with the earth, creates humankind. Thus 1,600 heroes sprung from a stone knife born of Ometeotl created a man and woman to repopulate the earth, after a recurrent cataclysm, by mixing their blood with the bones of former men brought from the underworld by Quetzalcoatl's twin Xolotl. Xolotl was identified with the Nahua dog of the underworld, equivalent to the Maya Pek, dog of lightning. The Mexicans thus shared with other mythologies the theme of life out of death.

Other parallels can be seen in the role of the wind-god in stirring up primeval formlessness. He woke the maiden Mayahuel, guarded by the old crone Tzitzimitl, from a profound sleep and aroused her love. On earth the couple became the Precious Tree, but Mayahuel's branch was shattered by Tzitzimitl and its pieces devoured by vengeful young gods, the spirits of inert nature. Nevertheless, Mayahuel's bones, buried by the wind-god, grew into vines, source of white wine. Throughout Mexican mythology runs the theme of dualities, but especially – and despite the effort to free the spirit from matter – the recognition that the material is the complement and basis for the spiritual, and is formed by forces such as love.

These relationships were symbolised by the four pillars supporting heaven: the Falling Eagle, heavenly power on earth; the Serpent of Obsidian Knives, sacrifice; Resurrection, the cycle of reincarnation; and Thorny Flowers, the universal duality of beauty and pain. Two further supports for heaven were Quetzalcoatl in his aspect as wind-god, the Precious Tree, pure spirit; and Tezcatlipoca, god of the smoking mirror, matter – at whose request Quetzalcoatl brought music to earth from the House of the Sun.

Animals were associated with the fundamental cosmic principles and gods. Thus the serpent represented time, and the green quetzal bird (of Maya origin though principally associated with the Nahua god Quetzalcoatl) symbolised the hope of release from time's bondage. The eagle, day-sun, was opposed to the ocelot, Nahua night-star and jaguar, which the Mayas associated with obsidian and with the embrace of heaven and earth. Owl and dog

247

were associated with death, the sea-snail and butterflies with rebirth and joy. Many other animals, familiar and exotic, had their own cosmic meanings.

In addition, each individual had his personal totem animal, his *nagual* who lived and died with him and became attached by the unfathomable workings of predestination. Some heroes could transform themselves into the shape of their *nagual*, and so travel from place to place instantaneously and invisibly, with supernatural powers. For most people, however, the *nagual* was a limiting guardian, often to be met in dreams of the dead. Predestination was governed by the calendar with its conjunctions of good and ill fate, but was tempered by the possibility of escape from time, which was immediate for women dying in childbirth and soldiers killed in battle and could also be approached through prayers, austerities and general courage. Liberated souls were transformed into birds of fine plumage fluttering among the honey flowers. Social distinctions persisted after death: the souls of nobles inhabited the higher animals and birds, whilst those of the common people inhabited various insects.

Just as the *nagual* died with the individual to which it was attached, so the sun of a given era was thought to perish with the degeneration of a species. Thus the present sun was said to be the fifth, born of all four elements, its predecessors having sprung separately from Earth, Air, Fire and Water. Men's efforts to attain wisdom and liberation–the sacrifice of hearts, spiritual or literal–was essential for the continuance of the present sun, and this was shown too in the continued search of the gods for a species capable of appreciating and praising their creator, and thus nourish and sustain the gods.

The famous Maya myth of Popol Vuh recounts the successive races of men created by the gods: the mindless clay men; the soulless wooden men, whose tools rose up in rebellion against them and who were turned into monkeys; and the giant Vucub-Caquix, whose pretensions and those of his sons were disposed of in epic struggles by the heavenly twins Hunapú, god of the hunt, and Ixbalanqué, 'the little jaguar', with the aid of four hundred warriors. The twins then descended to the underworld where they avenged their father's death there, first by playing a mystic ball game with its inhabitants the Xibalba, and then by allowing themselves to be twice burned to death and resurrected. The Xibalba rulers tried to perform the same feat and perished. Their people became outcasts.

Thereafter fitting men were created of maize seeds by the jaguar, coyote, parrot and crow. So successful was this creation that the gods decided to limit these men, clouding their intelligence. They were nevertheless still able through discipline and through the use of drugs to enter into communication with cosmic truth. The drugs included various hallucinogens, incense made from copal resin, tobacco, and tequila and pulque, both made from the maguey cactus, and all were under the protection of the goddess Mayahuel. The state they induced was associated with flowers, and considered a divine blessing, their proper use the secret of the priestly caste. Their misuse by pleasure-seekers may help to account for the degeneration of the ancient traditions, especially under the Aztecs.

Priests who had attained enlightenment were identified with Quetzalcoatl, undoubtedly the major figure of Nahua mythology. He may be based on a real Toltec ruler living near the time of Christ. In myth at any rate he was known as a lawgiver of great sanctity, unwilling to harm any human being, despite the temptations of demons to perform human sacrifice, and a culture-hero who introduced the use of maize and instituted the arts of the Toltecs (master-craftsmen). The roots of his name indicate a symbolic combination of the gentle quetzal bird of the Guatemalan forests and a water-serpent, time. The jade-coloured plumed serpent was god of wind and divine messenger and road-sweeper.

Quetzalcoatl represented the force of life and, in the form of a black ant, stole maize from the red ants for the benefit of mankind; but he also represented the possibility of transcending the material world. Quetzalcoatl's mother was Coatlicue, one of the five moon goddesses, and his father was the sun (also son of Coatlicue). Coatlicue's presence, wrapped in cloud, was discovered by magicians, and her agency permitted the materialisation of beings, a necessary step or foundation for ultimate release into the spiritual through her son. Like many another mother-goddess, Coatlicue had two aspects: life-giving and cruel (as had a number of other female deities in Mexico).

Antagonistic to Quetzalcoatl but not so utterly evil as some of the goddesses was Tezcatlipoca, whose four hundred sons killed Quetzalcoatl's father. As the boy grew older, magicians failed to persuade him to shed blood, so Tezcatlipoca first caused him to retreat by showing him his ravaged image in a mirror, and then to re-emerge by painting his face and dressing him in quetzal feathers and a turquoise mask. Demons then led him into a drunken orgy culminating in incest with his sister. In remorse afterwards Quetzalcoatl dressed himself in his finery and threw himself on a funeral pyre. After this self-immolation, he lay for eight days in a stone casket, symbolising a descent to the underworld, after which his heart rose to become the planet Venus as the morning star, which welcomed the hearts of the initiates who followed his spiritual example. He was later identified with the Aztec sun-god Huitzilopochtli, who demanded the literal sacrifice of hearts. As Venus, Quetzalcoatl's partner in the dualist system and twin in myth was the dog Xolotl, associated with death–though the partner of his form as sun was an ocelot, symbolising the sun's journey through the underworld.

Just as lesser gods such as the wind-god and the maize-god were aspects of Quetzalcoatl (or of his Maya counterparts Kukulcan or Kinich Ahau), so Tezcatlipoca had four aspects (Maya, Bacabs), corresponding to the four cardinal points. In the south, blue, was Tlaloc, the rain-god; in the east, red, was Xipe Totec, the flayed god, or alternatively Tonatiuh, the sun; in the north, black, was Tezcatlipoca himself; and in the west was his opposite Quetzalcoatl. A personal peculiarity of Tezcatlipoca was that his feet, which had been cut off by the primeval earth-monster, had been replaced by a mirror in the shape of a curled-up rabbit, symbolic of unpredictability. He was a stern judge of men, seeing all, and bore the dark mirror of obsidian, suggestive of the curved obsidian sacrificial knife; but he rewarded the good with feasting, and was assiduously propitiated.

An elaborate myth tells how he nearly vanquished Quetzalcoatl and dominated his people, the Toltecs. Adopting various disguises, Tezcatlipoca tempted Quetzalcoatl with wine, supposedly of rejuvenation; seduced his daughter; conquered his armies in battle; lulled his people into stupor with music; played with a puppet figure of Quetzalcoatl to amuse the people in the market place, then had the puppet-master stoned so that the body would pollute the land, and made it so heavy it could not be removed; caused a volcano; and finally, by roasting maize, food of Quetzalcoatl, in the market place, gathered

One of the great pyramids at Teotihuacán, Zapotec city of the gods, which later became a stronghold of Toltec culture. This Toltec pyramid, usually thought to be dedicated solely to Quetzalcoatl, was in fact shared by Tlaloc, the rain-god and an aspect of Tezcatlipoca. Eighth century AD.

all Toltecs for slaughter. Quetzalcoatl set out on a last pilgrimage back to the place at the centre, Anáhuac, in sorrowing old age. But despite temptations and obstacles he won through, sailing to spiritual eternity on a raft of serpents.

Though Tezcatlipoca represented the material that was to be overcome, he became enamoured of Xochiquetzal, goddess of gaiety and love and of flowers, which symbolised spiritual enlightenment. She was associated with the Aztec form of Quetzalcoatl, Huitzilopochtli, and envisaged with a retinue of fluttering butterflies and birds. Her husband was that other aspect of Tezcatlipoca, the rain-god Tlaloc. The fourth aspect was also associated with fertility. This was the god of spring Xipe Totec who, in a symbolic representation of the struggle of nature to regenerate and of the shoot to penetrate the seed husk, was seen as a pock-marked sufferer who allowed his skin to be flayed so that growth could proceed. With the shedding of his skin he emerged golden, brilliant light, pure spirit, Quetzalcoatl redeemed.

opposite
An Aztec funerary mask used in the burial of a person of high rank. Made of mosaic and jade, which in Mexican symbolism represented loss of life, or the deified heart sought by Quetzalcoatl. Tezcatlipoca once bedizened Quetzalcoatl with turquoise mask and red-painted lips.
below
The wind-god Ehecatl seen as an aspect of Quetzalcoatl, breathing life into a skeleton representing Mictlantecuhtli, god of the hell of boredom at the centre of the earth. To fulfil his liberating mission, the plumed serpent had first to descend to the underworld. *Codex Borgia.*

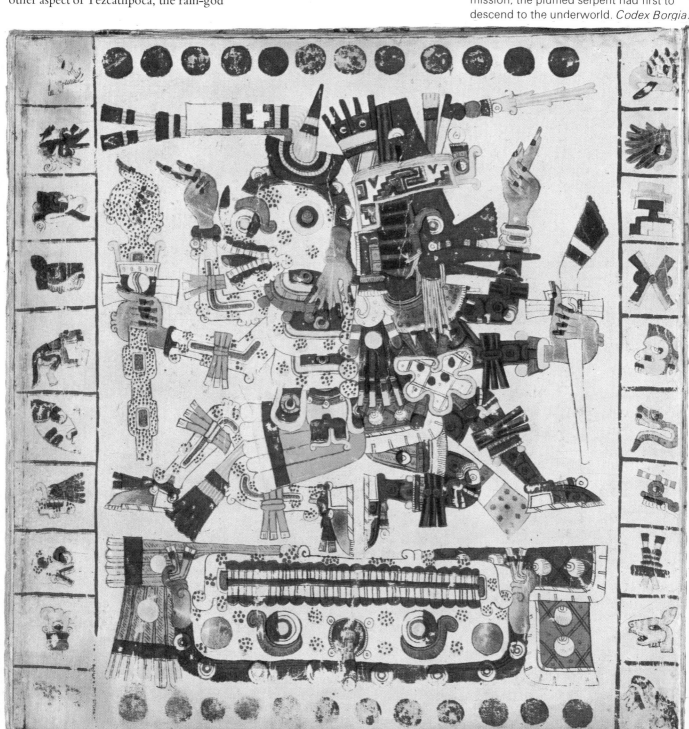

below
Chichén Itzá, largest of the Toltec-Maya sacred cities, dating from the sixth century AD. It is an example of the interpenetration of Nahua and Maya beliefs. In the foreground is the Temple of the Warriors, looking over to the pyramid of the plumed serpent, the god they served.

opposite
A Maya worshipper; pottery originally coloured blue, which indicates a connection with the month *Yaxkin*, when the fields were fired in preparation for sowing of the maize, and everything was coloured blue, the colour of Tezcatlipoca in his rain-god aspect. Late classic Maya. Campeche.

253

above
Tlaloc scattering seeds. God of rain, he wore a crown of heron feathers, had a face blackened with rubber and carried thunder-rattles. Like other fertility-deities, he had death associations and presided over a materialistic paradise. Mural painting from Teotihuacán.

opposite
A Maya priest, pottery figure from the island of Jaina, off Campeche on the western coast of Yucatán, which was an important culture centre in the sixth century AD. Like the nobility, the priesthood had its hierarchy, and was either hereditary or elective.

opposite
Xipe Totec, supreme example of the
Mexican gods who suffered for the
benefit of mankind, in the effort to
transcend the world of matter. He is seen
as a tortured penitent, with gashes down
his face. Zapotec pottery figure, eighth to
eleventh centuries AD.

below
The Maya sacred city of Uxmal, in
Yucatán, seen from the summit of the
House of the Magicians or Soothsayers,
and looking down on the quadrangle of
the 'Temple of the Nuns'. Magic and
divination were an important part of
cults among Nahua and Maya.
Eleventh century AD.

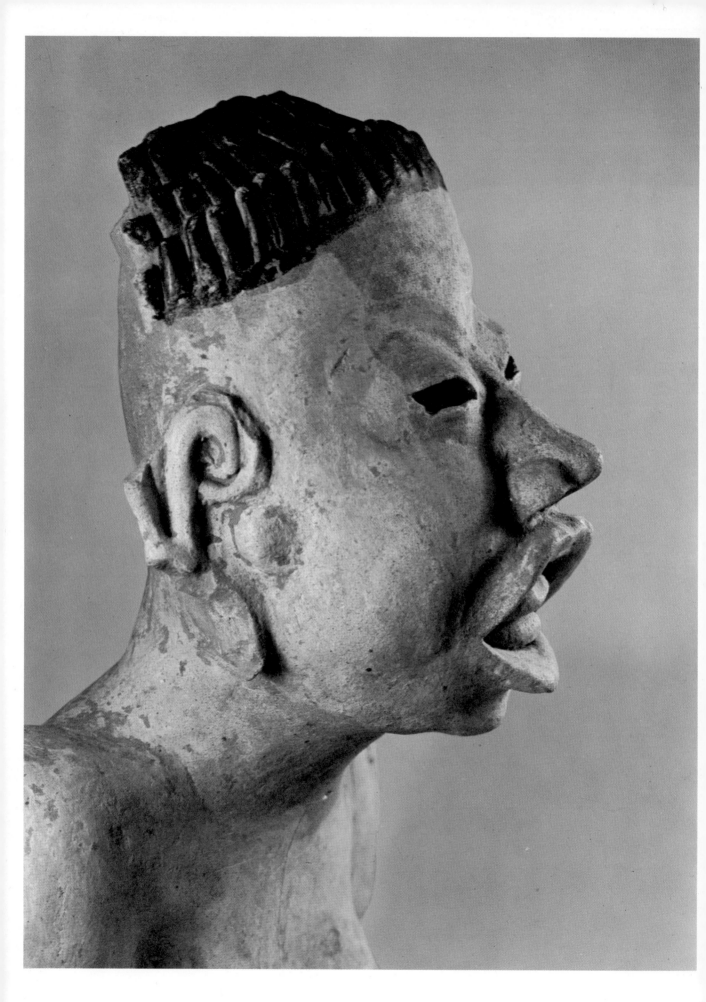

opposite
Xipe Totec, with the loosened skin of the
flayed god, was an aspect of the shabby
god Nanautzin whose self-sacrifice
created the fifth sun, of the present era.
Xipe's self-sacrifice allowed him to
emerge as god of spring, Quetzalcoatl
redeemed. Totonac painted clay,
Veracruz region.

right
Vase from Tula with an image of the
rain-god Tlaloc, with his characteristic
goggle-eyes. The fertilising, benign
aspect of Tezcatlipoca, his activity in
producing the material sustenance of life,
was as essential to man as the spiritual
benefits promised by Quetzalcoatl.

below
Aztec clay cup from Cholula. It was
probably used for pulque, which was one
of the many intoxicants used to facilitate
and enhance communications with the
gods. Their misuse hastened degradation
of spiritual sacrifice to a cult of cruel
blood-letting.

259

opposite
Tlacolteutl, fearsome goddess of carnal vice and eater of filth as symbol of men's sins. But she was also goddess of childbirth, here giving birth to one of her children, either Cinteotl, god of maize and an aspect of Quetzalcoatl; or Xochiquetzal, goddess of flowers. Aztec statuette.

page 262
Mictlantecuhtli, the Lord of the North and of Death, whose domain at the centre of earth was the destination of those dead not fitted for the various grades of heaven. The punishment was not torment, merely boredom. Mixtec gold pectoral, eighth to eleventh centuries AD.

above
Xolotl, twin brother of Quetzalcoatl in his aspect as the planet Venus (the evening star), when as a penitent he descended to the underworld. Xolotl too descended, as a dog, to bring forth bones for the creation of man. The two sides of this Aztec carving show the death-spirit and the sun.

page 263
Hunhau or Ahpuch, the Maya god of death, corresponding to Mictlantecuhtli. He was associated with the screech-owl, portent of death, and the dog, Pek, death and bringer of lightning. Pottery figure painted red, the colour of death, from Tikal, Guatemala.

below
Maya warriors triumphing over their enemies, perhaps in a raid to obtain prisoners for sacrifice. Warriors fought under the banners of animals symbolic of cosmos and gods, but tribal warfare was real enough, whatever the meaning attached to it. Eighth-century mural at Bonampak.

opposite
The Maya maize-god Yum Caax, as aspect of Kukulcan or Itzamná, who also brought the Mayas cocoa and rubber. His elongated head, representing an ear of maize, was artificially emulated as a sign of perfect beauty. Classic Maya, from Copán, Honduras.

above
Moan, the vulture harbinger of death. Late classic Maya tripod-legged bowl. It was vultures who informed Quetzalcoatl of the murder of his father the sun by the four hundred warriors of the Milky Way, sons of Tezcatlipoca, so enabling him to recover the bones.

right
The Maya wind-god emerging from a snail. Both Maya and Nahua wind-gods, aspects of Kukulcan/Quetzalcoatl, were linked with the tortuous shapes into which they could penetrate; but the sea-snail was also a symbol of death and resurrection.

opposite
The sun-god Kinich Ahau, Maya equivalent of Huitzilopochtli—the fire-bird or flash of illuminating light which would be extinguished if not nourished on human hearts. Cylindrical carving with the god wearing a massive symbolic headdress, from Palenque, c. AD 700.

267

A Maya warrior or priest, from the Temple
of Inscriptions at Palenque, which was
used as a mausoleum for nobles and
priests, both of whom served the divine
order in their allotted roles. The plumes
and flowers indicate a connection with
Kukulcan. Seventh century AD.

opposite
Wall-carving from Chichén Itzá in
Yucatán. The frieze shows a ceremony
before the sacred ball game, with the
figure on the left dressed for play.
The game probably symbolised man's
efforts to master cosmic forces, and
sacrifices were offered to the gods before
play on great occasions.

South America

The peoples of South America, of the same Mongoloid stock as the North American Indians, evolved vastly differing levels of civilisation. Despite theories of trans-oceanic influence, they most probably developed without significant outside influence until the arrival of the Spaniards in the sixteenth century. Though a common cultural heritage with the peoples to the north can be seen in some mythological themes (for example in the relationship of animal spirits to the tribes hunting them), no general pattern of mythology and culture can be discerned, even allowing for wide geographical variations of altitude, climate, fertility and natural resources.

Some scholars think, though it is only surmise, that the present-day beliefs of the more primitive peoples of South America may correspond to the cultural foundations of the higher civilisations. As so often happens, in most areas of South America where indigenous beliefs persist untouched – or emerge through the veneer of Christianity – myth, legend and folktale are inextricably mixed. It is true to say, however, that there is little evidence of elaborate mythology or of religious doctrine in these areas. They can be broadly divided, in ascending order of culture level, into Marginal and Semi-Marginal tribes inhabiting the Chaco, Patagonia, the Pampas, the upper Xingú in western Brazil, and eastern Bolivia; Tropical Forest peoples inhabiting the rain forests of Guiana, the Amazon basin, the Paraná delta, the Paraguay valley and parts of eastern Bolivia; and the Southern Andean tribes living in the Atacama desert, central Chile (Araucanians), northern Argentina (Diaguita), and parts of the Chaco.

The Marginal tribes, frequently nomadic hunters and food-gatherers without agriculture or domesticated animals and without weaving, pottery or developed building techniques, based their relations with an all-embracing spirit world on shamanism and magic. Rituals were based on family rather than society, and were mainly connected with the crises of birth, puberty and death, sometimes with weather and sickness. Though some had a supreme deity, sometimes sun or moon, the spirits of evil had a more important role, and the shamans themselves were closely involved with cults of the dead.

The Tropical Forest peoples, who developed slash-and-burn agriculture, simple pottery, weaving and basketry, transport via canoe and permanent village settlements, had similar practices, but a slightly more developed pantheon based on sun, moon, stars, rain and thunder, as well as the usual multiplicity of nature-spirits. Prime among these was a jaguar-spirit.

The Southern Andean tribes had fairly advanced agriculture, bred llamas, built in stone and worked metal. Shamanism and magic was again important, but they differed from the other primitive peoples in having simple communal rites of agricultural fertility, which included animal sacrifice.

The advanced civilisations of South America developed in the Central Andean region, modern Peru and Bolivia, and the coastal and valley districts to the west. These ancient civilisations spanned three millenia, from about 1500 BC to the Spanish conquest in AD 1532, during which time highly advanced agricultural, building and artistic techniques were evolved, fully fledged cities and temples were built, communication by road was developed, elaborate social and political systems were instituted.

Despite all this, no form of writing existed, and succeeding civilisations relied for transmission of the cultural heritage on the trained memories of wise men using mnemonic devices known as *quipus*, consisting of series of knotted and coloured strings. Unfortunately, though many *quipus* have survived, the art of understanding them died soon after the Spanish conquest, for the conquistadores methodically rooted out traces of idolatrous beliefs (and thereby enriched themselves with the loot that had given rise to the El Dorado myth). Indians or half-blood mestizos, converts by conviction or expediency, allowed the ancient lore to fade from memory, and sometimes even deliberately distorted the picture in the course, supposedly, of giving an account of the old beliefs. Such was the case with the chroniclers Don Felipe Guamán Poma de Ayala, who claimed royal Inca blood, and Garcilaso Inca de la Vega, who wrote later in Spain, who are among our chief near-contemporary sources for Inca mythology. For other regions we rely on fairly objective accounts by Jesuit missionaries of beliefs in the sixteenth century.

For earlier cultures, however, in the absence of writing, we have to turn to the archaeological record; and rich though the store of artefacts is – from architecture and sculpture to pottery and textiles – we cannot tell with certainty whether any given figure depicted is merely decorative or of spiritual significance, nor what the exact nature of the attached mythology might be. The archaeological record itself is no doubt still far from complete. One of the more important early cultures, for example, the Paracas, which flourished in the southern coastal zone of Peru from about 400 to 100 BC, and whose tombs have yielded astonishing pottery and textiles, their colours marvellously preserved by the dry atmosphere, was discovered only in 1925. And the roughly contemporary Nazca culture, which developed about fifty miles inland from the southern coast of Peru, was discovered in 1901.

At present we know little more than that there was a succession of impressive cultures in the central Andean region. In the north of Peru a civilisation centred on Chavín de Huantar, which may have been a place of pilgrimage and a cult centre for feline (jaguar), condor, snake and fish deities – though there is no proof – flourished c. 850–400 BC and exercised a powerful artistic influence on the northern coastal kingdoms that succeeded it. The Gallinazo culture was followed by the Mochica (roughly 300 BC–AD 500), whose great Huaca del Sol sun temple lies outside the modern town of Trujillo. Then, after a period of Tiahuanaco influence, the Chimu empire rose about AD 1000. Centred on the Chicama valley and the enormous walled capital of Chanchan, its influence extended over a coastal strip 600 miles long until the Inca conquest about 1400.

What knowledge we have of coastal mythology dates from this period, but it should be remembered that the Inca, like previous cultures, were in the habit of altering the record, partly because the mythopoeic faculty was still alive, and

Fishermen of the Suyá tribe in the tropical rain-forest area of the Xingú river, wearing ear-plaques. The beliefs of such tribes, actively researched by anthropologists, are better known to us than those of higher civilisations of former days.

partly to fit in with their imperial purposes. As in other American mythologies, early attempts at the creation of men were unsuccessful and they had to be destroyed. One such myth concerns a race of giants arriving on the coast in huge balsa boats who, since they exhausted local supplies of fish and game, were hated by the natives, and, since they had come without women, practised sodomy. Another, reminiscent of Mexican myth, tells of the rebellion of men's implements and animals and the disappearance of the sun for five days, followed by a deluge, of which advance warning was given by a llama (of which a number of variant myths survive). A new race was then born of five eggs on the mountain Condorcoto. They hatched into five falcons who turned into men, the god Pariacaca and his brothers. Pariacaca, a god of rain, flood and thunder, established his cult by driving the fire-god Caruincho into the jungle. The cult of Pariacaca was taken over and incorporated by the Incas as one of the many subsidiary nature cults centred on so-called *huacas*, a term of Aymara popular belief, indicating anything imbued with spiritual force.

Coniraya, a coastal creator god identified by the Incas with Viracocha, was said to have introduced terracing and irrigation to farmers and to have filled the sea with fish, as a result of thwarted desire for a daughter of Pachacamac, a creator god and culture-hero worshipped to the south of the site of Lima. Other stories of Coniraya tell of his love for the beautiful Cavillaca, who rejected him because he

Karaja tribesman wearing the feather headdress of boys' initiation. Rites of passage are the most important religious practice among the Marginal and Tropical Forest peoples, and they featured too in Central Andean lore, for example in the Inca origin myth.

page 274
Waura tribesman of the Amazon basin preparing feathers for ritual purposes. As among North American Indians, the spirits and powers of animals and birds can be magically used through possession of a token part of them. The sun's radiance is often connected with feathers.

page 275
Waura tribesman with a necklace of jaguar claws. A cult of the jaguar—but no known mythology—is attested among numerous tribes of eastern Bolivia, who connected its spirit with the powers of shamans. One caused eclipses by attempts to swallow sun and moon.

approached her in rags, but by whom he magically had a son. In fleeing him, both were turned into rocks in the sea. In common with other myths of the area, an account is given of special relationships with certain animals: Coniraya blessed the condor, puma and falcon, and cursed fox and parrot. But elsewhere, among the Cañaris near Quito, the parrot or macaw was said to be ancestress of the tribe, repopulating the area by union with survivors of a deluge.

Another aborted creation was attributed to a boneless man called Con, whose agility on his long legs was helped by his power to raise and lower mountains. Son of the sun, he created a race of humans in a land of plenty, but when they annoyed him, turned the land into desert, with just the bare amount of water to sustain life by hard work and irrigation. Con was eventually ousted by Pachacamac, also child of the sun—and of the moon, who changed Con's people into monkeys and created a new race of men.

Inland, on the highland plateaus known as the Collao, now the Bolivian Altiplano, an extraordinarily advanced and almost totally mysterious civilisation flourished from 300 BC to AD 400 and possibly as late as 1000 at Tiahuanaco by Lake Titicaca. Archaeological remains are abundant, including great megalithic buildings, some unfinished, stone carvings, and highly accomplished handicrafts with complex iconography. These all point to a powerful centralised society whose influence spread, possibly by conquest, as far as the Peruvian coast. Yet even at the time of the Spanish conquest the chroniclers could discover no record, memory or even definite legend associated with the culture. The most likely explanation seems to be systematic obliteration by conquerors. One Inca legend tells that the Collao fell to them because the area was torn by dissension between two rival chieftains, Cari and Zapana, possibly heirs to these conquerors. These people were also linked with tales of conquest of a white and bearded race at Lake Titicaca current in many parts of the Central Andes (South American Indians have no facial hair).

Other tales of a culture-hero named Thunupa or Con Ticci Viracocha describe him as a huge white man able to raise and lower hills and to make water flow, who arose, bringing sun, moon and stars, from Lake Titicaca after the sun had disappeared for some time. He travelled north working miracles until he reached Cacha, where the people threatened to stone him. Fire appeared in the sky and burned stones to a cinder, but he extinguished the fire when they worshipped him. Then he went on to

the coast and, holding his mantle, disappeared into the waves. Other versions relate that Viracocha, angered by men of a former creation, destroyed them. At his second appearance, after making sun, moon and stars, he modelled men, including their identifying forms of dress, from stone and distributed them throughout the land. Then he travelled north to Cuzco calling forth and vivifying the races of men from trees, fountains, caves, rocks etc., threatening those who refused him worship with fire, or punishing them with a flood. The Aymara Indians, modern descendants of these people, still worship features of the landscape, as well as anything associated with the dead, as *huacas*.

Myths specifically associated with Thunupa as culture-hero, clearly conflated with Christian and Inca themes, tell of his arrival from the north with five disciples. He bore a cross and preached a puritanical, pacifist doctrine, banished the former idols and forbade human sacrifice and was harried by those he could not convert. They left him for dead in a boat made of totora reeds on Lake Titicaca, and it drifted with such force against the banks that it cut the channel of the river Desaguadero, which bore Thunupa to the coast at Arica.

In the northern highlands, about AD 1200, the Incas developed their kingdom, known as the Four Regions (the four quarters of the world which met at their capital Cuzco). According to myth, and probably historically, their origin was not far from Cuzco. They were said to have emerged richly and strangely dressed from the Inn or Origin, Paccari-tambo, a cave or building with three exits. From the middle hole emerged four brothers and four sisters, ancestors of the royal Incas, who were to claim descent from the sun. From the other two holes emerged the common people. Thus the myth of origin explained the rigid hierarchy of Inca society, which allowed for no social mobility except perhaps for women. If beautiful, women could be chosen as one of the Virgins of the Sun, dedicated to tending the fire in the sun-god Inti's temple; or could become concubines of the supreme ruler, the Sapa Inca, son of the sun—or of his favoured nobles and warriors; or could be destined for sacrifice on special occasions, with the promise of a happy afterlife. The Mama Coya, one of their number, who was also sister of the Sapa Inca to ensure the purity of the royal blood, bore the successor to the throne of an empire that in the fifteenth century, under Pachacuti and his son Topa Inca, expanded into a vast, largely benevolent despotism.

An impressive structure of bureaucratic

below
Quimbaya gold pectoral from the Nariño lowlands of Colombia. Little is known of the advanced early civilisations in these parts. Among the Chibcha, there was a creator goddess Bachué, a supreme sun-god Bochica, a culture-hero Nemterequeteba, and his opponent Huitaca, the moon, wife of Bochica and goddess of indulgence.

opposite
Woven textile from a Paracas burial with an intertwined feline and snake motif. Images of a feline deity are common in remains of all the coastal cultures from 850 BC onwards (Chavín), and it is thought it may have been the supreme god, but precise evidence is lacking.

social control with a network of roads and imperial messengers was erected under the aegis of the royal sun cult, its important posts manned by the noble 'Children of the Sun', the other offspring of the Sapa Inca, who were marked out by special headdress and ear-plaques, whence their Spanish name Orejones. In his royal association the sun-god Inti was identified with order and justice; but as bringer of light and thus life in a highland region where crop success was precarious, he had an important agricultural role. Nevertheless he was not the official supreme god; this was the creator Viracocha, whose myth, of which there are many variants, we have already encountered in the Collao. The Incas also had gods of the moon, the stars and the weather, especially thunder.

Though the state cult was thus cosmological, *huaca* cults of locality continued, and were brought into service in explanations of the Incas' divine origin. Thus the Inn of Origin myth continues with an account of how one of the brothers angered the others by boastfulness so that they shut him up in the primeval cave by a ruse. He then appeared to them in a vision, adorned with ear-plaques, and exhorted them to found the capital at Cuzco (or alternatively instructed the first Inca ruler, Manco Capac, in maturity rites for Inca boys), and then turned himself into a stone on the mountain Huanacauri, later a cult object.

A different origin myth relates that after a flood sent to destroy the world, the sun-god sent his son Manco Capac and his daughter Mama Ocllo to earth to marry and to travel northwards from the Collao to Cuzco, teaching men the arts of civilisation and proper worship of the sun. It was they who founded the Place of Gold, Coricancha, the sun temple at the mystic intersection of the four quarters in Cuzco, from which radiated and depended the many provincial sun temples, the most important being that which displaced Pachacamac near Lima. Collao creation myths were clearly incorporated by the Inca after their conquest of that area; another claim was that Manco Capac alighted specifically on that island in Lake Titicaca where the inhabitants of the Collao believed the sun to have been created.

A more cynical or humorous account for the relation of the dynasty with the sun tells that Manco Capac dressed himself in a shining mantle of gold or beads which so impressed the people that they believed his story that he was the son of the sun; or that the mother of the second Inca ruler Sinchi Roca dressed him likewise, and by producing him from a cave practised the same deception. But this complexion put upon the myth may simply be an example of that paradoxical distortion of Inca myth by contemporary – and even Indian – observers.

Fragment of woven textile from one of the Paracas graves. Though probably symbolic of some belief—possibly, from context, a cult of the dead—no definite interpretation can be given. The figures seem to be demons with snake headdresses carrying a bent staff and knife or axe.

278

Detail from a woven textile of the Paracas necropolis. This appears to feature a killer-whale motif, and may be connected with a trophy-head cult in which the lips of a fetish of the defeated enemy were sewn up to prevent curses escaping, so that the victor could use its power.

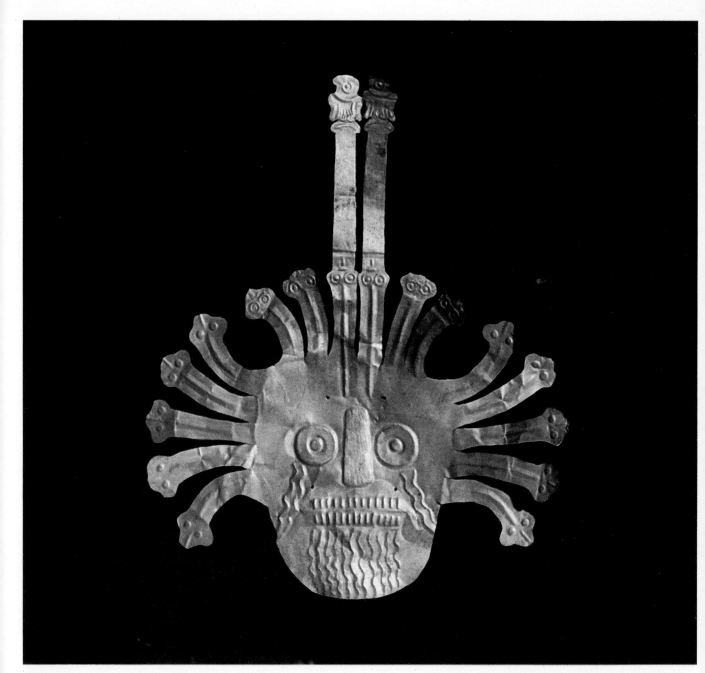

above
Beaten gold mask from one of the graves at Nazca. It may indicate a cult of the sun, the rays of the image terminating in stylised snake-heads. The suggestion of a beard is interesting in connection with the widespread myth of a white, bearded culture-hero creator.

opposite
Nazca vase in the shape of a man decorated with snakes and wearing a foxskin on his head. Among coastal Indians, the fox was said to have got a black tip to his tail by trailing it in the water when escaping one of the floods that periodically wiped out mankind.

below
Nazca jar decorated with rows of small heads in three colours and a large head, possibly that of a demon, and an arm holding a severed head. Too little is known of this southern Peruvian culture to tell whether head-collecting had a military or religious significance.

opposite
Figurine in terracotta of a female worshipper in an attitude of prayer or of adoration. Her hands, with their six digits, resemble an animal's paws, but too little is known of its place of origin, the central coastal valley of Chancay, to offer interpretations.

below
Woven textile from Chancay with a
pattern of felines (possibly pumas, the
South American lions), and birds.
It is said that at Chancay stylisation
reached a point indicating a weakening
of the mythological significance of such
motifs in earlier Chavín and Paracas art.

opposite
Mochica stirrup vase in the form of a
seated dignitary wearing large ear-
plaques. The pouch on his right wrist
may have been for coca leaves, chewed
to induce euphoria, used in
mummification and divination, and
among the Inca a divine plant reserved
officially for the nobility.

Carved stone figure from Chavín de Huántar with the nose and eyes characteristic of this culture, whose artistic tradition dominated coastal and highland Peru from 850 to 400 BC. Its tribal cult may be among the earliest with organised priesthood and temples.

below
Gold ceremonial knife decoration with a fan-type headdress with pendant birds and ear-plaques inlaid with turquoise. The powerful Chimu kingdom supported a capital, Chanchan, covering eight square miles, with an elaborate harbour and canals and aqueducts supplying verdant gardens.

opposite
Mochica ceramic figure of the first to ninth centuries AD. This type of figure, with the mace in the right hand, is usually called a warrior, but may be a nobleman or chieftain. With its naturalistic portraiture, it shows facial resemblance to present-day Quechuas.

opposite
Pottery jar decorated to represent a man
wearing a headdress, his body
quartered with stylised images of animals.
Though showing Tiahuanaco influence,
it comes from Pachacamac, cult centre
of the coastal creator god taken over by
the Inca sun-god.

below
The *Intihuatana* at Machu Picchu, a kind
of shadow clock connected with
observation of the solstices. As
observation by Inca wise men was central
to their sun cult, such stones were
usually broken off by the conquistadores;
but Machu Picchu remained
undiscovered until 1912.

below
Red-painted carved wooden face with shell eyes of the Inca period, perhaps a funerary offering for use in a 'mummy bundle', into which the body, flexed and packed with hot preserving sand and cloth, as well as various artefacts, was carefully roped.

opposite
A painted and lacquered beaker of the type known as a *keru*, with human, snake and bird motifs. Popular belief at all levels of culture in South America featured animals possessing supernatural powers, helping or hindering in creation and the bringing of civilisation.

The South Pacific and Australia

This area, along with Africa, has been and is the subject of the most intensive fieldwork by anthropologists, for its primitive societies still maintain traditional ways and a living mythology. Part of the reason for the continued vitality of mythology among many of these peoples is their isolation and freedom from the white man's influence–by government policy in pockets of the continent of Australia and in parts of New Zealand, or by force of geography: impenetrable terrain on a large island like New Guinea, or the scattering of innumerable islands elsewhere. The islands are of two main sorts: high and volcanic, or low coral atolls surrounding a lagoon. For all of them the Pacific Ocean is the major influence shaping the way of life, which in some cases involved shifting from one island to the other to reap the benefits of soil fertility. On the whole, however, the main migration completed, isolation has ensured the development of highly disparate beliefs which make classification and generalisation difficult, and has obscured themes that might have been common to peoples who most probably came in small groups from south-east Asia to populate the area over a period from about 20,000 years ago to about 1000 BC.

First to arrive were the negroid hunters and gatherers who pursued a nomadic way of life in Australia and New Guinea. About 3000 or 2000 BC a neolithic culture of settled farmers growing root crops and raising pigs, fowl and dogs spread through the area, except for Australia, New Guinea and parts of Melanesia. These were followed by the light-skinned Austronesians, who brought the double outrigger canoe which permitted long sea journeys. These, to an extent mixed with their predecessors in Melanesia, emigrated north to the Micronesian islands and east to Tonga and Samoa in Polynesia by 1000 BC. The Polynesians colonised the Society Islands and the eastern Marquesas by 200 BC. The Society islanders had settled the Hawaiian Islands by AD 100 and the Marquesas Easter Island in the far east by AD 300; but Polynesians did not reach south to New Zealand until after AD 1000. Though the incursions of European discoverers certainly caused changes, the societies thus formed remained fairly static until the major disruptions of the nineteenth century, with exploitation of labour and resources by white men, introduction of diseases, the stirring up of warfare, and the missionaries' battle for souls.

Some of the ancient beliefs survived, however, and the missionaries themselves, together with explorers, traders and colonial administrators, with greater or lesser skill and objectivity, recorded some before they faded from memory, or became too overlaid with a new mythology designed to explain the profound changes of life and of knowledge that had been wrought. From the middle of the nineteenth century Polynesians in Hawaii and New Zealand were recording and writing down their oral traditions, for they attributed their loss of power, political and spiritual (mana), to failure to maintain faith and ancient rituals.

This oral tradition was preserved by three main classes in Polynesian society. Firstly the priests, some of whom were full-time and some craftsmen who made canoes, fishing gear, houses and divine images, whose skill depended on supernatural as well as manual ability. At their head was the tribal chief, who claimed divine ancestry; there were also ceremonial priests, who made sure that the precise words of invocations of the gods were adhered to–for deviation invalidated them; and the inspirational priests, who sometimes worked as a force for change by developing new myths to fit in with new circumstances. The tradition was also maintained and sometimes elaborated by poets and bards, and by itinerant entertainers organised into guilds, through which they could obtain social advancement. They were known as Ka'ioi in the Marquesas, Arioi in Tahiti, and Hula in Hawaii. These musicians and dancers would often re-enact the story of creation in order to stimulate fertility.

The mythological past was called the Night of Tradition, and the various stories took place in the land of darkness or underworld, called Po; or in the land of spirits in the sky, which was also the western ancestral home, and was known variously as Hawaiki, Polotu, Kahiki (Tahiti), or the Land of Kane. The bards sang the praises of the traditional great chiefs, warriors and navigators, especially those who discovered new lands.

According to west Polynesian accounts of the creation of the universe, it was the work of the omniscient creator god Tangaloa or Tangaroa, who existed in a shapeless dark void, Po, and formed the islands by casting down rocks into the vast expanse of water. His messenger bird Tuli sought shade, so Tangaloa created the Peopling Vine, from which grew men. Alternatively the union of Po, inert darkness, and Ao, active light, brought about creation.

These forces were sometimes represented as Earth Mother and Sky Father, called Papa and Rangi in New Zealand. They created the other major gods: Tangaroa, father of fishes and reptiles; Rongo, father of cultivated foods; Haumia, father of wild plants; Tane, father of forests and their creatures; Tawhiri, god of storm; and Tu, the prototype of man. These gods were enclosed in darkness between their closely embracing parents and sought to escape. Tu wanted to kill them; Tawhiri wanted to leave them in peace; but the others agreed to try to separate them. Rongo, Tangaroa, Haumia and Tu tried and failed; at last Tane succeeded despite their protests, prising them apart, his feet raising the heavens, and his head pressing down the earth.

Tawhiri sought to avenge his parents by sending great storms, as a result of which Tangaroa's reptile offspring sought refuge in the forests of Tane. This was the origin of the never-ending quarrel between gods of sea and forest. The forest supplied Tu with the materials for fishing gear, while the sea swallowed up canoes and nibbled away at the land with waves, and emerged the more powerful brother. Rongo and Haumia fled into the earth, leaving Tu alone to defend the brothers' actions against Tawhiri. That is why Tu (man) exploits the creatures of sea and forest and consumes the wild and cultivated food born of the earth. Tawhiri's anger had created storms and flooding, but when he had been defeated by Tu, peace and light enabled creation to proceed. This basic creation myth was varied in order to give the decisive role to the god from whom

Maui, the hero 'of a thousand tricks' whose exploits were celebrated throughout Polynesia. Though semi-divine and a helper in creation, he chose to use his magical talents to alleviate the condition of man. This image in a Maori meeting house shows a fishing exploit.

below
Carved wooden figure from the prow of
a canoe from the Marquesas Islands.
The death's head figure with its feet
planted on skulls would be considered a
protective spirit for the fisherman,
perhaps a reminder of Tane's eternal
struggle against Tangaroa's ocean.

opposite
Wooden statuette, carved and patterned,
probably of an ancestor, from Aitutaki
Island, Cook Archipelago. The family had
to recover the body and perform proper
rites for their relatives: otherwise they
could not enter the ancestral spirit world
and haunted the living.

people in a given region claimed descent.

Tu (or Ku in Hawaii) was Tangaroa's chief assistant in the Society Islands and was offered human sacrifices as god of war under the name Oro, son of Tangaroa. But Oro became god of peace in Tahiti, where he was patron of the Arioi. Rongo, god of song and agriculture, was known as Ono in the Marquesas and Lono in Hawaii, where he was said to have descended on a rainbow to marry a mortal wife. Having jealously killed her, he instituted games, commemorated at a harvest festival, and departed on a canoe laden with foods; he was destined one day to return on a floating island of abundance. Rongo was known on Easter Island, along with Tangaroa as creator, but the most important deity there was Makemake, patron of the local bird cult of the egg-gatherers and creator of mankind in the role taken by Tane (Hawaiian Kane) elsewhere.

In New Zealand, according to a myth developed as late as the 1860s, Tane was not only creator of man, but the god who brought down from the highest of the ten heavens (inhabited by a new supreme god Io) the three baskets of all knowledge. Tane, as we have seen, created the space between heaven and earth, man's world. After being rejected by his mother Papa, and fathering various natural features on other beings, he also begot man on Hine or Hina, a woman he formed from red sand and vivified with his own breath. The first man was called Tiki or Ti'i (though the name was also given to Tane's procreative powers), who became the husband of double-faced Hina, first woman, patron of women's crafts and guardian deity of the dead. The Dawn-maiden, Hina's daughter by Tane, unknowingly committed incest with her father. When she discovered the truth she fled to the underworld and ever since has dragged down the children of man to the land of the dead. The offspring of Tiki formed marriage links with both gods and mortals, and from these unions sprang royal and noble lineages, and the demi-gods and heroes whose exploits form a large part of Polynesian mythology.

Undoubtedly the most famous was Maui, the trickster who aided the gods in creation. His mother was sometimes said to be Hina, who herself had a complicated skein of relationships and identifications with other female deities representing her dual nature, among them Haumea, goddess of childbirth, and her daughter Pele, destructive Hawaiian goddess of volcanic fire. Maui killed Hina's lover, an eel called Tuna from whose head sprouted the first coconut tree. Another dual-natured deity was Tinirau, alternately handsome youth and fearsome ocean-god whose mes-

sengers were shark and whale. The girl Hina-uri, sister of Maui, pined for and pursued her distant lover Tinirau to the spirit world of the ocean, but he eventually ill-treated and abandoned her. After the naming ceremony for Tinirau's son, the priest Kae killed his pet whale, and the retaliation for this instituted the practice of cannibalism.

Maui was more usually called son of Tangaroa and a mortal mother who abandoned him because of his ugliness. He made up for this in wisdom and magical skill. He helped to raise the skies; snared the sun and slowed down its course so that there was enough time for men to perform necessary tasks; fixed the stars in their positions and controlled the winds, thus helping sailors; fished up islands, sometimes using as hook the jawbone of his grandmother whom he killed for the purpose; stole fire for mankind from his ancestress in the underworld; changed his brother-in-law into the first dog; tried to obtain immortality for men by creeping through the body of his ancestress, Hina goddess of death. She woke and scotched the attempt; in this respect Maui's divine powers could not benefit mankind with whom he identified himself – and he himself was destined to die through men's disloyalty to a benefactor whose thousand tricks they sometimes found ridiculous or tedious.

The fate of all men was therefore death, where they might meet annihilation in the fires of Miru; or, if helped by relatives, living and dead, might join their ancestors in the spirit world. The pathfinders for this journey along a rainbow or creeper were the noble Tawhaki, descendant of a heavenly cannibal chieftainess, who sought to avenge his father Hema, killed by goblins; and his son Rata, who sailed after Tawhaki in a canoe made by forest-spirits.

left
Ironwood statue from Rarotonga usually described as Te Rongo and his three sons—perhaps ancestors of a tribe who considered Rongo chief god. It is more likely to be of Tangaroa, god of the ocean and fishermen, in his central and western Polynesian role as creator.

opposite
Figure from Easter Island to be placed near the door of a house in order to ward off malevolent spirits. It was fashioned of bullrushes covered with tapa cloth and decorated with tattoo patterns. Tapa cloth was made of paper mulberry bark beaten out by the women.

Such was the brutal exploitation of the products, trade facilities and people of the Micronesian islands and of much of Melanesia, with decimation, shifting or scattering of peoples, that the mythological tradition has been largely lost, or so fragmented and adulterated as to permit few generalisations in a short study. It seems, however, that there were many elements in common with Polynesian myth, though with less attention to myths of origin, and more on trickster figures, both semi-divine culture-heroes such as Olifat, Nareau and Motikitik, and animals. The tales lay down social patterns on matters such as property, gift exchange for status and incest – and include the usual themes of demon-slaying. There is also an important pair of brothers who taught the arts of navigation.

In Melanesia the picture is equally or more complex. With societies simpler, or at least less hierarchical than in other island groups, based on small villages and more widespread kinship groups—mostly isolated by geography, though bearing the imprint of a complex pattern of earlier population movement—mythology is mostly local. Spirit beings—of ancestors, of animals and of various aspects of nature, and culture-heroes confined to one locality or to one particular skill, are more prominent in everyday thought than great deities. These factors, plus the wealth of evidence from particular studies by anthropologists, especially among the undisturbed tribes of New Guinea, make it especially difficult to build up a general picture in Melanesia.

The mythical beings of the first time, who came from heaven or from underground, took part in creation and especially in releasing the sea. (In later myths, for example those supporting cargo cults, the release of the sea was the aftermath of breaking the social code, and resulted in the loss of precious objects, which the ritual sought to regain). Often they had animal helpers or mates who became clan totems. Snakes had a special role as emblems of fertilising rain and of aggression—storm, flood and earthquake.

Spirits inhabit all sorts of objects, and man himself is said at times to have been created from stones, or a tree, or maggots, eggs, blood clots, sand-drawings, clay or wood. All these myths tend to explain men's limitations or wants by comparison with the freedom of spirits. Many of these spirits inhabit a sky world similar to the earthly world but which controls the hunt, warfare and weather. Important heroes include Kembal (Keraki); Tudava (Trobriand Is.); Sido, pathfinder for the spirits after death (Kiwai, Papua); a number of

right
Maori *hei-tiki* jade pendant. The word *tiki* indicates its human form, for the first man was Tiki, husband of the dual-natured Hina. The first *hei-tiki* ornament was given by the man-shaped god Tane to his daughter Hineteiwaiwa, goddess of childbirth.

below
Maori carved jade ornament in the form of a fish curled into a spiral. Though Maoris were largely dependent on agriculture, after their arrival in New Zealand about AD 1000 they maintained the island tradition of attaching paramount importance to the sea and its creatures. North Island.

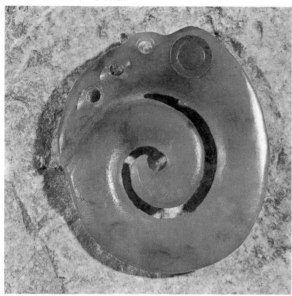

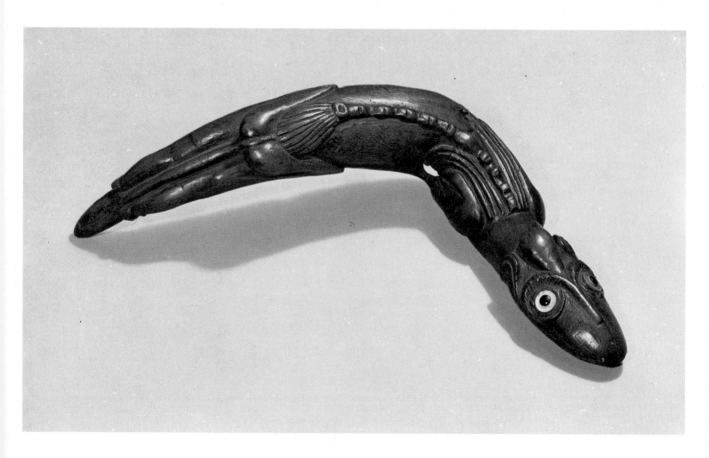

opposite, bottom
Wooden fish-man carving from Easter Island. Such ornaments and similar lizard-men were worn round dancers' necks at festivals. Celebrations, often lasting several days, were performed throughout Polynesia, the most common theme being a re-enactment of creation.

below
A short Hawaiian hula drum, supported by carved figures. Hula troupers used their entertaining puppet shows to make satirical social comment; but they had a religious role under the patronage of Laka, sister of Lono (Rongo), god of agriculture. Hooper Collection.

fatherless heroes who in childhood killed man-eating ogres, from whom emerged tribal ancestors; and various pairs of antagonistic brothers, often wise and foolish, the origin of good and evil, and the paradigm for clan rivalry. Sometimes one kills the other by crushing him in a posthole, a mythological representation of the sacrifice needed to initiate building or boat-launching. Other figures represent raw brutality – wandering heroes of war cults, with headhunting, cannibalism, sexual abuses, matricide, mass slaughter; these are generally exiled or ultimately deprived of power.

The aboriginal inhabitants of Australia, commonly considered nomadic survivors of the Stone Age, naked hunters and food-gatherers, were in fact influenced in their mythology and adaptation to their harsh surroundings by northern neighbours of more advanced culture. But only modern technology could successfully overcome the continent's aridity and consequently the aborigines remained fixed in a pattern where the prime objective is to control rainfall. The most common figures in the mythical past, known as the Eternal Dreamtime, which created and determined the condition of life and the details of initiation and ritual, are beings associated with thunder, lightning, clouds, and the frogs which proliferate after rain.

Nomadic like the aborigines, these include the wondjina of north-western Australia, and the Mamandabari of the Northern Territory desert region, who rose out of the earth. In south-eastern Australia and parts of the north-west, sky heroes are the primal beings who established the totemic relationship between men and nature, and gave form to the amorphous universe. In the interior the dominant belief is in totemic ancestors who rose from the ground. In all creation myths sun, moon and animals took an important part, especially the eaglehawk, crow and bat. Bat or moon invented the female sex, usually by castration. Such myths serve to reinforce the primacy given in these parts to the male creative role.

Everywhere there is the rainbow snake, who helped to shape the landscape, is identified with fertility, especially in the Arnhem Land mother cults, but who also punishes those who infringe taboos with disease or flood. One rainbow snake in the Northern Territory, for example, called Kunmanggur, was challenged in his role of sexual supremacy by his son Tjinimin the bat. Tjinimin raped his sisters, the green parrot women, and stabbed his father, who during a long journey to the sea in an attempt to staunch the blood, drew forth

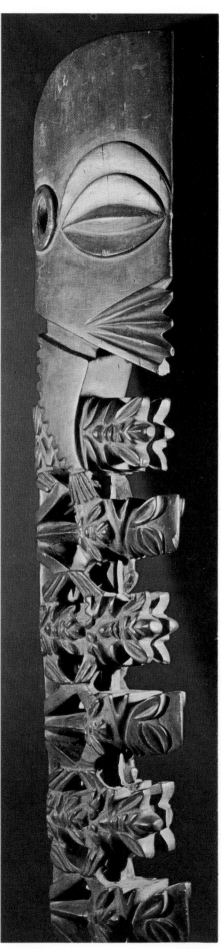

far left
Maori tiki gable ornament. These human-shaped carvings were called *tiki*, 'man', by the Maori after Tiki, the generative power of Tane. Elsewhere Tiki was first man and first to die, when his daughter-wife failed to use her magic to save his life. Hooper Collection.

left
Upper portion of a Rarotongan staff god representing Tangaroa or his son Oro. Beneath the profile head and body of alternate profile and full-face heads was a stick wrapped round with tapa cloth to a circumference of two to three yards and below it a phallus.

opposite, top
Colossal stone images on Easter Island, most easterly Polynesian island, where of the great gods only Tangaroa and Rongo were known. They are probably connected with the bird-man cult. The white man's exploitation, smallpox, famine and warfare largely effaced Easter Island tradition.

opposite, bottom
One of the rock-carvings on the cliff-top at the sacred village of Orongo, Easter Island. Makemake, who first appeared in the form of a skull, drove the birds to sanctuary there to protect them from egg-gatherers. The first egg collected each year was a talisman of fertility.

life-giving water, and ultimately entered the sea, having gathered the fire of the world to use as a headdress. Later the kestrel invented the use of firesticks. The rainbow snake is a bi-sexual and ambiguous fertility symbol.

Another primal being is the Great Mother, origin of land, plants, animals and humans, of the Northern Territory coast. In north-eastern Arnhem Land her role is filled by the two Djanggawul sisters, beings of Dreamtime who with their brother, by whom they were forever pregnant, came across the sea to the site of modern Port Bradshaw, the Place of the Sun, from the land of the dead. By striking earth with sacred rangga sticks (phallic symbols but also representing their progeny) they brought forth water and all plants, trees, edible roots and animals. The prolific wombs of the sisters were symbolised by the sacred dilly bag they brought, which contained ritual paraphernalia that they taught men to use correctly. However, their control of ritual passed into the hands of men, who stole the sacred objects from them and truncated their genitals to make them purely female.

The daughters of the older sister came from the south and were known as the Wawalag sisters. At a waterhole, often a sacred site, they angered the great rainbow snake Yurlunggur, who repeatedly swallowed and regurgitated them, to be revived by green ants, each time marking a ceremonial ground for ritual connected with the myth. A similar myth of an old woman who swallowed young men and vomited them up again was the basis for a Great Mother cult from Arnhem Land through to Western Australia.

opposite
Malanggan carving from New Ireland, representing a fish accompanied by a flying fish and a snake, ridden by the male and female forms of Solanang and led by the semi-divine Lamesisi. Esoteric knowledge suggesting such images often comes from ancestral or other spirits.

below
A spirit canoe manned by ancestral figures wearing totemic devices. Carving made in northern New Ireland for a Malanggan ceremony, which combines commemoration of the dead with initiation rites for young men—an occasion for prolonged celebrations and feasting.

opposite
In eastern Melanesia social status is
dependent on wealth, which buys the
feasts and gifts that gain a man
admittance to the various grades of
society. Pigs with these artificially
enlarged and curved tusks are the
currency for such dealings in the New
Hebrides. British Museum.

right
Protective spirit prow ornament with the
characteristically male forehead and jaw
of the area: Bougainville Island,
Solomons. In these parts men are thought
to have two souls, that not destined for
the afterworld being at large on earth or
in the sea. But some spirits are non-
human.

left
Wood carving from San Cristobal, Solomon Islands, of an *adaro*, a malevolent fish-man sea-spirit who travels in waterspouts and uses rainbows as bridges. *Adaro* shoot men with flying fish, and they can recover only if an offering of a flying fox is made in time. British Museum.

opposite, left
Seated wooden image decorated with mother-of-pearl from Mala or Ulawa, Solomon Islands. With its bared teeth and fearsome tattoo marks, it probably represents a malevolent spirit. Equally common in Melanesia, however, were spirit helpers. British Museum.

opposite, right
Wooden image of Ukaipu, made by earth from a wild-ginger stem as a wife for Ivo. Ivo came from earth but visited the sky to bring back knowledge of the ritual practices of the people descended from him and Ukaipu, the Orokolo of Papua. Horniman Museum.

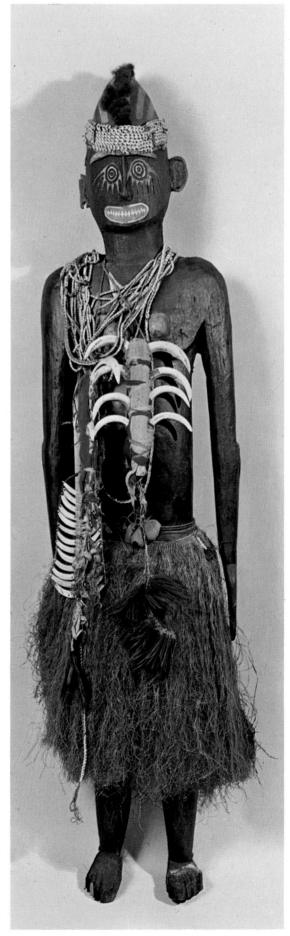

opposite
The protective spirit of a canoe in the form of a prow ornament. Carved wood blackened and inlaid with mother-of-pearl, from the Maravo lagoon in New Georgia, Solomon Islands. Benevolent spirits imparted secrets of wealth, strength, magic power and ritual.

right
A ceremonial axe with jadeite blade, a chief's symbol of authority in New Caledonia. It is thought to have been used in rain-making ceremonies. Spirits of a sky world are believed to control the weather, those of snakes being specially associated with rain.

opposite

Bark painting by the artist Kneepad from Groote Eylandt, off the eastern coast of Arnhem Land. It represents a creation story. The east wind is pushing up the morning star, precursor of the sun. With daylight comes earth, man, rocks and the rest of creation. Rex Rienits Collection.

bottom

Bark painting by the artist Bunia of Groote Eylandt, illustrating a fight between a wallaby and a dingo. An eagle is hovering above waiting for the spoils of battle. Such animals, birds, and insects were taken as totems by the various clans. Rex Rienits Collection.

below

Bark painting by Bunia of Groote Eylandt showing the path of the spirit after death to reunion with the Eternal Dreaming. Top left, a man lies dying; top right and bottom left, didjeridu (drone pipe) playing and dancing until he dies; then he crosses the great snake and, bottom right, kills a fish as food for the hazardous journey. Rex Rienits Collection.

311

opposite
Wooden images by different artists at Yirrkalla. On the left is Laindjung, an ancestral being of eastern Arnhem Land, who rose out of the sea, his face white with foam and body marked with salt water. The other two figures are the Wawalag sisters. Australian Institute of Anatomy, Canberra.

right
Carved wooden image of the Djanggawul brother, from Yirrkalla. Together with his sisters, he came to the Place of the Sun from the island home of the dead, and the dots represent sea foam. He wears the dilly bag containing the ritual paraphernalia he stole from his sisters.

Africa

Truly African mythology stretches south from a band reaching from Morocco through to Ethiopia (whose culture is primarily Islamic or Christian), passing through equatorial and tropical latitudes to the Cape. The mythology is a compound of diversity because of geographically condioned isolation, and themes that spread wide because of past great empires and the migration of peoples. Another factor making for similarities is racial. The majority in 'black' Africa are negroes, though there are other groups: the light-skinned Hamites in Ethiopia and Sudan, who brought Islamic influences south; Bushmen (including Hottentots), who came from the north and had reached the Cape when the first Europeans arrived; and Pygmies or Negritos in the Congo forest region.

The lingua franca of these people before any of them had writing was art, and this was the common vehicle for expressing deep feelings about birth, life, death, and the triumph of the spirit over it–the subjects of mythology. The commonest art form was sculpture, especially in wood, terracotta and bronze, though occasionally in stone. Paintings on cave walls and rocks abound, especially the ancient East and South African Bushmen paintings, which often seem to be connected with hunters' sympathetic magic, though too little is known of the ancient beliefs to permit sure interpretation. Personal adornment remains a common expression of feeling about life, and especially the life-enhancing power that is the basis of much African religious thought.

The numerous studies that have been made of traditional African ways of thought in the past century reveal that the mainspring is dynamism. The cycle of life for the individual and for his extended family is subject to the play of forces, spiritual and otherwise, which he must try to direct to his benefit. Man is affected by and answerable to the fount of this dynamic structure, a supreme creative being (who existed independently of Christian or Islamic influence). He must also keep on good terms with the lesser gods and, equally powerful, the ancestors. And, through magic and medicine, he must propitiate the lowest spiritual beings, which may take as their vehicle animals or various objects in nature. Many of the countless legends and folktales of Africa

concern these lower forces, in everyday contact with men's daily lives, such as the many tales of animals–how they gained their shapes and abilities, how they came to serve or hinder man, how they showed their astuteness or foolishness. Such tales are common throughout the world where man lives close to nature. Many other popular tales are basically legendary history. The stuff of mythology proper in Africa deals with the mysteries of human life and involves the higher spiritual beings: creator, gods and ancestors. It is also concerned with the way in which men organise their lives on earth: sexual, marriage and family patterns; their means of livelihood and skills, and the way their society is governed.

Almost all African peoples believe in a supreme god who created the universe. The deity is omniscient and immanent in all creation, the life-affirming principle: in other words corresponding to a philosophical notion for which there is no temple cult. Yet this deity is also personalised in mythology, usually a bi-sexual or non-sexual being, father and mother of all creatures, arranger of their customs and builder of every detail of earth. Sometimes his universal nature is further personalised, and he is said to have a wife and an old mother with whom he lives in heaven. From heaven he sends rain and judges all men. Though benevolent, his ways are inscrutable, and he also sends men their ills –although often enough men are said to have squandered the gifts the creator gave them through stupidity or improvidence. His wisdom and patience are sometimes symbolised by identification with the clever spider. Anansi, the trickster spider of West Africa, sometimes called the creator's chief official, is the hero of innumerable tales. Given the omnipotence of the creator, one might imagine a monotheistic faith, but there are of course other divine beings in African belief. The creator's names vary from region to region and are especially numerous in West Africa, but in East Africa the general name is Mulungu, in central Africa Leza, and in the western tropics Nyambe.

Heaven and earth are symbolised by a round calabash or hollowed gourd, the horizon being formed by a cut across its middle. Sometimes earth is thought of as a smaller calabash floating on waters within the lower half. According to the Yoruba

of Nigeria, the gods who lived in heaven sometimes came down to earth on spiders' webs, but there were no men, for earth was marshy. The supreme god Olorun ordered the Great God Orisha Nla to create solid ground. He descended to the site of the sacred city of Ilé-Ifé and, scattering earth from a snail shell and allowing a chicken and pigeon to scratch it over a wide surface, he created dry land. On the fourth day a sure-footed, large-eyed chameleon reported back to Olorun that the task was complete. The four days were commemorated by a four-day week, the fifth day being set aside for worship of Orisha Nla, whom Olorun sent back to plant four precious trees, including the palm, whose nuts the Yoruba use for oil and drink, and to create other goods and wealth for mankind. Olorun sent rain to water the plants and then instructed Orisha Nla to fashion men from earth. But he would not divulge the secret of how he vivified these creatures, and this so angers Orisha Nla that he disfigures some humans.

In nearby Dahomey, the Fon speak of Mawu, the moon, and her twin brother Lisa, the sun, as joint creators. Their union, in an eclipse, produced seven more pairs of divine twins, the most important being connected with earth, storm, and iron. The iron twins cleared the forests to make cultivable land and gave men tools and weapons for hunting and war. The length of men's lives is fixed by the sky-gods, who inform the creator about men's deeds and prevent men from seeing the other gods. The Fon believe that the world was gathered together and is supported by the snake, universal symbol of eternal rejuvenation because of skin-sloughing, and especially as conceived by the Fon, swallowing its own tail: the image of flowing, cyclic movement–and of the circular pad used to carry burdens on the head. This African Atlas, living in the sea, where he is fed iron bars by monkeys, causes earthquakes whenever he shifts position, and one day, it is said, he will no longer bear

An Ibo from eastern Nigeria with his two wives and children, about to sacrifice a fowl to the spirit of the yams. Such offerings are made by the Ibo and by the Ashanti of Ghana to the earth-spirits before sowing. Ala, the Ibo earth mother, was usually represented with a child.

the weight of the earth, which will sink to the bottom of the ocean.

Thus while each people has its own particular creation myth—and for space reasons it is impossible to go further into them—the general idea of a supreme creative principle is well-nigh universal. Another general theme—this time common to mythologies all over the world—is that men obtained fire by stealing. Among the Pygmies, who claim to have discovered fire before the negroes, divine displeasure at the theft was punished by the institution of death. Among the Dogon of Mali and Upper Volta, the Nummo, spirits of water and light and children of the creator and earth, chased the Dogon ancestor who stole fire from their heavenly smithy; he slid down a rainbow to earth so precipitately that he broke his bones, and that is why men's limbs have joints. Another divine benefit, understandable in sun-baked lands, was the coming of darkness. According to the Kono of Sierra Leone, there was perpetual warmth and light in the beginning. The creator entrusted a basket containing darkness to a bat, who through carelessness allowed the darkness to escape; that is why the bat flies at night, chasing darkness.

Though benevolent, the creator was human enough to get tired of men's constant requests for gifts great and small. Myths among many African peoples tell how he was particularly irritated at the importunacy and familiarity of women and children, and that is why he brought an end to the golden age when he had lived in close proximity to men, and removed himself and heaven to on high. In early times the link between earth and heaven was a tree, or more often a rope or spider's web. When god had finally ascended to heaven he had the link severed.

Animals, on the other hand, often had freer access to heaven, and a number had an important role in the creation of man or possessed the secret of immortality. Thus in the Sudan the Shilluk say that men and beasts used to live together and that men could be rejuvenated by being trampled on by cattle; and the Dinka associate the primal man Garang with a snake and the sun, and his consort Abuk with a snake and water. In Buganda the first man, Kintu, had animal helpers to

A female ancestor mask of the Mpongwe people of the Congo (Brazzaville). Carved of wood, with hair dressed high and the characteristic lozenge-shaped forehead decoration, the face was whitened with kaolin. In many places the first men are said to have had light skin.

persuade the creator Gulu to allow him to marry his daughter and so become the founder of the Dinka people. Kintu used trickery which, together with magic, could often be used to extract benefits from heaven. The creator spirit of the Bushmen took the form of a mantis. The Pygmies relate that the first man and woman were released from a tree, together with a flood of water, by a chameleon.

The link with animals at the time when patterns of life and civilisation were being laid down was one of the reasons why the creation of many of the gods was by animal-like multiple births: a series of pairs of twins. Among the Ashanti—as among peoples all over the world—it was a snake, the non-poisonous python, that taught the first couple the mysteries of procreation, for almost universally myth held that the first men were childless since they had been left in ignorance of sex. The Pygmies—aside from typically claiming that they had to inform the negroes of these matters—thought the original instruction took place in heaven, where moon taught lightning how to consummate his marriage with a woman whom, after her death, he himself married. With its waxing and waning the moon was associated by the Hottentots with renewed life—but also with death.

Death was thought to be equally unnatural, for the creator sent messengers to men to tell them they should not die, or that they might seem to die but by following the correct procedure they would be revived after a short time. The messengers, often animals, through a mistake failed to give the correct message or had it stolen from them. Thus among the Lamba in Zambia death escaped from a Pandora's Box bundle sent by god to a leader who had asked for seeds to enable him to adopt a settled way of life as a farmer. In Burundi the coming of death was attributed to a woman who obstructed the creator when he was chasing death away. Among the Dinka in Sudan and the Luyia in Kenya permanent death was the result of the survivors' unwillingness to accept back the resurrected. The curse of a chameleon not given proper hospitality by their ancestor was another reason given by the Luyia for death. And among the Zulu the chameleon's slowness in bringing a message of life allowed the lizard to arrive first with a message of death—a theme paralleled among the Mende of Sierra Leone with toad and dog messengers. The Kono people, also of Sierra Leone, blame the dog as well—because he allowed a snake to steal the skins of rejuvenation intended for men.

To the Nuba of eastern Sudan the fault was man's, for instead of obeying the

creator's instructions he took the advice of a hare and buried a corpse before god could revive him next morning. Similarly the Ila of Zambia say that the first man and woman were foolish enough to choose the brighter of two bags offered them by the creator, and so chose death for their children; they then forfeited a second chance of life by failure to keep a fast. Likewise foolishness caused a boy ancestor of the Krachi in Togo to apply to the eye of the giant Death a magic rejuvenating drug with which he had reversed the giant's handiwork. Previously the giant had required the boy's help, rewarded by delicious food, to obtain victims; afterwards he had merely to open his eye for a human to die. A number of myths elsewhere also tell of defiance of death, by men or gods; death was successful only because of some act of foolishness or malice, or of a combination in the breaking of a taboo. Despite all this the land of death, either beneath the earth or in the sky, was often considered a place where one might obtain riches.

Relatively little mythology attaches to the heavenly bodies, though sun and moon are sometimes described as marriage partners—their disputes, or elsewhere their union, causing eclipses. Sometimes their offspring are called the stars, while at other times the ancestor of a people is said to have married a child of sun or moon. The earth-spirit, usually female, is sometimes the consort of the creator, sometimes his opponent. The dual connection of earth with fertility and death, and thus with morality too, is seen clearly in the Ibo earth-goddess Ala in eastern Nigeria. Other earth-spirits are connected with specific mountains, such as Mount Kenya or Kilimanjaro, or with forests and hunting. Spirits of water are naturally important in Africa. The Nigerian sea-god Olokun has an underwater kingdom second only to that of the creator and is more often propitiated than him by the Yoruba and Benin peoples, for he once destroyed most of earth. Elsewhere the spirits of lakes or rivers are powerful and are propitiated by fishermen and before and after crossing. In Buganda rivers are the offspring of ancestors or of gods.

Most important of all nature-spirits are those of storm. The Dinka in Sudan see their divine ancestor Deng as a Zeus-like figure whose club is lightning and who brings rain and fertility. The Ashanti in Ghana call thunderbolts the axes of Nyame, the creator. Elsewhere lightning is seen as various animals: a bird, usually a fish-eagle, in southern Africa; and a dog in the Congo basin. Kibuka is god of war and of storm in Buganda, as is Shango, a

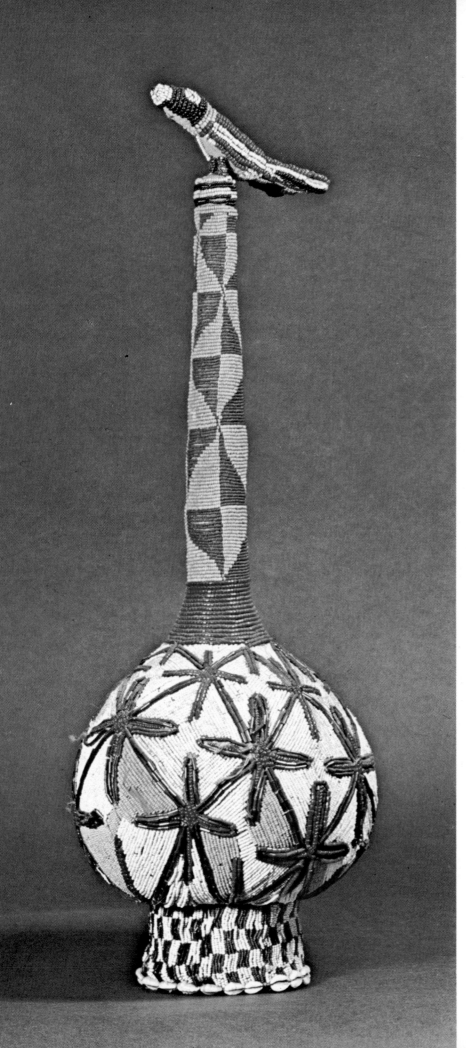

mythical early king of the Yoruba in Nigeria. He was possessed of magic powers and could kill people by breathing fire, but was dethroned by disloyal ministers and hanged himself. Since then he has ruled from heaven by thunder, symbolised by the bellowing of a ram, the animal sacred to him. To the Fon the rainbow, seen as two snakes, promises a crock of gold; but more usually rainbows possess dangerous magical powers which attack men.

The secrets of communication with the ancestors, whose powers equal those of the lesser gods, are held by closed societies of initiates, whose celebrations resemble divine mysteries of many other peoples. The members are almost always exclusively male, though often women first learned the secrets. They relinquished their knowledge when frightened by masks or by bull-roarers invented by the men – a theme paralleled in Australia.

It is difficult for ordinary men to understand supernatural powers, or to communicate with the gods, for each has his own language, which only priests and medicine-men are inspired to understand. The most accomplished interpreters of these languages were various men-gods who instituted oracles or taught methods of divining, for example by divining bowls or by throwing of nuts. Among the best developed systems was that of the Yoruba in Nigeria where the demi-god Ifa set up his oracle at the sacred city of Ilé-Ifé to guide men in matters of medicine and

left
A royal calabash from Cameroun, decorated with beadwork. Some such calabashes are used as musical rattles; others to hold the bones of ancestors. Used for utilitarian and ritual purposes, the calabash is likened to the universe in Dahomey. Horniman Museum.

opposite, top
Incised gold anklet of an Ibo woman from eastern Nigeria. Such decorations, sometimes in copper or brass, and extending up the whole leg, were worn from the initiation of adolescence onwards and could be removed only with difficulty, by a smith. Horniman Museum.

opposite, bottom
Zulu beadwork necklace from South Africa, and other ornaments from Uganda. Both men and women wear colourful and intricate jewellery. Personal decoration, like art, is valued for the way it expresses the life-affirming dynamic of African thought. Horniman Museum.

sacred lore and to set the world in order. He is sometimes identified with a god of mercy, Orunmila, who descended to earth to help men after the attacks of the sea-god Olokun. Similarly merciful was the oracular demi-god Mukasa in Buganda. A recurrent and interesting figure of African myth is a sort of combined archangel-trickster: intermediary between gods and men, whom he protects; but at the same time delighting in mischief-making – often leading to the withdrawal of the creator from earth. Such were Eshu among the Yoruba, and among the Fon Legba, who taught the art of interpreting the Fa oracle.

While medicine and magic are protective of men, witchcraft is invariably evil. Sorcerers hide their telltale characteristics – or indeed change into animal or other form – to perpetrate their secret evildoing. Other malevolent creatures include ghosts of men, animals or trees; diminutive imps or evil fairies; half-men whose false half is made of stone or wax; and man-eating beasts who take human form to lull suspicion.

It will be seen that in the continent which produced the first men and which contains some of the last areas in the world which sustain a living mythology there are as many myths as peoples – or more – but many common themes. And the themes have affinities with mythological motifs from every region of the globe, from creation, to the unleashing of uncontrollable and mysterious forces by man, to the ways in which man seeks to control his environment through ritual and its mythological substructure. For knowledge of many ancient and classical mythologies we owe the greatest debt to archaeology or to literature. In the case of Africa, social anthropology finds a rich field, intricate and still a powerful cohesive force in a land of geographical and political diversity and change.

left
Yoruba king's headdress from Dahomey, the beads cascading curtain-like to veil the face of authority from public gaze. Kings held power from the supreme god and were subordinate to him. But even the ancestral former rulers, founders of the people, are not fully deified.

opposite
One of the many stylised antelope heads carved by the Bambara people of Mali and used in rites for human and agricultural fertility. The creator sent the antelope as his messenger to the people to teach them to grow corn. The patterns on the cloth represent the universe.

opposite
Brass Kuduo box used during a man's
lifetime when 'washing the soul' and in
commemoration of the ancestors of the
clan; and at his death buried with him,
with offerings of gold dust and beads.
The cover is decorated with a leopard
attacking a deer. Ashanti brass, Ghana.

right, above
Hare climbing up the back of a Yoruba
mask. African fable abounds with tales of
how the clever hare bested the lion or
the spider-trickster Anansi. The slave
trade brought him to south-eastern
North America where, mixed with tales of
the rabbit creator, he became Brer Rabbit.
British Museum.

right
Man and woman with the sacred python,
support of the world, symbol of eternity
and rejuvenation, essential helper in
creation, say the Fon, and teacher of the
art of procreation. Advancing
sinuously, it represents the flowing
movement of water. Yoruba bowl. British
Museum.

opposite
Animal mask of the Bapende people, Congo. Humans, animals and even inanimate nature possess spirits. The power of the animal's is concentrated in the head, and an animal mask can endow the wearer with the strength of the animal in resisting evil attack. British Museum.

above
Carved wooden headrest of the Luba people of the Congo. With their identical fan-style hair and sinuous, interlacing limbs, the miniature figures are examples of a common theme of African art: interdependent man and woman as the fount of human society. British Museum.

page 326
A skin-covered helmet mask of the Ekpe or Egbo secret society in eastern Nigeria. The light-skinned female face, looking into the future, is balanced by the dark male face, with closed eyes: dead ancestors ensure continued life for the peoples they founded. Ikoi people.

page 327, left
Ancient painted wooden figure of the Dogon of Mali. The Dogon have a highly complex mythology, well researched, but little is known of these spirit images kept in granaries and given offerings, except that the open hand calls down rain and the closed hand stops it.

page 327, right
Mask of the Mossi people of Upper Volta. The lower half is a stylised antelope head, the upper a naturalistic image of the earth-goddess. In cult use it has a universal combination of functions: funerary and protective of the produce of the earth.

opposite
Priest sitting in the temple of Shango at Ibadan, Nigeria, which contains thunderstones which this Yoruba god of storms and war hurls down during tropical tornadoes. Sometimes thunder is seen as a double-headed axe, the symbolic headdress of Shango cult figures.

right
Carved and polished wooden ancestor figure of the Fang of Gabon. It surmounted a reliquary for the ancestor's bones. Paradoxically, such remains are treasured as part of a cult maintaining that the ancestors continue to live, in triumph over death. British Museum.

page 330, left
Wooden cult figure of the Bakongo people, living near the mouth of the Congo river. With the aid of the circular head-pad—likened to the snake supporting the earth—the figure carries a kettle drum on which coils a snake, and another snake in the hands. Horniman Museum.

page 330, right
Spirit image from the club house of the Ekpe secret society. The club house is the gathering place for initiates of such societies, whose main purpose is to worship the ancestors and to ensure fertility by maintaining the traditional ways of society.

page 331
Carved ebony figure of a medicine-man or witch-doctor from Mozambique. Both physical and spiritual remedies are needed to cure the sick: a medicine-man is familiar with the secrets of nature, while a witch-doctor can counteract the effects of bewitchment.

below
Mask used by members of the Poro
society among the Mende people of
Sierra Leone and Guinea in masquerading
as spirits. The chief spirit is the Gbeni
and may be seen only by full initiates
after ritual death and rebirth in the
sacred bush outside the village.

opposite
Rock painting from Mtoko Cave,
Rhodesia. In the past, when they were
widespread over the continent, Bushmen
made numerous such paintings, some
thousands of years old. With the realistic
detail of the animals, this was probably
intended as hunting magic.

above
Canoe prow from Douala, Cameroun,
which includes European figures
wrestling with snakes and, at the tip, a
battle between snake and bird. With five
centuries of contact, Europeans have
entered African mythology, usually in
unflattering roles. Museum für
Völkerkunde, Munich.

opposite
Shamba, king of the Bushongo in the
Congo c. AD 1600. Legend makes
Shamba a culture-hero famous for wise
judgments, who travelled abroad to
bring his people new inventions and
crops. He introduced more humane
weapons and replaced gambling with
Mankala, the Arab game he is here
playing.

opposite
Antelope headdress patterned with seeds used by the Kurumba of Upper Volta to disperse ancestral spirits after mourning. In Angola the Mbundu explain the limitation of mourning by King Kitamba's resignation after attempting to bring back his wife from the land of the dead.

right
Man-bird mask of the Senufo, Ivory Coast. On the back of its wings are genealogical figures. In neighbouring Guinea the mask images were first revealed to women, but only men had the courage to master their secrets and so communicate with ancestors and spirits.

page 338
Benin bronze of a soldier playing on a pipe. The kingdom of Benin was founded in myth by the youngest son of the creator, his eldest son having founded Yoruba Ifé to the north. Brass-casting came to Benin from Ifé in the fourteenth century and became well known through Portuguese traders.

page 339
Yoruba mask from Dahomey used in an ancestor cult society. It has the motif of the circular snake of eternity being attacked by a bird—which is recurrent not only throughout Africa but in parts of the world as diverse as Scandinavia, India and North America.

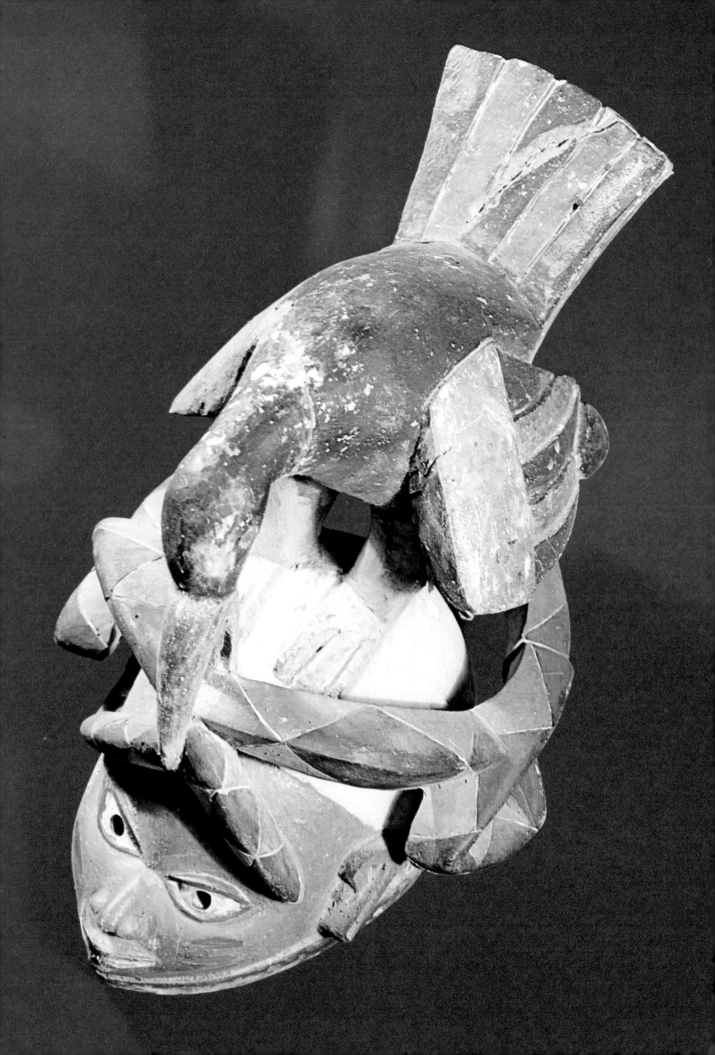

GENERAL

Everyman Dictionary of Non-Classical Mythology. J. M. Dent, London and E. P. Dutton, New York, 1952

Frazer, Sir James **The Golden Bough.** 1 vol. ed. Macmillan, London, and St Martin's Press, New York. 1922

Graves, Robert **The White Goddess.** Faber & Faber, London, 1948 *MacCulloch, John A. and Gray, Louis H.* **The Mythology of all Races.** 13 vols. Cooper Square Pubs. Inc, New York. 1922

New Larousse Encyclopedia of Mythology. Hamlyn, Feltham. 1968

Parrinder, Geoffrey **Man and His Gods.** Hamlyn, Feltham. 1971

Standard Dictionary of Folklore, Mythology and Legend. 2 vols. Mayflower Pub. Co., London and Funk & Wagnalls, New York. 1951

THE NEAR EAST

Drioton, Etienne **The Religion of the Ancient East.** Burns & Oates, London. 1959

Driver, G. R. **Canaanite Myths and Legends.** T. & T. Clark, Edinburgh. 1956

Gray, John **Near Eastern Mythology.** Hamlyn, Feltham, 1969 **The Canaanites.** Thames & Hudson, London. 1964

Gurney, O. R. **The Hittites.** Penguin Books, Harmondsworth. 1953

Harden, D. E. **The Phoenicians.** Thames & Hudson, London. 1962

Hooke, Samuel H. **Babylonian and Assyrian Religion.** Hutchinson, London. 1953

James, E. O. **Myth and Ritual in the Ancient Near East.** Thames & Hudson, London. 1958

Kramer, S. N. **History begins at Sumer.** Thames & Hudson, London. 1958

EGYPT

Cerny, J. **Ancient Egyptian Religions.** Hutchinson, London. 1952

Desroches-Noblecourt, C. **Tutankhamun.** Penguin Books, Harmondsworth. 1965

Gardiner, Sir Alan H. **Egypt of the Pharaohs.** Oxford Univ. Press. 1961

Griffiths, John Gwyn **The Conflict of Horus and Seth.** Liverpool Univ. Press. 1960

Herodotus **The Histories** trans. by Aubrey de Selincourt. Penguin Books, Harmondsworth. 1954

Ions, Veronica **Egyptian Mythology.** Hamlyn, Feltham. 1968

Murray, M. A. **The Splendour that was Egypt.** Sidgwick & Jackson, London. 1949

Plutarch **Isis and Isiris.** (Vol. V in Plutarch's **Moralia**). Ed. and trans. by F. C. Babbit. Leob Classical Library, London. 1936

PERSIA

Ghirshman, Roman **Persia, from the Origins to Alexander the Great.** Thames & Hudson, London. 1964 **Iran. The Parthjans and Sassanians.** Thames & Hudson, London. 1962

Hinnells, John R. **Persian Mythology.** Hamlyn, Feltham. 1974

Vermaseren, M. J. **Mithras, the Secret God.** Methuen, London. 1963

Xaehner, R. C. **The Rise and Fall of Zoroastrianism.** Weidenfeld & Nicolson, London. 1961

INDIA

Basham, A. L. **The Wonder that was India.** Sidgwick & Jackson, London. 1954

Dowson, J. **Classical Dictionary of Hindu Mythology.** Kegan Paul, London. 1961

Humphreys, C. **Buddhism.** Penguin Books, Harmondsworth. 1951

Ions, Veronica **Indian Mythology.** Hamlyn, Feltham. 1967

Jaini, J. **Outlines of Jainism.** Cambridge Univ. Press. 1940

Riencourt, Amaury de **The Soul of India.** Jonathan Cape, London. 1961

Weber, Max **The Religion of India.** Allen & Unwin, London. 1958

Zaehner, R. C. **Hinduism.** Oxford Univ. Press. 1962

GREECE

Cook, A. B. **Zeus.** Cambridge Univ. Press. 1940

Cottrell, Leonard. **The Bull of Minos.** Evans Bros., London. 1954

Graves, Robert. **The Greek Myths.** 2 Vols. Penguin Books, London. 1959

Mylonas, G. **Eleusis and the Eleusinian Mysteries.** Routledge & Kegan Paul, London. 1962

Pinsent, John. **Greek Mythology.** Hamlyn, Feltham. 1969

ROME

Bloch, Raymond. **The Origins of Rome.** Thames & Hudson, London. 1960

Grant, Michael. **Myths of the Greeks and Romans.** Weidenfeld & Nicolson, London. 1962 **The Roman World.** Weidenfeld & Nicolson, London. 1960

Perowne, Stewart. **Roman Mythology.** Hamlyn, Feltham. 1969

Rose, H. J. **Ancient Roman Religion.** Hutchinson, London. 1949

Warner, Rex. **Men and Gods.** Penguin Books, Harmondsworth. 1952

THE CELTS

Branston, Brian. **The Lost Gods of England.** Thames & Hudson, London. 1958

Jones, T. & G. (Trans.) **The Mabinogion.** J. M. Dent, London, and E. P. Dutton, New York. 1963

MacCana, Proinsias. **Celtic Mythology.** Hamlyn, Feltham. 1970

Ross, Anne. **Pagan Celtic Britain.** Routledge & Kegan Paul, London and Columbia Univ. Press, New York. 1967

Sjoestedt, Marie Louise. **Gods and Heroes of the Celts.** Methuen, London. 1967

Yeats, W. B. **Mythologies.** Macmillan, London. 1959

SCANDINAVIA

Branston, Brian. **Gods of the North.** Thames & Hudson, London. 1955

Ellis Davidson, H. R. **Gods and Myths of Northern Europe.** Penguin Books, Harmondsworth. 1964

Scandinavian Mythology. Hamlyn, Feltham. 1969

Jones, G. **Eirik the Red, and other Icelandic Sagas.** Oxford Univ. Press. 1961

Oxenstierna, E. G. **The Norsemen.** Weidenfeld & Nicolson, London. 1965

Vries, J. de. **Heroic Song and Heroic Legend.** Oxford Univ. Press. 1964

CHINA

Christie, Anthony. **Chinese Mythology.** Hamlyn, Feltham. 1968

Harvey, E. D. **The Mind of China.** Yale Univ. Press. 1933

Reincourt, Amaury de. **The Soul of China.** Jonathan Cape, London. 1959

Watson, W. **China.** Thames & Hudson, London. 1961

Werner, E. T. C. **Myths and Legends of China.** Harrap, London. 1922

JAPAN

Anesaki, Mahasaru. **History of Japanese Religion.** Kegan Paul, London. 1930

Aston, W. G. **Nihongi: Chronicles of Japan.** Allen & Unwin, London & Oxford Univ. Press, New York. 1956

Kidder, J. E. **Japan.** Thames & Hudson, London. 1959

Piggott, Juliet. **Japanese Mythology.** Hamlyn, Feltham. 1969

Watts, Alan W. **The Way of Zen.** Thames & Hudson, London. 1957

THE AMERICAS

Burland, Cottie. **The Gods of Mexico.** Eyre & Spottiswoode, London. 1967

North American Indian Mythology. Hamlyn, Feltham. 1965

Bushnell, G. M. S. **The Ancient Peoples of the Andes.** Penguin Books, Harmondsworth. 1949

Macmillan, C. **Glooskap's Country.** Oxford Univ. Press. 1956

Martin, Paul Sidney. **Indians Before Columbus.** Chicago Univ. Press. 1947

Mason, J. A. **The Ancient Civilisations of Peru.** Penguin Books, Harmondsworth. 1957

Morley, S. G. **The Ancient Maya.** Oxford Univ. Press. 1946

Nicholson, Irene. **Firefly in the Night.** Faber & Faber, London. 1959

Mexican and Central American Mythology. Hamlyn, Feltham. 1967

Osborne, Harold. **South American Mythology.** Hamlyn, Feltham. 1968

Peterson, Fredrick. **Ancient Mexico.** Allen & Unwin, London. 1959

Vaillant, G. C. **The Aztecs of Mexico.** Penguin Books, Harmondsworth. 1952

Von Hagen, Victor W. **The Ancient Sun Kingdoms.** Thames & Hudson, London. 1962

The Desert Kingdoms of Peru. Weidenfeld & Nicolson, London. 1965

THE SOUTH PACIFIC AND AUSTRALIA

Beckwith, M. **Hawaiian Mythology.** Yale Univ. Press. 1940

Berndt, R. M. **Djanggawul.** Routledge & Kegan Paul, London. 1952

Kunapipi. F. W. Cheshire, Melbourne. 1951

The World of the First Australians. Angus & Robertson, Sydney. 1965

Grimble, Sir Arthur. **A Pattern of Islands.** John Murray, London. 1952

Grey, Sir George. **Polynesian Mythology.** Whitcombe & Tombs, London and Christchurch. 1965

Heyerdahl, Thor. **Aku-Aku.** Allen & Unwin, London. 1958

McConnel, Ursula. **Myths of the Munkan.** Cambridge Univ. Press. 1957

Metraux, A. **Easter Island.** Andre Deutsch, London. 1957

Poignant, Roslyn. **Oceanic Mythology.** Hamlyn, Feltham. 1968

Suggs, R. C. **Island Civilisation of Polynesia.** Mentor Books, London. 1960

AFRICA

Cardinall, A. W. **Tales Told In Togoland.** Oxford Univ. Press. 1931

Fugi, A. **Fourteen Hundred Cowries.** Oxford Univ. Press. 1962

Idowu, E. B. **Olodumare. God in Yoruba belief.** Longmans, London. 1962

Itayemi, P. and Gurrey, P. **Folk Tales and Fables.** Penguin Africa Series, Harmondsworth. 1953

Parrinder, Geoffrey. **African Mythology.** Hamlyn, Feltham. 1968

West African Religions. Epworth Press, London. 1949

Rattray, R. S. **Religion and Art In Ashanti.** Oxford Univ. Press. 1927

Smith, E. W. and Parrinder, E. G. **African Ideas of God.** Edinburgh House Press, London. 1967

Acknowledgements

Illustrations are reproduced by courtesy of the following owners, collections and museums:

Acropolis Museum, Athens 118 top; American Museum of Natural History, New York 234; American Numismatic Society, New York 57; Archaeological Museum, Eleusis 125 bottom; Archaeological Museum, Teheran 61 bottom; Ashmolean Museum, Oxford 14; Australian Institute of Anatomy, Canberra 312; Sir Harold Bailey 64; Bayerische Staatsbibliothek, Munich 59; British Museum, London 10, 21, 22, 33, 48, 49, 52, 58 bottom, 62, 101, 108 left, 109 bottom left, 109 bottom right, 110, 114, 115, 118 bottom, 121, 122, 141 top, 153 bottom, 167, 168 top, 168-169, 169 top, 182, 183, 184 top, 185, 193, 194, 195 bottom, 210, 217 right, 218 top, 218 bottom, 221, 222, 231, 233 top, 233 bottom, 239 top right, 239 bottom right, 241, 242 top, 242 bottom, 250, 287, 296, 298 bottom, 304, 306, 307 left, 307 right, 315, 323 top, bottom, 324, 325, 329, 338; Chester Beatty Library, Dublin 60, 73; Chicago Museum of Natural History 229; Dumbarton Oaks, Robert Woods Bliss Collection, Washington 253, 260, 265; Egyptian Museum, Cairo 29, 41, 45; Freer Gallery of Art, Washington 85; Frobenius Institute, Frankfurt-am-Main 333; General Post Office, Dublin 154; Guildhall Museum, London 138; Hermitage Museum, Leningrad 61 top; Historisk Museum, Bergen 156; Hooper Collection 294, 299, 300 left; Horniman Museum, London 187, 309, 318, 319 top, 319 bottom, 330 left, 330 right; Institute of Archaeology, Oxford 175 right, 177 top; Iraq Museum, Baghdad 18, 23; Islamisches Museum, Berlin 96; Kabul Museum 58 top; Kemper Collection, London 278, 281, 282, 283, 285, 286 left, 288, 290, 291; Kyoto City Government 209 left; Linden Museum, Stuttgart 302-303; Louvre, Paris 11, 13, 16, 17, 19, 20, 50, 111, 139; Metropolitan Museum of Art, New York (Gift of Alexander Smith Cochran) 72; Metropolitan Museum of Art, New York (Harris Brisbane Dick Fund, 1934) 120; Metropolitan Museum of Art, New York (Rogers Fund, 1907) 124; Musée Borély, Marseilles 148; Musée Calvet, Avignon 147; Musée de Chartres 146; Musée Guimet, Paris 71, 83; Musée de l'Homme, Paris 280, 316, 320, 339; Musée Municipal, Lambaesis 144-145 bottom; Musée National du Bardo, Tunis 141 bottom; Musées Royaux d'Art et d'Histoire, Brussels 117; Museo de Oro, Bogota 276; Museo Nazionale, Reggio 108 right; Museo Nazionale Romano, Rome 136 top, 136 bottom left; Museo Nazionale, Taranto 109 top; Museo Nazionale di Villa Giulia, Rome 28, 132 left; Museum of the American Indian, Heye Foundation, New York 228, 230, 232, 238, 240 top, 240 bottom; Museum of Antiquities of the University and Society of Antiquaries of Newcastle-upon-Tyne 65 bottom, Museum of Navajo Ceremonial Art, Santa Fé 237 top, 237 bottom; Museum of Religion, Ulan Bator 192 top left; Museum für Volkerkunde, Basel 303 top, 305; Museum für Volkerkunde, Hamburg 293; Museum für Volkerkunde, Munich 295, 298 top left, 298 top right; Museum für Volkerkunde, Vienna 336, 337; National Museum, Aleppo 12, 24 top; National Museum, Athens 25 top, 125 top; National Museum, Guatemala 263; National Museum of Anthropology, Mexico City 245, 247, 251, 256, 258, 259 left, 259 right, 266 top, 266 bottom, 267, 268, 269; Nationalmuseum, Copenhagen 150 bottom; 150-151, 151 bottom, 164-165, 166; Peabody Museum, Harvard University, Cambridge, Massachusetts 264, 297; Mrs. Margaret Plas, Philadelphia 332; Private Collection, 198; Rheinisches Landesmuseum, Bonn 149; Rex Rienits Collection 310, 311 top, 311 bottom; Seattle Art Museum 190, 191; Sheffield City Museum 171 top; Staatliche Antikensammlungen und Glyptothek, Munich 116; State Regional Museum of Archaeology, Oaxaca 262; Statens Historiska Museum, Stockholm 169 bottom, 171 bottom, 177 bottom; The Board of Trinity College, Dublin 155; Universitetets Oldsaksamling, Oslo 172, 173 bottom; Victoria and Albert Museum, London 81, 82, 84, 86, 90, 94, 97, 99, 179, 184 bottom, 188, 189, 192 bottom, 195 top, 196, 197, 201, 202, 203, 204 top, 204-205 bottom, 206-207, 208, 209 bottom right, 211, 212-213 top, 212 bottom right, 213 top right, 213 bottom right, 214 top right, 214-215, 216-217 top, 216 bottom left, 217 left, 219; Wellcome Historical Medical Museum, London 1, 181, 186, 192 top right; Würtemburgisches Landesmuseum, Stuttgart 261.

Photographs

Ferdinand Anton, Munich 279; Dr. P. H. Beighton 301 top, 301 bottom; Bemporad-Marzocco, Florence 143; W. Bruggmann-Holle Verlag, Baden Baden 321, 322, 326, 327 left, 327 right; C.D.O., 284; Camera Press, London 235, 236, 243; Yves Coffin, Paris 205 bottom right, 209 top right; J. E. Dayton, London 69 top, 70 top, 70 bottom; Fondo Editorial de la Plástica, Mexico City 255; W. Forman, London 40; Photographie Giraudon, Paris 35, 127; Irmgard Groth-Kimball, Mexico City 254; Hamlyn Group Picture Library 136-137 bottom, 140, 144 top left, 156-157, 249, 300 right; Gudmundur Hannesson, Reykjavik 176-177; André Held-Ziolo, Paris 131, 137 top; Hirmer Verlag, Munich 118-119; Holle Bildarchiv, Baden Baden 69 bottom, 173 top, 175 left; Irish Tourist Board, Dublin 153 top right, 158 bottom, 159 top left, 159 top right, 159 bottom; A. F. Kersting, London 32, 34; Kungl. Vitterhets Historie och Antikvitets Akademien, Stockholm 161; Karel Kupka 313; M. L. Lancaster, London 328; Joan Martin 205 top; Middle East Archive, London 25 bottom, 26 top, 27 top, 27 bottom; W. K. Müller–Bavaria Verlag, Gauting 102, 112-113; I. N. Nalawala, Bombay 88, 89; Office of Public Works, National Monuments Branch, Dublin 153 top left, 157 top, 158 top, 158 centre; M. Pedone–Bavaria Verlag, Gauting 104-105; Antonello Perissonotto, Padua 55; Pictorial Press, London 128-129; Picturepoint, London 106, 123; Axel Poignant, London 162, 170-171, 174, 308; Paul Popper Ltd. London 75, 257; Josephine Powell, Rome 68; Réalités, Paris 199; Réalités, Paris–H. Gloaguen 286 right; Scala, Antella 47, 66-67, 132-133, 142; R. V. Schoder, Chicago 134, 135; Harald Schultz 271, 272, 274, 275; Shell Photographic Unit, London 31; J. C. Spahni, Geneva 289; Stattliche Museum zu Berlin, Islamisches Museum 93; M. Stapleton, London 133 right; Henri Stierlin, Lausanne 246; Wim Swaan, New York 76, 79, 87; Uni-Dia-Verlag, Grosshesselohe 26 bottom; Leonard von Matt, Buochs 98; R. Wood, London 30, 36, 37, 38, 39, 42, 43, 44, 46, 51, 53, 54, 56, 63, 65 top; Professor Yigael Yadin, Hebrew 104-105; Antonello Perissonotto, Padua 55; Pictorial Press, London 128-129; University, Jerusalem 24 bottom; Zodiaqe, Saint Léger Vauban 152.

Index